This Sunrise of Wonder

Michael Mayne

THIS SUNRISE OF WONDER

Letters to my grandchildren

Foreword by Ronald Blythe

NEW AMERICAN EDITION

2012

Parson's Porch Books   Cleveland, Tennessee

Parson's Porch Books
121 Holly Trail Road, NW
Cleveland, Tennessee 37311

This Sunrise of Wonder: Letters to My Grandchildren
© 1995, 2008, 2012 by Michael Mayne. All rights reserved.

New American edition. Published 2012. First published in 1995 by
HarperCollins Religious; new edition published 2008 by Dartman,
Longman & Todd, Ltd.

Printed in the United States of America.
ISBN 978-1-936912-44-5

To order additional copies of this book, contact:

Parson's Porch Books
1-423-475-7308
www.parsonsporchbooks.com

Cover photograph (Sunrise at Sharp Top Mtn.) and book design by
John Eric Killinger for *Ars Intermundia Expressusiæ*.
Cover photograph © 2012 John Eric Killinger.

FOR ADAM AND ANNA

With gratitude to David and Pauline Summerscale who, by lending us their Swiss chalet, made it possible for me to write these letters in a place of beauty and tranquility; and to my son Mark, observant and encouraging critic.

Contents

Foreword

A N AMERICAN FRIEND LIKED this little joke about wills. "What did he leave?"—"He left it all." Where our money is concerned we shall certainly leave it all. Yet most of us do take great riches to the grave with us. These are the literature, music, art, and personal responses to nature which formed our philosophy and culture, and which created our joy. Some lives have been transformed by a single poem or novel or author, or by seeing a Monet, or by listening to Mozart, but usually they become fulfilled by a gradual build-up of private discoveries. For Michael Mayne it is not enough that his grandchildren will be able to say that he was fond of reading, enjoyed the theatre, visited art galleries, went to concerts, was sensitive to the natural world, etc.; and that these pleasures enhanced his faith and became part of his ministry. He needs to tell them what books, what songs, which moment when the butterfly settled on the flower or the evening blackbird was heard. He also needs to put together for himself, as well as for future generations, an inventory of his joy, a list of what exalted his spirit, or what opened his eyes, or what produced in him contentment (or unrest), and what made him what he was. So delightful and important to him were these things that he unapologetically urges them on his children's children with a "don't miss this" and a "do read that." There is no moralizing, no talk of improving one's mind; just an offering of his collective inspiration.

It would have been easy for Michael Mayne to have simply arranged his reading and cultural life generally as an anthology, or a day-book for others, but the strength of *This Sunrise of Wonder* lies in its candid autobiographical setting. It is a confession of how he came to unify his outer and inner worlds, the ordinariness and yet the extraordinariness of everything. Both, he realizes, need the voice of autobiography. There is no detachment and no divorce of his religion from the wonders of writing and painting.

The artist John Nash once told me that when he was about ten years old he was given a book entitled *Eyes and No Eyes* so that he would learn to be observant on country walks. This little volume was filled with lessons which he never forgot and when he was old he was to write: "The artist's main business is to train his eye to see, then to probe, and then to train his hand to work in sympathy with his eye. I have made a habit of looking, of really seeing." Michael Mayne is anxious—eager—passionate, even—that those who come after him should have a trained eye. What a disaster to pass through our one and only earthly life and to miss its glories, is what he is saying. These are of many kinds, yet, added up, they amount to nothing less than the only treasure we can ultimately possess which is worth calling a treasure.

It is harder for priests than for most of us to "will" their spiritual gains. Popular shifts in Christian attitudes and beliefs have a way of dating the aspirations, tastes, and ideals of an earlier generation. Whilst Michael Mayne is steadfast in presenting his "wonder" as that of a man of the late twentieth century, he successfully draws on the timelessness of many of the things which constantly provided it for him. In some respects this keenly argued book confronts today's fashionable cynicism and despair, and thus has a message for the current moment when the *experience* of ageing, or environment, or of those complex skills and emotions which go into the creation of poetry or stories or music, are all distorted or ignored in favour of what is called "reality," but where the highest thought and achievement are concerned, is not at all real. *This Sunrise of Wonder* is not optimistic in the sense that it would have us turn away from the grim facts of the world to see "beauty," but it does prove that, as well as tragedy or just plain dreariness, there exists for anyone to find, given the fuller vision, an illimitable universe of plants, creatures, prayer, art, music, and, most of all for Michael Mayne, for we each have our inspirational preferences, books. In some ways all his books are prayer-books. This letter-book for his descendants, no less. Thumb through it, he asks. Discover what I discovered, only from your own heights.

Ronald Blythe

I

By Way of Explanation

Growing, Flying, Happening

Say the soft bird's name, but do not be surprised
to see it fall
headlong, struck skyless, into its pigeonhole—
columba palumbus and you have it dead,
wedged, neat, unwinged in your head.

That the black-backed tatter-winged thing
straking the harbour water and then plummeting
down, to come up, sleek head a-cock,
a minted herring shining in its beak,
is a *guillemot*, is neither here nor there
in the amazement of its rising,
wings slicing the stiff salt air.

That of that spindling spear-leaved plant,
wearing the palest purple umbel,
many-headed, blue-tinted, stilt-stalked
at the stream-edge, one should say briefly
angelica, is by-the-way (though grant
the name itself to be beautiful).
Grant too that any name
makes its own music, that *bryony, sally-my-handsome*
burst at their sound into flower,
and that *falcon* and *phalarope* fly off in the ear,
still,
names are for saying at home.

The point is the seeing—the grace
beyond recognition, the ways
of the bird rising, unnamed, unknown,
beyond the range of language, beyond its noun.
Eyes open on growing, flying, happening,
and go on opening. Manifold, the world
dawns on unrecognizing, realizing eyes.
Amazement is the thing.
Not love, but the astonishment of loving.

ALASTAIR REID[1]

I want to beg you . . . to be patient towards all that is unsolved in your heart and try to love *the questions themselves* like locked rooms and like books that are written in a very foreign tongue. Do not now seek the answers, that cannot be given you because you would not be able to live them. And the point is, to live everything. *Live* the questions now. Perhaps you will then gradually, without noticing it, live along some distant day into the answer.

RAINER MARIA RILKE[2]

I don't think that it is always necessary to talk *about* the deepest and most private dimension of who we are, but I think we are called to talk to each other *out* of it, and just as importantly to listen to each other *out* of it, to live out of our depths as well as our shallows.

FREDERICK BUECHNER[3]

Henry Thoreau said: "I should not talk so much about myself if there were anybody else whom I knew so well," and like Walt Whitman, he devoted his life to presenting his enthusiasms, assuming that they had universal application.

EDWARD HOAGLAND[4]

20 May

BRITISH RAIL RECOGNIZE ME as a senior citizen; London theatre box offices don't. I am sixty-three, a son of in-between age when you look older than you feel. You, on the other hand, are experiencing the new-minted wonder of childhood. Why should I think these letters should be, in some remote and unpredictable future, of any use or interest to you? Not because I claim to have learned much wisdom on my human journey. When John Betjeman was asked in a radio interview on his appointment as Poet Laureate, "Do you not think, Sir John, that you are arbitrary and irrelevant?" Betjeman replied "Yes, thank goodness!" And in one sense I go along with that. Whatever role we are invited to play, whatever job we do, is pretty irrelevant in the light of eternity; and yet . . . it is my journey, and you are (at one remove) bone of *my* bone and flesh of *my* flesh. And if I have learned anything it has to do with the wonder and the value of each unique and particular creature, for no living person or thing is either arbitrary or irrelevant.

I only knew one of my grandparents, a remarkable grandmother who played bridge and snooker every day to the age of ninety-nine and died aged a hundred-and-one. Nor did I ever know my father. He must have known a lot about pain and anguish secretly borne, for one day in May he climbed the church tower in the village where he was rector, threw himself down, and was killed almost instantly. I was three, the same age as you, Adam, are now. Sometimes I wonder what they were like, those whose genes I carry, and I long to know what they cared about and believed to be of value.

Only children, especially fatherless only children, are often (understandably) somewhat private people, so even if I live to the age when you are old enough to understand those things which speak to me most deeply in the mystery of my life, I find it easier to write about them, and to do so now. "The impulse to keep to yourself what you have learned," writes Annie Dillard, "is not only shameful, it is destructive. Anything you do not give freely and abundantly becomes lost to you. You open your safe and find ashes." After Michelangelo died a piece of paper was found in his studio. In an old man's hand he had written this to his apprentice: "Draw, Antonio, draw, Antonio, draw and do not waste time."[5]

So I must not waste time. Ezra Pound was right:

> And the days are not full enough
> And the nights are not full enough,
> And life slips by like a fieldmouse
> Not shaking the grass.[6]

I have come to a dark wooden chalet with brick-red shutters standing high above a small village in the Val d'Anniviers in the Swiss Alps. On a fine day, if you climb a bit, you can see the Matterhorn, and as the winter snows melt and the Alpine flowers begin to appear I am spending just over a month trying to share with you what, in looking at the world about me, I have found of value. "Study leave" they call it; but the study has been done: over the years by reading books and observing people, by watching and listening, by giving attention and learning to make connections. I did not have to look very far once I had spotted the thread I wished to pursue, for it runs through the work of most artists and many scientists and some theologians, and it is the theme of this book. For these letters are, above all, about wonder.

"I want to write a novel about silence," says a character in Virginia Woolf's *The Voyage Out*, "the things people don't say. But the difficulty is immense."[7] Substitute "wonder" for "silence" and the difficulty doesn't diminish, for wonder knows no boundaries and is as slippery and imprecise a word as you can find. Perhaps G. K. Chesterton best defines the sense in which I want to explore it. He writes of how, following a period of depression, he is granted an insight he never forgot:

> At the back of our brains, so to speak, there is a forgotten blaze or burst of astonishment at our own existence. The object of the artistic and spiritual life is to dig for this sunrise of wonder.[8]

I want only to speak of what I know on my own pulse, those things I have proved to be true for me. Just as an artist praises the world by seeing it with his or her own clear vision and setting it down in paint or lucid prose, giving it form in stone or wood, or imaging it in poetry, so I should like to call attention to the world into which you have been born, whose potential is breathtaking, whose beauty has an unchanging validity, and in which every object (let alone every person) has its own stubborn uniqueness. Yet I only have words with which to explore the mystery; and I must juggle the twenty-six letters of the alphabet in such a way that they take the shape of my gradually clarifying thoughts and convey them to you. (That a and b and c and d may combine to communicate the imagination of Shakespeare, the wisdom of Aristotle, and the holiness of St. Augustine is a pretty knockdown cause for wonder in itself.)

But then communication is not just about finding intelligible words. It is also about giving something of yourself. It has validity only if, like Edgar in Lear, we "speak what we feel, not what we ought to say." But communication may go deeper still and be about a desire to say, and a yearning to receive, something which words can only point at. We sense there is something more. Words are always approximate: they hint at the reality some call God. Words point to the experience of love, but never entirely capture it. It needs to be enfleshed. Words struggle to describe the beauty of a primrose. It needs to be seen. What words sometimes do is to exclude. Perhaps by being technical, and a book on computers or a book on the Trinity may be equally nonsensical to one who has not learned that particular language.

In writing about wonder I am writing above all of what it means to be human. I happen to be a Christian. So often Christians write as if they possess a privileged insight into what it is to be human and go on to speak a language that only the enlightened will understand. But if it is true (as I profoundly believe) that we are each made in "the image of God," that we are bodies and we are also spirits, embodied spirits that have qualities not found in inanimate nature, then "human" and "Christian" are not mutually exclusive terms, nor is a Christian called to be anything other than human. Each of us is unique, yet the story of any one of us is in some measure the story of us all.

What a Christian claims to have is a different frame of reference, and in later letters I shall be describing what that is, and how I believe it may enable us to become the kind of people God calls us to be. But I am not assuming that when you grow up you will want to affirm such a belief for yourselves, and I want above all to avoid in these letters any sense of exclusiveness. Beliefs that are exclusive are usually wrongheaded and always unattractive.

How then, should I write? "Write," says Annie Dillard, "as if you were dying. At the same time, assume you write for an audience consisting solely of terminal patients. That is, after all, the case. What would you begin writing if you knew you were to die soon? What would you say to a dying person that would not enrage by its triviality?"[9]

I would say: "Open your eyes; both your physical eyes, and what William Blake called 'the inward eye.' Learn how to see, for to see is the beginning of wonder." Artists know this. So do many scientists. But I struggle more with the latter and most of those I shall call upon in these letters will be painters and writers. I have always been attracted to that concept of priesthood that likens a priest to an artist. Keats spoke of the poet as a "priest." one who experiences the joys and suffering with and on behalf of others and who understands the reality and the truth of the things of the spirit. The most awesome task of an artist is to help us to see, to say, "Look! Pay attention!"

Alan Ecclestone points out that some linguistic scholars believe the root "lig" in the word "religion" means "to pay attention," "to give care"; and he suggests that a religious attitude is that which is careful "to pay full attention to people and things in the process of learning to love them."[10]

The true artist does not manipulate or indoctrinate us: he doesn't have to. He simply shows us how (in his eyes) things truly are. It was William Blake who saw the artist as one who conveys to others the perception of things in their true essence and points to a divine reality beyond himself.

A priest as pastor tries to do the same, helping people to make sense of the raw material of their lives by building on whatever glimpses they may have of goodness or beauty or suffering or love. I shall hope to show you in a much later letter how the Christian Gospel is all about seeing with changed eyes. For van Gogh, Christ is the supreme artist "disdaining marble and clay and colours, working in the living flesh." Those who write of the impact of Jesus upon them are saying: "Look! Listen! A child is born and a man dies, and in the story of that birth and that life, in images of water and bread, in damaged lives healed and in people forgiven and set free, and on a wooden cross and in an upper room a new way of living becomes possible, a new creation is set in being, and a whole new understanding of God is revealed."

For me, this too begins with giving attention, learning to see, and it ends in wonder and gratitude. I hope you will be suspicious of those who attempt to diminish you by imposing views that are too narrowly restrictive or untrue to your own experience of life. It's as important to sniff out the bogus in the religious field as in any other. Equally, I hope you will look with particular care at those whose work has to do with the creative imagination: painters and poets, novelists and playwrights, sculptors and musicians. An artist cannot afford to dabble in the bogus. He must work within the limits of his own authentic vision. "There must be no 'ought to know' or 'try to feel,'" writes David Jones in the preface to that distillation of the British spirit, *The Anathemata*, "for only what is actually known can be seen *sub specie aeternitatis*"[11] (by which he means "life as God sees it, with all its imperfections removed"). So listen with your full attention to those who, as it were, touch your sleeve and invite you to see what the landscape and the journey look like to them. And most especially those who have a kind of reverent and infectious wonder.

Inevitably I have thrown my net wide, called on a lot of witnesses and done a fair amount of plundering. But what is life about if not to tap others' wisdom; to make connections; and to celebrate with gratitude those who help us to see? I have placed Alastair Reid's poem "Growing, Flying, Happening" at the start of these letters. It says memorably what will be my repeated theme:

> *The point is seeing—the grace*
> *beyond recognition, the ways*
> *of the bird rising, unnamed, unknown,*
> *beyond the range of language, beyond its noun.*
> *Eyes open on growing, flying, happening,*
> *and go on opening . . .*
> *Amazement is the thing.*
> *Not love, but the astonishment of loving.*

Dag Hammarskjöld, the United Nations Secretary General killed in a plane crash in 1961, wrote in his personal journal:

> God does not die on the day when we cease to believe in a personal deity, but we die on the day when our lives cease to be illumined by the steady radiance, renewed daily, of a wonder, the source of which is beyond all reason.[12]

If I could have waved a fairy grandfather's wand at your birth and wished upon you just one gift it would not have been beauty or riches or a long life: it would have been the gift of wonder. One of the wisest Jewish teachers of my time, Abraham Joshua Heschel, a refugee of the Nazis, said towards the end of his life: "I did not ask for success: I asked for wonder."[13] That seems to me the best of all epitaphs, and I hope that these letters, which come to you with so much love, show you why.

II

The Mystery That Is Me

Sir,

My husband, T. S. Eliot, loved to recount how late one evening he stopped a taxi. As he got in, the driver said: "You're T. S. Eliot." When asked how he knew, he replied: "Ah, I've got an eye for a celebrity. Only the other evening I picked up Bertrand Russell and I said to him: 'Well, Lord Russell, what's it all about?' and, do you know, he couldn't tell me."

Yours faithfully,
Valerie Eliot[1]

You would pluck out the heart of my mystery.

HAMLET[2]

[Music plays] Now is his soul ravished. Is it not strange that sheeps' guts should hale souls out of men's bodies?

BENEDICK[3]

YESTERDAY THE MID-MAY SUN caused the snow to come crashing down the mountain gullies with a noise like distant thunder, the new green of the larches shimmered in the breeze, and in the meadows the deep blue trumpet gentians startled the eye and the waxy, yellow globeflowers and cowslips were thick on the ground. Today everywhere is white, muffled in snow, an extraordinary transformation of summer into winter. Even the birds are subdued. A good time for writing.

My subject is wonder, and my starting point so obvious it often escapes us. It is me, sitting at a table looking out on the world. It is the fact that I exist, that there is anything at all. It is the *givenness* that astonishes: the fact that the mountains, the larch tree, the gentian, the jay, exist, and that someone called *me* is here to observe them. It is what the Cambridge philosopher Wittgenstein called "existential wonder," and there is nowhere else to begin. Not with theories of the Big Bang, nor with what subatomic physics tells us of the nature of matter, but with the most disarming fact of all: the world *is* and it might not have been. It is: I am. That is the first wonder: what do we make of it?

When you look at yourself and the world about you with as objective and dispassionate an eye as you can, do you see both (including the "you" doing the seeing) as phenomena to be understood, analysed and classified in a logical scientific way; or do you view what you see with a sense of awe? Do you have a sense of mystery? No generalization can be pressed too hard, but it does seem as if there is a thick sheet of glass placed, not between people of different creeds and cultures, but between those who have a sense of mystery (properly, a religious sense) and those for whom wonder is a luxury they can do without. We can see each other through the glass, but we can't hear each other for we're talking a different language, those with the capacity to see the extraordinary in the ordinary and to acknowledge the mystery, and those who don't or won't.

Now here I must walk as one who walks on eggshells, for we are on the brink of the often impenetrable worlds of philosophy, theology and aesthetics; and that is as alarming to me as it may be to you. So let me define what I mean by "mystery."

Mystery is a word with a past. In ancient Greece the mysteries were initiation ceremonies through which the initiates (the "mystics") gained a secret knowledge of divine things and entered into what was holy and timeless. They were not allowed to speak of what they had learned. Later, not long before the birth of Christ, the word had come to have a different meaning. It had come to mean a particular way of approaching reality through the use of our intuitive, as well as our intellectual, faculties; the belief that much of philosophy, art, poetry, and music are inspired by a sense of something that lies beyond and unseen, something over and above the world as we perceive it with our five senses, though interwoven with it; if you like (to use Bonhoeffer's phrase about God), the "beyond" in our midst.

In what is called the mystical tradition, both in the East and in the West, this consciousness of the "beyond" is present, often in an intense form. The most mystical of the New Testament writers, St. John and St. Paul, speak of certain specific mysteries about the being and nature of God which have been revealed in Christ, truths which we should not know unless they had been so revealed and which we can only partially understand; mysteries which I will come to much later, and which were taught to those to be initiated into the Christian faith by baptism.

A mystery in the religious, as opposed to the P. D. James sense, is not some truth that can be fully understood once the wit and cunning of our brains have fathomed it out. It is implicit in life itself, and above all in the mystery that is me. "Mysteries," it has been said, "are not truths that lie beyond us; they are truths that comprehend us." But which we do not comprehend. Let me name just some of them: timeless, daily human mysteries we can't escape. The mystery that you are uniquely you. One of you a boy called Adam, the other a girl called Anna. But there are thousands of other Adams and Annas. Your names are a convenience, a kind of shorthand, but they don't even begin to define the mysterious beings you are. Your body will utterly change before you are old enough to read my words, yet you will retain your own unique chemical mix, your own irreplaceable self, recognizably *you* until the day you die.

Then there is the mystery of your birth. We know the gynaecological facts. Scans can show us the embryo in the uterus, and over the months the developing eyes and limbs. But the mystery of how this sperm unites with that egg to produce the miracle which is you would be (were it not so familiar) mind-blowing. There is the mystery of the relationship between two persons: what the marriage service in the Prayer Book calls "the mystery of one flesh," a man and a woman who, through growing together by the daily unspoken giving and receiving of love in small ways, find that over the years each has been invaded and shaped by the reality of the other, in a way that does not diminish, but rather enhances, each of them. There is the mystery of love, then; and also those moments of human crisis that are in some way linked to our freedom: sickness, undeserved pain, accident, death, which leave us asking "why?"—and learning to expect no very satisfying answer. And there is the mystery of evil and how, by what is called redemption, its poison may be countered and even (most mysterious of all) good brought out of it.

But these are large and difficult questions; so I turn and look at the rather safer chaffinch that is at this moment perched on a rock outside my window. In Alastair Reid's poem he says that if I say the bird's generic name it may "fall headlong, struck skyless, into its pigeonhole" and that I need to see the mystery of this particular bird, its "growing, flying, happening . . ." as children do, when each new thing is *itself*, accepting what is given in this moment, wondering at its uniqueness and singularity. Yet what is this thing into which the chaffinch launches itself that I label "sky?" What is this mystery that is without form or substance, seemingly empty, yet which swarms with light? "How do you know," wrote William Blake, "but every bird that cuts the airy way is an immense world of delight clothed by your senses five?"[4] Perhaps even the chaffinch is not as safe as he seems.

All of which raises all kinds of questions about the nature of reality, about the nature of what I see. The twentieth century has seen a dangerous reductionism that seeks to reduce everything to certain material, mechanical principles. There are physicists who explain everything in terms of atoms obeying their own mechanical laws, biologists who explain life purely in terms of physics and chemistry, and doctors who appear to treat the body as a machine, parts of which need to be manipulated when they go wrong without much reference to the holistic entity each of us is. There are behaviourists who analyse my psyche purely in terms of mechanistic causality and neurochemistry, repressed appetites and desires; and biologists who claim that blind chance is the only origin of the fact that we are conscious, creative beings. The *reductio ad absurdum* of attempts to explain the higher in terms of the lower would be to describe a Mozart sonata in terms of technical expertise in the use of catgut and vibrations in the air. Not only does such an approach find no place for wonder, but it flies in the face of those aspects of ourselves that make us most authentically human.

The Head of Science at Westminster School spoke recently in Westminster Abbey about why he would call himself a religious man:

> It is because I find a description of the universe based solely on scientific terms unbelievable. I cannot believe that the original hot Big Bang contained all the necessary information to determine why I am now here talking to you. When I hear a moving piece of music, I cannot believe that my emotions can completely be described in terms of impulses sent to my brain from the hair cells on my basilar membrane.
>
> I cannot believe that the pleasure one gets when successful and the pain one gets when one is not, are solely explained by the release of endomorphins in my hypothalamus. I cannot believe that I know I am Peter Hughes purely because of some programming of a complex neural network associated with my hippocampus. That is why I need science and religion . . . firstly, something that I can believe in because it is seen to

work, and secondly, something I can believe in because it fits in with my experience.[5]

The mystics (and I use that word fairly loosely to encompass those who have sought seriously to contemplate the mystery of our existence, those who in every age and culture speak of encounters which for them touch on the very source of reality itself unite in believing that the world of matter, the world perceived by our five senses (which in themselves are always selective in what they see and hear) is only a partial aspect of reality. They claim that the material world is pervaded by, and finds its explanation in, a transcendent reality: that is to say, a reality that surpasses or goes beyond itself; that underlying all we are and know is (for want of better words) a Divine Ground. Until the sixteenth century this formed the basis for a universal philosophy among religious thinkers in the East and West often known as the Perennial Philosophy. The transcendent reality of which it spoke was known to the Chinese as the Tao, to Buddhists as the Void, to Hindus as the Brahman, to Muslims as the Reality; and to Christians as the Godhead or the Supreme Being.

A second belief commonly held in the mystical tradition was that we can only realize the Divine Ground by intuition, by the kind of creative, imaginative insight that is as valid and as central to any concept of being human as our other faculties; and that when we explore that which is beyond us we may sense a kind of unity between what we seek and our questing selves.

Let me put it like this. When I try to analyse who or what I am, I am conscious of experiencing two worlds: a visible material world outside me which I make mine by using my eyes and ears and hands and brain; and an invisible inner world which is utterly different and which consists of my thoughts and feelings. The question is: how are they connected and which one is the *real* world? Origen, one of the great Christian teachers of the second century, was in no doubt: "The real world is within." At this point I have to speak of "matter" and "spirit," even though each is mysterious; and to affirm that there is indeed in me a strong need to explore, to reach out to what is beyond me, to explore the world before my eyes and the world only accessible to the inner eye. I am challenged by the transcendent mystery beyond me, and I can only make sense of what I feel about myself and how my outer and inner world relate if for this mystery I use the word "God." For the present I am using "God" as a kind of shorthand for that which is beyond, transcendent in the sense that it surpasses the bounds of observable fact; it is different from and other than the visible world of people and things; it is that to which they (as well as I) would seem to point, and what must be true of me must be true of you and of everyone else.

Awareness of the transcendent is a large phrase for a simple fact. It is something a child may know intuitively. It is what those who belong to what we (rather patronizingly) call "primitive cultures" know in their bones. I know, then, with a conviction I can no more deny than fly, that in the depth of myself, in stillness, I am aware of the "other" that is not me and yet, paradoxically, is the very ground of my existence. And I believe that it is precisely this intuitive sense of the transcendent, the muffled presence of the holy, that makes me human.

The phrase I have just used "in the depth of myself," needs spelling out a little further. It is interesting how many of the illuminating discoveries of twentieth century psychology bear out the beliefs of so many spiritual teachers in both East and West that I am a kind of double person. I am conscious of my self in terms of my ego, that ego which is so demanding, so clamorous, that it can deceive me into thinking that it is all that I am. But (they would claim) this is not so, for there is another self, an inner, eternal self, my spirit, that spark of divinity which links me to the Divine Ground; and it is the purpose of my life to discover and identify myself with this true self, until outer and inner reality are one and I achieve an integrity whose marks will be an inner stillness, unity and peace of mind.

Few of us achieve such integrity. A man of 95 wrote the other day to a friend of mine:

> I have this imaginary "I" which feels no praise could be sufficient to meet the wonder that I am. And another which dismisses me as worthless because I have never lived up to my possibilities. I finish up, after all this egoism about my unimportance, in a daily gratitude to the Almighty for my wonderful life and the privilege of being allowed to live it out as if I had deserved it.

One of the greatest of the German mystics of the Middle Ages, Meister Eckhart, was a Dominican friar, a man greatly admired for his saintly life and his gifts as a scholar, preacher and director of souls, although (like so many people ahead of their time) he was to be accused of heresy. His great concern is with the union between the soul and God which rests upon the fact that we are created in God's likeness. He spoke of how it is necessary, if we are to be persons in the fullest sense, to become aware of "a transcendent abyss" within ourselves. He spoke of God as having an infinite capacity for giving, and each human soul having an infinite capacity for receiving. He wrote of how each one of us must discover "our own ground," our capacity, little by little, to detach ourselves from the all-demanding ego, and begin to reflect the divine purpose that lies at our very centre. That suggests that the deepest mystery about me is that I can find God in the depths of myself; and having begun to do so I am then enabled to find him everywhere

So I am a kind of double person on a double journey. The outer journey, the public one, has to do with the outer reality, with people and places and events, with what I do and achieve in my life. The inner, private journey has to do with a different kind of exploration, and it needs different words with which to describe it; words like faith (in the sense of trust) and wonder. Words which have to do with that giving attention that is the nerve centre of all religious belief, for it is as we exercise our faculty of wonder that we become aware of the beyond in our midst. D. H. Lawrence writes:

> The sense of wonder
> that is the sixth sense.
> And it is the natural religious sense.[6]

The most likely way in which my outer journey and my inner journey may conflict is in the confusion between what I do and what I am. A good example of how doing and being can get confused, and how important it is to match our private journey to our public journey, came for me a few years ago when I was ill for a tiresomely long time and later wrote a book about it. One of the critical moments in that illness was when a holistic doctor to whom I had gone for help questioned me on the stresses of my job as a very busy parish priest. Priests, rightly or wrongly but like many other professional people, often find themselves acting out a kind of role, either because we can feel unconfident without its protective cover, or because people's expectations demand it of us. "The trouble is," he said, "your inscape does not match your landscape" (my inner world and my outer world). He was using Jungian terms, but Eckhart would have understood. One of our most Godlike characteristics as transcendent beings is to learn how to be, for there is a still centre at the very deepest part of you where you are yourself without subtraction. But it is a sacred place, and sacred places are a little scary.

Because these letters are about what it means to be human, many of them will have to do with this idea of the transcendent: with the fact that I am conscious of an inner mystery that goes beyond me; with the transcendent reality to which I give the name God; and with the fact that I can transcend myself. I know that I may be formed from the dust of the earth and that my body will one day return to it, yet I am dust capable of a transcendent creativity, capable (to give the most common example) of transcending myself, going beyond myself, in the give-and-take of love. And, not least, I am surrounded by the witness of those in every age who have used the words and sounds and images that spring from the creative imagination. This too is mystery. Certain combinations of words, the way paint is placed on a canvas or notes on a score, have the power to move me because they speak of something beyond; they transcend time and space and, in some inexplicable way, heart speaks to heart.

George Steiner, for all his sometimes opaque and rhetorical style, has written a brilliantly perceptive book called *Real Presences*. He makes no claim to traditional Christian belief, but argues passionately that

> the wager on the meaning of meaning, on the potential of insight and response when one human voice addresses another, when we come face to face with the text and work of art or music, which is to say when we encounter the other in its con-

dition of freedom, is a *wager on transcendence.* . . . (For) where God's presence is no longer a tenable supposition and where his absence is no longer a felt, indeed overwhelming weight, certain dimensions of thought and creativity are no longer attainable.[7]

Steiner's whole essay proposes that "any coherent understanding of . . . the capacity of human speech to communicate meaning and feeling is, in the final analysis, underwritten by the assumption of God's presence."[8] He goes on to argue his "wager on transcendence," on "otherness," by demonstrating how in art or music or literature there is a freedom of giving and receiving, a space in which giver and receiver are themselves transcended, and which makes the creative experience the guarantor of our proper human stature.

[Yet] we flinch from the immediate pressures of mystery in . . . aesthetic acts of creation as we do from the realization of our diminished humanity. . . . Like sleep-walkers, we are guarded by the numbing drone of the journalistic . . . from the often harsh, imperious radiance of sheer presence.[9]

So much of what I want to share with you in succeeding letters could be summed up by saying: to ask "What is art?", "What is poetry?", "What is music?" is one way of asking, "What is a human being?" For I believe the mystery of what I am and what you are has to do before all else with our capacity to create, and be possessed by, such things. It is a sharing in the creative act that is no less than God-like, and that, too, is a source of wonder.

III

The Transfigured Commonplace[1]

[I believe] there is nothing more needed by humanity today ... than the recovery of a sense of "beyond-ness" in the whole of life to revive the springs of wonder and adoration.

JOHN V. TAYLOR[2]

My fiftieth year had come and gone,
And I sat, a solitary man,
In a crowded London shop,
An open book and empty cup
On the marble table-top.

While on the shop and street I gazed
My body of a sudden blazed;
And twenty minutes more or less
It seemed, so great my happiness,
That I was blessèd and could bless.

W. B. YEATS[3]

A certain minor light may still
Leap incandescent
Out of kitchen table or chair
As if a celestial burning took
Possession of the most obtuse objects now and then——
Thus hallowing an interval
Otherwise inconsequent
By bestowing largesse, honour,
One might say love.

SYLVIA PLATH[4]

THE SNOW MELTED AWAY overnight, and yesterday I deserted you and walked high in the Alpine pastures. Everywhere you turn in this place seems to be uphill. It's hard work climbing through forests of pine and larch, but when you emerge onto flower-strewn slopes the view of the mountains is more than worth it. These letters feel to me a bit like that, for I fear there's some early climbing still to do, and that I cannot say "Come and see the view" without a good bit of foot-slogging first.

My last letter was about the mystery, the "beyond" in our midst, the experience I have—when I give attention to the world before my eyes or to the work of creative artists—of what I can only call the transcendent.

Most people know something of this. It seems to be part of the gut feeling of being human to experience a sense of yearning, even of loss, a restless, seeking spirit which can feel like a kind of homesickness. There are times when we ache for that which will fulfill and complete us; a longing, it may be, for the lost state of innocence, the Eden of our childhood, or for a future when all questions are answered and we are home at last. This sense of a lost freedom "hammers at the far threshold of the human psyche" (Steiner again). "We are creatures at once vexed and consoled by the summons of a freedom just out of reach."[5] Certainly in the presence of beauty we may have a sense both of delight and longing.

At its simplest (though nothing about it is simple) it is a feeling that there is a "something more" that transcends the everyday world of sights and sounds and surface chatter. Philip Toynbee, whose questing exploration of Christianity is recorded in the diary he kept in the last years of his life, writes:

> The notion that what we happen to apprehend directly with our five senses is all the reality there is now seems to me to be almost grotesquely parochial. And this conviction is the bedrock of whatever religious faith I have: there must be more than this.[6]

In what proved a seminal book, *The Idea of the Holy*, Rudolph Otto first used the word "numinous" to describe the "otherness" of religious experience. He also coined a somewhat grandiose phrase for this "otherness": he called it *mysterium tremendum et fascinans*, by which he meant something wholly other than man (mysterium), something awesome and overpowering (tremendum), and something which draws and fascinates us in spite of ourselves (fascinans). He was describing the utter transcendence of God, but in using the word "numinous" of our experience of that "other," from the Latin verb *nuo*, "I nod" in recognition or command, he was suggesting that in some mysterious sense we are approached by this presence, invited to pay attention, to notice. We are invited, as it were, momentarily to step outside the taken-for-granted reality of everyday life.

Bishop John Taylor, who has explored this area in three
of his books with great sensitivity and insight, writes of how

> the mountain or the tree I am looking at ceases to be merely
> an object I am observing and becomes a subject, existing in its
> own life, and saying something to me—one could almost say
> nodding to me . . . The truly numinous experience is not
> marked only by primitive awe in the face of the unknown or
> the overwhelming, but occurs also when something as ordi-
> nary as a sleeping child, as simple and objective as a flower,
> suddenly command attention . . . I am face to face with the
> truth of it, not merely the truth about it.[7]

It would seem that not only am I capable of being open to mystery, but the mystery appears to have given us some tiny element of its own essential nature so that we can speak both of
our need to search and of a sense of being met. In the words of
the poet Rilke, "everything beckons to us to perceive it."[8]

Now I am not about to take off into some mystical flight
of fancy. On the contrary. What I am speaking of could not be
more common in the experience of earthbound (though not
"ordinary," no-one is that) people like us. It would seem—and
the evidence is overwhelming—that many, perhaps most, people have experiences of the transcendent, numinous experiences
which may or may not be recognized by those concerned as authentically religious. Some are quite commonplace, others more
striking. Sometimes these moments are so unexpected and revealing that people remember them all their lives: moments of
transcendence which John Taylor calls "annunciations," and
which usually take the form of a brief heightened perception
of reality. He writes:

Experiences of God are experiences of the ordinary seen in the context of an otherness which enfolds them all and lies within them all. . . . The secularization of the human outlook may have banished the supernatural from the day-to-day conversations and calculations of millions of people, but that is no reason for supposing that the beyondness at the heart of things discloses itself any less widely or frequently.[9]

P. J. Kavanagh, poet and novelist, describes in his book *People and Places* a number of experiences that followed the early death of his first wife, Sally.

What I saw and understood was oddly familiar, as though I was remembering something I already knew . . . (It was as if) the experience *rapped on my windows and drew my attention.* . . . It came unsolicited, involuntarily, and went away when it wanted to, leaving behind a residue in which it was impossible not to believe.

It is best described . . . in terms of colours. I was invited to the country for a few days, and stood on a little bridge in Gloucestershire . . . (and I was) suddenly astounded by the variety of greens that unfolded themselves in front of me, layer upon layer, tone upon tone. On top of the extraordinary spring vitality of the sight before me, and contained in it, was a certainty of benevolence, which was there to be co-operated with or not, as I chose. . . . *It was all wholly innocent and good.*

Nor was it only when confronted by a fortunate landscape that this sense of an innate and mysterious tenderness arrived. (Later in London) I was halted by the sight of an advertisement-hoarding. Successive posters had partly peeled off, they were faded, rain-stained, wind-tattered. It was entirely beautiful, and *gave the impression of waiting for this to be noticed.* [My italics throughout.][10]

Kavanagh writes that he has had no such experience since that time, but that it was wholly and undeniably good, a glimpse of something within yet outside him, a briefly revealed reality, and he draws attention to a passage in Coleridge's *Notebooks* in which the poet describes how, when looking at nature while he is thinking, he seems rather to be "seeking, as it were asking, a symbolical language for something within me that already and for ever exists, than observing anything new."

Strangely, Sally Kavanagh's mother, the novelist Rosamond Lehmann, had a similar experience of transfigured reality when she was deep in her grief. She was staying with friends when she became aware of the piercing beauty of a bird's song. She goes to the window and

> beheld a visionary world. Everything around, above, below me was shimmering and vibrating. The tree foliage, the strip of lawn, the flowerbeds—all had become incandescent. I seemed to be looking through the surface of all things into the manifold iridescent rays which, I can now see, composed the substances of all things ...

Later in the day, driving with friends, the experience continues:

> ... Hills, woods, groves, clouds, cornfields, streams and meadows—all were moving and inter-relating ... as if in the ineffable rhythm and pattern of a cosmic dance. I was outside, watching the animating, moulding, eternal principle at work, at play, in the natural world; and at the same time I seemed to be inside it, united with and partaking in its creativity.[11]

Some years ago the biologist, Alister Hardy, one-time Professor of Zoology at Oxford, founded a Religious Experience Research Unit (now the Alister Hardy Research Centre). He invited "all who have been conscious of, and perhaps influenced by, some power, whether they call it the power of God or not, to write a simple and brief account of these feelings and their effects." The Research Centre now has five thousand accounts collected over twenty years. Most people are shy of speaking of such things. Not only are they deeply personal but they fear they may be ridiculed or thought a bit odd. It was not surprising that people found it difficult to put words to experiences that belong neither wholly to the objective world of fact, nor wholly to the subjective world of feeling. What was interesting was the consistency of the experience of the sense of a numinous reality. In the 1970s and 1980s David Hay undertook further surveys for the Research Centre and in a nationwide poll, in answer to the question, "Have you ever been conscious of a presence or power other than your everyday self?" thirty-three per cent of the people asked said they had. In a survey of a hundred and seventy people in one city, where there was a detailed follow-up questionnaire the figure rose to sixty-two per cent, and similar research in the United States produced similar results.

Of course it is easy to make figures prove almost anything, and to dismiss such experiences as "all in the mind" (whatever that may mean), yet the body of evidence that this is a valid and central human experience is remarkably impressive. The American philosopher, William James (brother of Henry), lecturing in Edinburgh at the turn of the century, coined the phrase "religious experience" and later wrote the classic book on its varieties. Perhaps it is better to call them transcendent experiences, for they have to do with a different order of knowing and are often "religious" only in the broadest sense of that word. James speaks of four elements that are characteristic of such experiences: there is about them something ineffable (we have not the right language adequately to describe them); they convey a sense of a different order of knowing; the experience is short-lived; and they come whatever the person may be doing. (A friend in Suffolk once told me of an old lady who claimed she was joined one day by Jesus who took a dishcloth and helped her with the washing-up. "What do you think it means?" he asked her. There was a long, brooding silence. "I think," she said eventually, "it means it's going to rain.")

Two common features of such recorded experiences are that time seems to be temporarily suspended (or transcended) and that you are in harmony with the whole creation. You lose your sense of self, you are united with a greater whole. The two commonest triggers for such times of heightened perception are nature (most take place out of doors) and music; and (like Patrick Kavanagh) almost all those questioned felt the experience to be life-affirming and good. Like Julian of Norwich, the medieval anchoress who had a series of mystical "visions" of Christ which resulted in her deep conviction that, despite much that was painful and destructive in her life, in the end "all shall be well, and all shall be well, and all manner of thing shall be well," many who write of their experience use very similar words to describe something that is positive and strengthening.

What the Alister Hardy Research Centre confirms is that there is nothing unusual about these heightened moments when our sense of the numinous is overwhelming.

> He never saw again what he saw that morning, [writes Tolstoy] the children on their way to school; the silvery-grey pigeons that flew from the roofs to the pavement; the little loaves of bread some invisible hand had put out, all seemed to him divine.[12]

> There are moments [Philip Toynbee writes in his journal] when the outer world is seen with an almost pristine wonder

. . . Sudden brilliance of the chestnut tree across the road. Bright yellow leaves in the sun. How enlivening, enspiriting they are—those unexpected shafts which strike into the heart from the outside world.[13]

How shall I find the words to describe to you, my dear Timothy [writes Victor Gollancz in his autobiographical *Letters to his grandson*] what I felt in my year of wonder? I had a heightened perception of everything, and everything was perceived as beautiful and good. But it was more than a perception; it was a meeting, for which I had gone out to the other and for which the other had gone out to me. . . . The meeting (which was not in time but in eternity) was with the greenness, the freshness, the littleness . . . the sun accepting-ness, of the benign and far-reaching grass. With the trees in their various stages, and with every branch and every twig and every leaf of them . . . And with people. I would sit, going up to London, in a crowded railway-compartment, and know myself as in every one of my fellow-travellers, and know every one of them as in me. . . . (One day) I was standing on an escalator at Paddington. Just behind me a little girl of six or seven was looking round us and up; and (on her face was) such a glow of enchantment at the wonder of things that I went on my way as if from watching the dawn, or looking at crocuses in grass, or hearing a melody by Haydn.[14]

One morning, when I was well over sixty [writes Mark Rutherford], I was in a wood and something happened which was nothing less than a transformation of myself and the world. All my life I had been a lover of the country, and I had believed that the same thought, spirit, life, God which was in everything I beheld was also in me. But my creed had been taken from books. . . . I was looking at a great, spreading, bursting oak. The first tinge from the greenish-yellow buds was just visible. It seemed to be no longer a tree apart from me. The enclosing barriers of consciousness were removed and the text came to my mind, *Thou in me and I in thee*. . . . The distinction between self and not-self was an illusion . . . I do not argue. I cannot explain. It will be easy to prove me absurd, but nothing can shake me.[15]

My first hearing of Bach's great Toccata and Fugue in D Minor [writes the scientist, J. W. N. Sullivan] may prove to have been the cardinal experience of my life. . . . I experienced, quite literally, a revelation. All great art is . . . the record of a spiritual achievement . . . that cannot be conveyed in any other terms. . . . Never satisfactorily rationalized, nor ever communicated to others. It is also an experience that cannot be denied. No account of life that denies its supreme importance can be even remotely true. In this . . . however much it may seem to conflict with my liking for clear reasoning based on very viable premises, I am quite unshakeable. I have heard, and I know.[16]

The high-walled garden of Daniel's Cottage [writes Rosemary Sutcliff in her autobiography] was flickering in the coloured flame points of crocuses, white and purple and lilac and gold; each crocus opening to the sunlight seemed to me at once a star and a grail; a cup brimming with light. It is one of the Mysteries, surely, this sense of light shining *through* rather than on; the whole world becomes faintly translucent and the light of the spirit shining through its substance, that comes with being in love. One has it as a child, but in childhood one knows nothing else and so is not conscious of it, till the heightened awareness is given back for this one time.[17]

Proust's illuminations, in his massive *À la Recherche du Temps Perdu*, are always involuntary, a gift from the gods, sudden apprehensions of reality in the midst of illusion. Towards the end of the book Proust's narrator steps on an uneven paving stone and experiences an intense joy which takes away all his anxiety and fear of death. Proust sees this moment as set free from the order of time. The poet Elizabeth Jennings writes of such a Proustian moment:

It wasn't a moment. It
Was not possessed by time. Just now a shaft
Of broad sun shone and set
All Rome before me caught in memory's net.
I wish I knew the craft

Of Proustian moments when
Five senses link and smell is what we see,
Light is heard. Again
Touch could strike lightnings in that April rain
And Rome was palpably

About me, all the great
Churches and ruins rose in the broad-sweet air.
How do we open the gate
To this? We cannot, we can only wait
Until again we hear

Nostalgic powers making us surrender
All but attention and an ancient wonder.[18]

Not all such moments of heightened perception have to
do with the natural or artistic world. The Trappist monk,
Thomas Merton, is among those for whom such a moment altered his perception of people:

> In Louisville, at the corner of Fourth and Walnut, I was sud-
> denly overwhelmed with the realization that I loved all these
> people, that they were mine and I theirs. . . . It was like waking
> from a dream of separateness . . . to take your place as a mem-
> ber of the human race. I had the immense joy of being man, a
> member of the race in which God himself became incarnate.
> If only everybody could realize this. But it cannot be ex-
> plained. There is no way of telling people that they are all
> walking round shining like the sun.[19]

But what do such "annunciations" mean? Wordsworth
knows this country. He speaks of

. . . objects recognized
in flashes, and with glory not their own.[20]

As a child he had seen the mountains, lakes and meadows around him "apparelled in celestial light," and had to cling to a tree as a reminder that material things are not visions; and he used the phrase "surprised by joy" which C. S. Lewis then took as the title for his autobiography. In an earlier essay Lewis had spoken about such Wordsworthian moments with some guardedness, believing them to be but the purveyors of a beauty we cannot fully grasp and not the thing itself: "They are only the scent of a flower we have not found, the echo of a tune we have not heard, news from a country we have never yet visited. . . . We remain conscious of a desire which no natural happiness will satisfy."[21] He describes that sense (which may come from music or a landscape glimpsed in a certain light) of belonging to a world just beyond our reach, like a message we have overheard. For him, "joy," as distinct from pleasure, must have "the stab, the pang, the inconsolable longing," and in his description of such moments (as a child in a garden by a flowering currant bush on a summer's day, as a young man walking in winter on a lonely hillside) he comes to understand that they were about desire, yet not a desire to possess but rather to be possessed. The yearning is not just for glimpsed beauty or for joy itself: the yearning (he comes to see) is for the Other (and for Lewis it is very clearly with a capital O). Such experiences only make sense because

we have, so to speak, a root in the Absolute, which is the utter Reality. And that is why we experience Joy: we yearn for that unity which we can never reach except by ceasing to be the separate phenomenal being called "we." . . . These experiences . . . were the pointer to something outer and other.[22]

What such beguiling and unshakeable experiences suggest is a kind of momentary lifting of the veil between a seen and an unseen world, sudden moments of illumination which are gratuitous and unsought for, when things seem transfigured. But they are glimpses of a destination that we shall never know fully until we reach it. The poet Ruth Pitter describes her life-long aim: "To capture and to express some of the secret meanings that haunt life and language ... the silent music ... the hints of echoes and messages of which everything is full."[23] So she can write of one such moment:

> All was as it had ever been—
> the worn familiar book
> the oak behind the hawthorn seen,
> the misty woodlands look:
>
> The starling perched upon the tree
> with his long tress of straw—
> when suddenly heaven blazed on me,
> and suddenly I saw:
>
> saw all as it would ever be,
> in bliss too great to tell;
> for ever safe, for ever free,
> all bright with miracle.[24]

Let me sum up what most would recognize to be the characteristics of these rare, life-changing moments of seeing or hearing things with heightened perception. They seem to have a rightness and inevitability about them; they feel like an experience of reality, though of a different order from what we normally perceive; there is a sense of communion: for a moment you feel you are one with what you see or hear; they appear to transcend time as we know it (and sometimes place as well) and have a universality about them; and they leave you with a joyful sense that ultimately "all is well." There may also be in them what some have felt bound to describe as a sense of recognition. That might be because the experience is linked with memory traces of the experience of childhood, that time when we observe each object with a pristine sense of delight: if so, the two experiences may come together to produce something new and full of wonder. They almost always happen when a person is alone, and they come when they come and cannot be created.

In 1954 Aldous Huxley experimented with the drug mescaline, as others had before him, and wrote an entertaining book as a result called *The Doors of Perception.* "[I saw] Eternity in a flower," he wrote, "infinity in four chair legs and the Absolute in a pair of flannel trousers. Mescaline is the most extraordinary and significant experience available to human beings this side of the Beatific Vision."[25] W. B. Yeats once tried the same drug and became fascinated by an advertisement for Bovril on the Thames Embankment. He beheld gorgeous dragons "puffing out their breath in front of them in lines of steam on which white balls were balanced." Such hallucinogenic drugs may, in Steiner's phrase, "crack the crust of walled self-sufficiency," but they are dangerous as a way towards inner experience. The experience may come as a revelation in terms of how we perceive reality, or how it is possible to be at one with the universe, exploring the wonder of a leaf or a tabletop. "The user of drugs feels liberated to perceive the world more nearly as artists, mystics and primitive people perceive it," writes Donald Allchin, "the world is more alive, more personal, more resonant with unity, more terrifying, full of variety, of complexity, an astonishing surprise."[26] The language of doing gives way to the language of being.

Yeats's "gorgeous dragons" were harmless, but "here lie

dragons" and dangerous ones at that. The psychological reorientation after taking drugs can be extremely frightening and, over a period, destructive of the human psyche. And spirituality means growing into the kind of being God has created you to be. It is not simply a matter of widening our consciousness of reality (which drugs may do) but of coming to a more profound and rich awareness of things; not an altered consciousness but a new attitude to life, and a growth in love because you have learned how to see with new eyes.

You may be wondering why I have laid such stress on what at best might come to each of us a handful of times in a lifetime. (Few people could claim Victor Gollancz's whole year of wonder). It is because I believe such experiences are among the most valid insights we have into our transcendence: like Sullivan listening to Bach or Rutherford standing aghast before his great elm-tree: "I have heard and I know; I cannot explain . . . but nothing will shake me." And because such moments are authentic we must, as it were, keep faith with what we have seen when (however briefly), there has been a lifting of the veil at the horizon of the known.

> Joy [writes Rilke] is a moment, unobligated, timeless from the beginning, not to be held but also not to be truly lost again, since under its impact our being is changed chemically, so to speak, and does not only, as may be the case with happiness, savour and enjoy itself in a new mixture.[27]

Have I known such utterly convincing moments? Yes, a few. There was such a moment some forty years ago, when swimming in a translucent sea off the Dalmatian coast; another twenty years later high on a hill on a summer night in Iona; a third in the stillness of a Romanesque church in Burgundy.

These are moments that remain as vivid in my mind as on the day I first felt them. But there are few people whose lives have not been touched by joy—and I mean joy, not simply happiness. Like others, I have sometimes scented an intimation of the holy and wondered at it in the theatre or the concert hall, or standing before certain pictures. A little earlier I spoke of the almost "beckoning" nature of the numinous and the transcendent, a feeling that I am being invited—though in the gentlest, most reticent of ways—to respond. This is especially true of what George Steiner calls the "chemical bonding" between a work of art, a poem, a piece of music and ourselves, gradually, "perhaps unconsciously, of being possessed by that which we come to possess."[28] Mysteriously, it feels almost as if we had met before, as if words or notes placed just so answer something in me I have always known.

Like others, too, I have known the intoxicating joy of finding myself loved and loving in return, when suddenly the whole horizon tips, and your perception of the world takes on a different hue. But, you may protest, being moved deeply or being in love is surely not the kind of visitation you have been describing; how can you bracket an experience that is so common and everyday with that which seems extraordinary? If you do feel that, maybe you're right and maybe you're not: either way, it has grown dark and that question must wait for tomorrow.

* * *

And there I left it, and later last night I picked up John Fowles's novel, *Daniel Martin*, and read a scene in which the newly-married Daniel, with his wife Jane, her sister Nell, and her husband Anthony, all of them freshly down from Oxford, are visiting Italy. Daniel is an atheist, Anthony a Roman

Catholic. After a day visiting the exquisite Etruscan tombs at Tarquinia, they go for a swim towards midnight in a sea full of phosphorescence. Up to their necks in water, they form a ring, take each other's hands and begin to circle gently.

Perhaps the beautiful tomb-walls somewhere inland behind the beach; perhaps the fact that the holiday was near its end; no, something deeper than that, a mysterious union, and strangely uncarnal, in spite of our naked bodies. I have had very few religious moments in my life. The profound difference between Anthony and myself—and our types of mankind—is that I did for a few moments there feel unaccountably happy; yet I could see that for him, the supposedly religious man, this was no more than a faintly embarrassing midnight jape. Or I can put it like this: he saw me as the brother-in-law he liked, I saw him as the brother I loved. It was a moment that had both an infinity and an evanescence— an intense closeness, yet no more durable than the tiny shimmering organisms in the water around us.

I tried repeatedly in later years to put those moments into my plays—and always had to cut them out. It took me time to discover that even atheists need a sense of blasphemy.[29]

IV

The Given and the Glimpsed

We had the experience but missed the meaning.

T. S. ELIOT[1]

To be religious is to know that the facts of the world are not
the end of the matter.

LUDWIG WITTGENSTEIN[2]

Not everything has a name. Some things lead us into the realm
beyond words. . . . It is like that small mirror in the fairy-
tales—glance in it and what you see is not yourself; for an instant you glimpse the Inaccessible, where no horse or magic
carpet can take you. And the soul cries out for it.

ALEXANDER SOLZHENITSYN[3]

Rationalists, wearing square hats,
Think, in square rooms,
Looking at the floor,
Looking at the ceiling.
They confine themselves
To right-angled triangles.
If they tried rhomboids,
Cones, waving lines, ellipses—
As, for example, the ellipse of the half-moon—
Rationalists would wear sombreros.

WALLACE STEVENS[4]

I AM DISTRACTED BY A woodpecker, a greater spotted by
the sound of the short and spasmodic drilling coming from
the larches below my windows. Though I keep a pair of
binoculars on the table he continues to elude me.

Last night I was writing about those key moments that
are like epiphanies, and I imagined you questioning whether
by including such a common experience as falling in love I
wasn't beginning to shift the goal-posts. Here are a couple of
passages from two recent novels by A. N. Wilson and Susan
Hill.

The hero of Wilson's novel has fallen in love, deeply, for
the first time.

> Loving Ann transfigured existence, it changed everything. I
> found all bodily sensations were quickened.... My apprecia-
> tion of the way things looked was so profoundly enhanced
> that I felt in many respects that I had only begun to "see" since
> knowing her. Sometimes... when I cycled into Soho, I would
> find myself dismounting and staring with wonder at quite or-
> dinary sights, a tree, a bird on a window-ledge, sunlight on a

building which I had seen a thousand times but suddenly saw
for the first time.... (Now) I was seeing through the eye, seeing into the life of things, so that act of vision became a Vision,
and morning bike-rides an occasion for alleluias.[5]

The reference to seeing through the eye is to William
Blake, mystic, prophet, poet and painter, who wrote:

> We are led to believe a Lie
> when we see with, not thro' the Eye.[6]

In Susan Hill's novel, the hero is somewhat older, a celi-
bate, middle-aged don who, on the brink of being elected Master of his college, sees and falls deeply in love with a much
younger girl, Kitty. They go for a day by the sea. Suddenly, as
they walk on the beach,

> all of his past, the old interests and concern, dropped quite
> away from him, and his old self was sloughed off, like the skin.
> And looking about him, he saw the world re-created, all things
> were strange but new, brave and infinitely rare and beautiful
> to his eyes. He looked at sea and sky, at the stone beneath his
> feet, and the shimmer on the far horizon, and the bird bal-
> anced on the post ahead, and he had never seen their like be-
> fore, all were miraculously new to him.[7]

My point is that this kind of heightened perception, while
there may be for some certain highly dramatic, knock-down
moments (Kavanagh, Gollancz, Pitter), is not only commoner
than we might suppose (the Research Centre's evidence) but
also far more ordinary, if any such experience can be so
termed—and part of the purpose of these letters is to try to
persuade you that it can't I suspect that the American novelist
and theologian, Frederick Buechner, is right in thinking that

for the man in the street, any street, wherever his religion is a matter of more than custom, it is likely to be because, however dimly, a doorway opened in the air once to him too, a word was spoken and, however shakily, he responded. . . . We have seen more than we let on, even to ourselves. Through some moment of beauty or pain, some sudden turning of our lives, through some horror on the news, some dream . . . we catch glimmers at least of what the saints are blinded by.[8]

Yes, beauty and pain, for in every life, as Blake wrote,

> Man was made for Joy and Woe,
> And when this we rightly know,
> Thro' the World we safely go.
> Joy and Woe are woven fine,
> A clothing for the soul divine.[9]

There are in every life, except perhaps in the most severely diminished by disability or circumstance, days when we cannot avoid the transcendent and mysterious. The most obvious have to do with birth and falling in love, illness and death. These times may be at once deeply spiritual and deeply carnal experiences, putting us in touch with levels of experience that we sense but may find it difficult to describe. To hold your newborn child in your arms for the first time is something wholly different from awaiting its arrival and imagining what it will look like. To see a living creature emerge with ears and fingernails, and a palm engraved with the lines he or she will carry to the grave, and to know that without you this tiny human being who is unlike any other who has ever been born, with a unique personality and a unique destiny, simply would not be, must be a cause for wonder.

As is falling in love, especially when that leads to a deep and lifelong commitment; and to give yourself without reserve to that particular mystery is to trust that you are able to be lifted out of the narrowness of self in the give-and-take of love, and in so transcending yourself become more, not less, what you truly are.

But the key moments of our lives are not all happy ones: they are often moments of darkness and confusion. Inevitably as a priest I have had a lot to do with people facing darkness and pain of different kinds: sickness, or the loss of work, or the death of one who means more to them than life itself. At those points of crisis it is hard to escape questions about what a human being is and what hidden depths lie within us, and I have been amazed and humbled by the inner resources of courage and self-sacrifice human beings can call upon at such times. People have not been taught to think of their response to crisis or their coping with pain or—and this is the most significant gift—their natural compassion, as a mark of their God-likeness, but insofar as they enlarge our potential to give our loving attention to others, then they are precisely that; and there are innumerable ordinary experiences which have the quality of transcendence because they have taken us beyond our own egoistic selves.

Not so many today watch with people as they die, and that is a loss, for nothing can make you so aware of the mystery of life than to be present when a person, in an instant, becomes a thing. Like the moment of birth, you cannot properly imagine it in advance. What is still (however deeply unconscious) an embodied spirit at one moment is at the next something quite other: a corpse from which not only the breath but also the mystery has gone.

In Christopher Fry's play *The Dark Is Light Enough*, an Austrian Countess is arguing a deserter's case with a Colonel of the Hungarian army, and he speaks of respecting "the facts."

She answers:

> Facts? Bones, Colonel.
> The skeleton I've seen dangling in the School of Anatomy
> Is made of facts. But any one of the students
> Makes the skeleton look like a perfect stranger.[10]

Such experiences, which are the stuff of every human life, may also be the stuff of transcendent wonder for those who have eyes to see.

I believe, too, that most of us are moved by the beauty of the natural world. We consciously respond to that which is greater than ourselves yet a part of us, part of the kaleidoscope of colour and light and form that has pressed upon our senses from the day of our birth but which most of the time we take for granted. Epiphanies, if we did but know it, lie like unopened gifts at every turn of the road and every stage of our journey, for it is in and through the daily events and the given world that what is hidden may be sought and found. What is mysterious and ineffable may be discovered, or at any rate glimpsed, as much in the common as in the magnificent. "What is 'common' about the common life?" asks Mr. Sammler in Saul Bellow's novel, *Mr. Sammler's Planet*. "What if some genius were to do with 'common life' what Einstein did with matter? Finding its energies, uncovering its radiance."[11]

These small epiphanies may not have the momentously breath-taking power of those experiences I wrote about earlier, but they suggest that neither we nor the world we inhabit are as straightforward as we may think.

"The only justification I shall ever find for exploring my past life," wrote Philip Toynbee in his *Journal*, "is to find moments, episodes, annunciations which can be made to blaze

with the light of some universal truth and meaning. . . ." And
he lists a number of such moments, both of crisis and delight.
"Such moments of joy and horror are not just episodes in my
life but openings into the light and darkness everyone else has
seen."[12] But you have to pay attention: you have to learn how
to see if you are not to miss the meaning. It is all too easy to be
blind to the mystery and what it may be indicating about the
kind of world in which we live and the kind of people we are,
and the importance of keeping faith with whatever insights may
have been ours.

Franz Kafka, whose work centres on his portrayal of acute
suffering, once wrote some surprising words:

> You do not need to leave your room (to find enlightenment).
> Remain sitting at your table and listen. . . . Do not even listen,
> simply wait. . . . The world will freely offer itself to you to be
> unmasked; it has no choice, it will roll in ecstasy at your feet.[13]

When I read that, part of me nods in agreement (how
could I not, sitting at this window, looking at such an idyllic
scene?), yet part of me knows that such words must sound absurd to those for whom the world appears far from benign,
those whom life takes by the scruff of the neck and shakes until
their teeth rattle. And I am well aware that I have been making
a case and using words (transcendence, annunciations, mystery,
heightened perception) that may seem more at home in a pulpit
or a university lecture room than in the flats of the Peabody
Estate round the corner from the Abbey, or on the council estate that I was serving when your mother was born.

The point I am making in these two letters is that this is
not so. An Archbishop of Paris, fifty years ago, said that it was
the pastor's job "to keep the mystery of God present to man,"

that is, to point to the mystery, the transcendent reality, that other dimension that pervades all living things. It is a concern that people may become persons in the fullest sense, and so live their lives (to quote the Archbishop again) "that (it and they) would be inexplicable if God did not exist."[14] That has got to mean working with the raw material each of us is given, the stuff of daily experience, and (whatever our given circumstances may be) helping one another to build on whatever glimpses we may have had of the reality of God at the heart of our own lives. For almost certainly those glimpses will be authentic, if unrecognized, experiences of the transcendent reality in which our lives are rooted.

Frederick Buechner puts it much better than I can:

> There is no event so common-place but that God is present within it, always hiddenly, always leaving you room to recognize him or not to recognize him. . . . If I were called upon to state in a few words the essence of everything I was trying to say both as a novelist and as a preacher, it would be something like this: Listen to your life. See it for the fathomless mystery that it is. In the boredom and pain of it no less than in the excitement and gladness: touch, taste, smell your way to the heavenly and hidden heart of it because in the last analysis all moments are key moments, and life itself is grace.[15]

V

The Otherness and
the Nearness of God

Who, surveying the whole scheme of things, is so childish as
not to believe that there is divinity in everything, clothed in it,
embracing it, residing in it? For everything that is depends on
Him-who-is.

GREGORY OF NYSSA [1]

I find you, Lord, in all Things and in all
my fellow creatures, pulsing with your life;
as a tiny seed you sleep in what is small
and in the vast you vastly yield yourself

The wondrous game that power plays with Things
is to move in such submission through the world:
groping in roots and growing thick in trunks
and in treetops like a rising from the dead.

RAINER MARIA RILKE [2]

I learned, I learned, when one might be inclined
to think, too late, you cannot recover your losses—
I learned something of the nature of God's mind,
not the abstract Creator but he who caresses
the daily and nightly earth; he who refuses
to take failure for an answer till again and again is worn.

PATRICK KAVANAGH [3]

In our anguish we struggle
To elude Him, to lie to Him, yet His love observes
His appalling promise; His predilection
As we wander and weep is with us to the end.
Minding our meanings, our least matter dear to Him.

W. H. AUDEN [4]

25 May

THE WOODPECKER IS AT it again, and I have pinned him down to one of two trees, and every time I'm stuck for words I gaze in his direction; but still he eludes me.

All I have written so far has arisen from the mystery that is me, sitting at a desk looking onto a world that, on a morning such as this, ravishes the senses. What I have said implies certain assumptions about the nature of God as well as the nature of the world, so let me now tell you that I understand of these mysteries.

First, God, who seems easy; for he is at first sight quite simply indescribable. However much you twist the a and b and c of it, how can there be words to express the unknowable? But that leaves me with a paradox, for I am conscious at the heart of me of a Presence which at moments is more real to me than anything else, and to which I give the name "God." I cannot know God as I can know other things or other people. Yet it is desperately important to speak about God as truly and as accurately as possible for, as Archbishop William Temple said, "If you have a false idea of God, then the more religious you are the worse it is for you, and it were better . . . to be an atheist."[5]

Isaac Bashevis Singer, the Jewish novelist, used a good metaphor for where we stand in relation to God:

> It is as if you were to ask a bookworm crawling inside a copy of War and Peace whether it is a good novel or a bad one. He is sitting on one little letter trying to get nourishment. How can he be a critic of Tolstoy?[6]

Here, then, is the paradox. "God is of no importance unless he is of supreme importance" (Heschel), and for many he is simply given, as self-evident as light, without whom nothing could exist. Kart Rahner speaks of religion as "presence to the transcendent mystery . . . at the very heart of our existence," and it is his transcendence that makes God utterly "other" than ourselves, unlike anything we can name or experience. This idea of the transcendence of God is not uniquely Christian; it is shared by Muslims and Jews, who have a profound sense of God's "otherness." I cannot stress enough the importance of grasping this idea of "otherness," for the wonder we may come to feel when the other face of the coin is revealed is in direct proportion to our sense of awe at the One who is the very ground of everything that exists and holds it (holds me) in being at every instant in the continuing act of creation.

God is a hidden God, and again and again in the records of the Jewish people that form the Old Testament it is said that you cannot see God. "And the Lord said to Moses, 'My face you cannot see, for no mortal may see me and live.'" That is their way of stressing that he is transcendent mystery. Yet it is the discovery of God that emerged from the experience of the people of ancient Israel that is a landmark in religious understanding. Not only is there one God, and not a multiplicity of deities—an unheard of novelty at the time—but he is encountered in personal terms as a God who speaks to his creatures and makes of them certain ethical demands. God may be transcendent but he is not wholly inaccessible.

Here, then, is the breakthrough: the beginning of an understanding that, while God may be utterly "other" and transcend every human concept and analogy, yet by transcendence we do not mean *spatial separation*, we mean *difference*. God is not unknowable because he is "out there," wherever "there" may be. God's unknowability, his transcendence, is the *otherness* of Creator from creature, but he is a God whose creation is imbued at every point with signs of his presence. In other words, I can only encounter the Creator within his creation; but I can only do that because I am made in his likeness and there is that which is of God within the mystery that is me. St. Augustine, whose search for God is movingly told in his *Confessions*, tells how he ranged far and wide, questioning all the objects of the natural world who would say to him: "I am not He, but He made me. . . ." Finally he comes to find God within himself. "Too late have I loved Thee, O Thou beauty of ancient days, yet ever new! Too late have I loved Thee! And behold, Thou wert within, and I abroad. Thou wert with me, but I was not with Thee."[7] Again, in his *City of God*, he writes:

> God shall be so known and conspicuous unto us, that he may
> be seen by the spirit of every one of us, in every one of us; may
> be seen in one another . . . and in every creature . . . whither-
> soever the eyes of the spiritual body shall be directed.[8]

Commenting on these words a century ago, Bishop Ullathorne wrote:

> Let it be understood that we cannot turn to God unless we
> first enter into ourselves.... God is everywhere but not every-
> where to us; and there is one point in the universe where God
> connects with us and that is the centre of our own soul. There
> he waits for us: there he meets us. To see him we enter our
> own interior.[9]

Religious writers and mystics of different traditions down
the centuries have juggled with ideas of God and how he may
be found. All are agreed that he is a reticent, even diffident sort
of God who invites, never imposes; who leaves hints of his presence, never miraculous signs; such is the nature of our freedom
and his love. Julian of Norwich describes God as "utterly kind
and unassuming"; and the American novelist John Updike in
his autobiography writes:

> Like the inner of two bonded strips in a thermostat, the self
> curls against Him and presses. The need for "I" to have its
> "Thou," something other than ourselves yet sharing our sub-
> jectivity ... survives all embarrassment, all silences ... The sen-
> sation of silence cannot be helped; a loud and evident God
> would be a bully, an insecure tyrant ... instead of, as He is, a
> bottomless encouragement to our faltering and frightened
> being.[10]

Many in their praying and writing have followed two ways
in speaking of God: a negative and an affirmative way. The first
stresses his seeming absence, the second his presence: the first
darkness, the second light. The "negative" way, which has its origin in the Eastern Church, believes that God is so unknowable
that he is best defined in terms of negatives: "What dost thou
prate of God?" writes Meister Eckhart. "Whatever thou sayest
of Him is untrue"; and St. Bernard asks: "What is God? I can
think of no better answer than He who is." The two ways, neg-

ative and affirmative, are not opposed but the attempt to hold together complementary truths (and never fall for the "either/or" merchants: truth almost always means holding together both this *and* that). Yet even writers like Eckhart who so stress God's transcendence face us with the paradoxical truth that there is within each one of us a kind of "transcendent abyss" where God is present, and Eckhart can write of "the Ground of the Soul, the True Image of God in man."

I warned you we were in for some steep climbs, and once again the trees are pretty dense and the view patchy, for it is as impossible to capture in words exactly what is meant by the *immanence* of God as it is to express his transcendence. Immanence is what I meant by saying that we can only encounter God through the world and within ourselves, that it is in God that all that exists "lives and moves and has its being." That is not to say in any sense that God equals nature. It is not pantheism. Wordsworth's pantheism, claimed William Blake, gave him a severe stomach ache. But if God is not to be identified with nature then neither (as one of the greatest Christian writers, Irenaeus, insisted in the second century) may he be removed from it. He is the condition and ground of all that exists, expressed in, but not limited by, the natural world. The belief that everything is in God and that he can be sensed within all that is means that the Being of God includes and penetrates the universe, but that God is infinitely more than the creation and is not exhausted by it. What that also means is that any attempt to think of God simply in terms of religion (as opposed to life), or solely to identify that part of me I call "religious" with God, is nonsense. God loves matter. He created it: it is his language. To divide the holy from the common is a totally false distinction once you understand that everything is a sign of the presence of the God

... who caresses
the daily and nightly earth[11]

if only we have eyes to see.

This is, in part at least, the kind of God in whom I believe. One who is the core of my being and of all being, closer to me than I can conceive. Either that is true or I do not believe in God at all. In the breeze that is stirring my papers at this moment; in that teasingly elusive woodpecker; in the mountains thick with snow ("the peaks of the mountains are his also" I say each day at Morning Prayer); in the ant that has just scurried across my page ("He can hear the footfall of an ant" wrote the Hindu teacher, Ramakrishna, and when I once gave a sermon that title the local press, famous for its misprints, changed the second "f" in footfall to a "b"); in the immense sky full of fleecy clouds; in every person I have ever encountered and in me: God is the source of their being and all things point to him by their unique and particular presence.

Yet not everything is created in God's likeness in the sense that you and I are: we alone are self-conscious, aware of moments of transcendence, drawn to explore and celebrate the mystery of our being. We alone are potentially co-creators with God. We alone can choose to open ourselves to that intimate union between our most secret, hidden selves and the spirit of God.

I said that Jews and Muslims and Christians were at one in sharing a profound sense of the transcendence of God. The God who is the ultimate reality in which all we experience is grounded; the one glimpsed in all that is beautiful, true and good. There is a further truth. It is that God can (as it were) transcend himself, that he can so identify himself with his creation as to *give himself away*. What is uniquely Christian is not simply the belief that God meets us in personal encounter, but the belief that this hidden, reticent God was once revealed in the only language we can understand: in human language and in a human life. It is the belief that Jesus, alone of all our race, looked full at the transcendent mystery and said his name was Father.

But that is another story.

VI

The Creation as Sacramental:
The Holy in the Common

ANNE DE VERCORS: Did you mean this world? Or is there another?

VIOLAINE: There are two of them and I tell you there is only one of them and it is enough.

PAUL CLAUDEL[1]

There is another world, but it is in this one.

PAUL ELUARD[2]

It is not outside, it is inside; wholly within.

MEISTER ECKHART[3]

I am constantly aware that there is another reality which interpenetrates our own. "Turn but a stone and start a wing."

PHILIP TOYNBEE[4]

Love all God's creation, the whole of it and every grain of sand in it. Love every leaf, every ray of God's light. Love the animals, love the plants, love everything. If you love everything, you will perceive the divine mystery in things.

FYODOR DOSTOEVSKY[5]

... Word traced in water of lakes, and light on water,
Light on still water, moving water, waterfall
And water colours of cloud, of dew, of spectral rain,

Word inscribed on stone, mountain range upon range of stone,
Word that is fire of the sun and fire within
Order of atoms, crystalline symmetry,

Grammar of five-fold rose and six-fold lily,
Spiral of leaves on a bough, helix of shells,
Rotation of twining plants on axes of darkness and light,

Instinctive wisdom of fish and lion and ram,
Rhythm of generation in flagellate and fern,
Flash of fin, beat of wing, heartbeat, beat of the dance,

Hieroglyph in whose exact precision is defined
Feather and insect-wing, refraction of multiple eyes,
Eyes of the creatures, oh myriadfold vision of the world,

Statement of mystery, how shall we name
A spirit clothed in the world, a world made man?

KATHLEEN RAINE[6]

They ran in that resonance which is the world itself and
which cannot be spoken but only praised.

CORMAC MCCARTHY[7]

26 May

TODAY THE COWS, STABLED far down in the valley during the winter months, have come up to the Alpine pastures. They fall on the sweet new grass with what passes in cows for enthusiasm, and indeed it must be like smoked salmon and caviar after the long, boring months of eating hay. Each wears its individual bell, and their gently jangling music links with the sound of the distant waterfalls and streams.

"God likes matter," it has been said, "he invented it." Matter: rock, water, wood, grass, birds, corn, grapes, cells. Not only does God like it, but he clothes himself in it. It is one of his languages. When I spoke about the mystery which is me writing to the mysteries which are you I wrote about our ability to transcend ourselves because we are embodied spirits (or ensouled bodies): not physical cages in which canaries sit waiting for their eventual release, but mysterious, irreplaceable entities capable of acts of courage, creativity or unselfish love. These are spiritual qualities, yet we are only able to express ourselves or

relate to other people through our physical bodies and our
sense of sight and hearing, touch and taste and smell. I went
on to spell out what it could mean for us to experience the transcendent in our daily lives, whether or not we think of it as
such—not simply in terms of transcending ourselves, but in
experiences of the "numinous," not least of the God who is beyond our rational understanding and yet within our hearts; and
by my "heart" I mean that which lies at my centre, that which
best expresses me as I truly am.

If it is true that we must find God within the only world
we have (how else?), then this link I know in myself between
"matter" and "spirit," the holy and the common, must be true of
all that is created. Certainly those who wrote the books of the
Old Testament believed this to be so: they speak of God blessing everything he creates, making all creation the sign of his
presence. If spirituality means the way we grow into the kind
of being we are intended to be, then the starting point is not a
striving after another world, but a deepening awareness of the
true nature of this world and our place within it. For by and
large our sense of the perception of things has withered away:
what remains is mere recognition. "The habit of ignoring Nature is deeply implanted in our times," wrote the painter Marc
Chagall. "This attitude reminds me of people who never look
you in the eye. I find them disturbing and always have to look
away."[8]

Gerard Manley Hopkins writes that ours is a world

>...charged with the grandeur of God,
>It will flame out like shining from shook foil[9]

and Isaiah writes that: "the whole earth is full of his glory."[10]
William Law, perhaps the greatest of the English post-Refor-

mation mystics, writes:

> All that is sweet, delightful and amiable in this world, in the
> serenity of the air, the fineness of seasons, the joy of light, the
> melody of sounds, the beauty of colours, the fragrancy of
> smells . . . is nothing else but heaven breaking through the veil
> of this world, manifesting itself in such a degree and darting
> forth in such variety so much of its own nature.[11]

Ours is a world that is unimaginably more than the ordered
mass of atoms and molecules obeying the rules of their separate
fields. For it is a world in which matter is capable of being the
bearer of spirit—which is what people mean when they use yet
another of those tricky words that need unpacking and talk of
a "sacramental" universe. The word "sacramentum" began to be
used in the Latin West about the third century, the equivalent
of the Greek word "mysterium." While the latter spoke of a hidden or veiled reality, discovered by means of initiation, "sacramentum" was a term applied to any action or object which was
believed to mirror the Divine.

To talk of a sacramental world is not to appeal to magic,
but to describe another aspect of the mystery. For material objects, the world of bodies and things, the only world we know,
are the raw material for what gives life meaning. Spirit can only
speak through matter. When I was born my physical body became the vehicle of the spiritual being I know myself to be, and
what is true of a person is true of the world about us.

Quite ordinary material things have the potential to convey truths which carry for us the most value and the deepest
significance. The small band of gold I placed on your grandmother's finger in Southwark Cathedral all those years ago is a
comparatively trivial thing in itself, yet its meaning for us is
powerful. Many people don't fully grasp the language of sym-

bols and sacraments, yet they live as if they did. When people kiss or even shake hands, when they write a letter or give each other presents, when they create a work of art, they are giving value to material things by using them to express what are essentially spiritual, non-physical truths, bearers (if you like) of ourselves, our presences.

All I have tried to say so far about mystery and transcendence stems from my deep belief that the whole world is sacramental and the whole creation marked with the signature of its Creator, and that the only way to find the holy is in the ordinary; that the ordinary is far more extraordinary than we think. At the heart of all great art and all creative science lies this assumption, and there is nothing material that does not have both significance and value. What I aim to do in the rest of my letters is to call witnesses to this truth: not people who are professionally religious and might be expected to press such a case, but those most perceptive of people, creative artists. One who combines the role of priest and poet, R. S. Thomas, puts it like this:

> We are beginning to see
> now it is matter is the scaffolding
> of spirit; that the poet emerges
> from morphemes and phonemes: that
> as form in sculpture is the prisoner
> of the hard rock, so in everyday life
> it is the plain facts and natural happenings
> that conceal God and reveal him to us
> little by little under the mind's tooling.[12]

"Don't brood too much," wrote Margaret Schlegel to her sister Helen in E. M. Forster's *Howard's End*. "Don't brood too much on the superiority of the unseen to the seen ... our business is not to contrast the two but to reconcile them."[13] The world of the senses is meaningless unless such a reconciliation has been made. I believe a Christian understanding of God and the sacramental nature of the world makes it, beautifully and incomparably (as I hope eventually to show you), but that it is to artists above all that we must look for their showing of how "matter is the scaffolding of spirit," and how (as T. S. Eliot wrote in "The Rock")

Out of the formless stone, when the artist unites himself with stone,
Spring always new forms of life, from the soul of man that is joined to the
    soul of stone . . .
Out of the sea of sound the life of music.[14]

And this is so because we are a certain kind of being, made in the likeness of the Creator, and because this is a certain kind of world: a visible sacrament of the invisible, a place where God is to be known and loved in and through all he has made, and where those things are to be known and loved in him. In another of Christopher Fry's plays, *The Firstborn*, a play about Moses preparing to lead the Israelites into the wilderness, Aaron says:

> Is it not possible to be plain men,
> Dealing with a plain situation? Must we see
> Visions?

Moses answers:

> Shall we live in mystery and yet
> Conduct ourselves as though everything were known?
> If, in battle upon the sea, we fought
> As though on land, we should be more embroiled
> With water than the enemy. Are we on sea?
> Or land, would you say?

Sea? Land? [says Aaron] for pity's sake
Stay with reality.

To which Moses replies:

If I can penetrate
So far.[15]

Artists are those who look at reality as if for the first time
and try to see it with eyes which see beyond the surface appear-
ance: with, you might say, sacramental eyes, finding wonder in
a world full of mystery. Edwin Muir, one of this century's finest
poets, was a man who more than most understood this kind of
double vision, of seeing the holy in the ordinary, sensing how
matter is the vehicle of spirit. He can write

That was the real world: I have touched it once,
And now shall know it always.[16]

His body lies in the churchyard at Swaffham Bulbeck
near Cambridge and on his gravestone are the words chosen
by himself

. . . his unblinded eyes
Saw far and near
The fields of Paradise.

There is a sense in which children, who live on what is
given anew at every moment, have this kind of vision too. As
do those whose religious experience we condescendingly call
"primitive," for there has been a loss in the religious journey
from primitive man to ourselves. A loss of intensity, of contact

with the world of nature, a loss above all of a numinous awareness of the sacramental that is everywhere about us. Last year
we explored those parts of New Mexico which form part of the
Navajo Indian reservations. In Monument Valley, site of the
finest of the John Ford Westerns, we visited a hogan, one of the
small round dwellings in which a Navajo family lives, a fire in
the centre of the floor, the door always facing east to frame the
rising sun, so that you may always live properly oriented to the
world of nature. In the ceiling there is a smoke-hole, the only
other source of light. The Navajo's concern is to live always
"within the sacred," and for them not only the smallest moments of life are sacred—there are no past or future tenses in
their language, only the present tense, so that both past and future are simply "present-not-here"—but the smallest stones of
the earth are sacred too.

A Navajo will recreate the world afresh every morning.
Billy Yellow, a Navajo medicine man for whom Monument Valley is the centre of the world, chants the world into being daily,
just as he believes his Ancestors did in the very first hogan. His
aim is to "grow old in 'hozho,'" which means "beauty," and he
chants the world into being by chanting the beauty,

> speaking to the holy people every day who are everywhere and
> in everything. . . . Many times there is a need to make a door
> between the two parts of the world, inner and outer, for unless
> you think there is no word; unless you speak there is no world;
> unless you move there is no life. Walk in beauty outside and
> you walk in beauty inside.[17]

"Hozho" really means more than simply "beauty." It refers to
the total environment (ho) that includes beauty, harmony, happiness and everything that is positive.

There are strong similarities here with other tribal religious beliefs, like those of the Aboriginal "Dreamtime," about which Bruce Chatwin wrote in his book Songlines. The Aborigines also believe in the two aspects of the world, the physical world in which they live and another, linked world from which it is derived. This other world is the Dreamtime, and for them it is utterly real, for not only does it describe the period when the original Ancestors created the world by singing it into being, with its birds and animals and rocks and plants and rivers, but it is parallel to the everyday world of now. It is a kind of quantum physics concept of the simultaneous nature of different kinds of time. Past, present, and future fuse together. The stories the Ancestors sang *are* the land itself, and modern Aborigines walk what Europeans call the Songlines and Aborigines call the Footsteps of the Ancestors, and sing the songs and so (like Billy Yellow in Monument Valley) play their part in the continuing creation. The songs are not composed afresh; they come from the Ancestors and are handed down through the generations, "the cosmic rhythms and melodies that give the everyday world its form."

In the beginning was the Song: it is a concept as poetic and full of mystery as the story of creation in Genesis, or St. John's affirmation: "In the beginning was the Word."

> I have a vision of the Songlines stretching across the continents and ages, [writes Bruce Chatwin] that wherever men have trodden they have left a trail of song (of which we may, now and then, catch an echo); and that these trails must reach back, in time and space, to an isolated pocket in the African savannah, where the First Man opening his mouth in defiance of the terrors that surrounded him, shouted the opening stanza of the World Song, "I AM!"[18]

I think of Caedmon, who died in 680 and who is memorialized in Poets' Corner in the Abbey as the first known poet of Anglo-Saxon England. He was a cowherd in the employ of the Abbess Hilda of Whitby, and one night he had a dream in which he was commanded to sing. He replied that he was poor and useless and that singing was not in his line. "Sing!" he was told, and when he asked what he should sing he was told to sing of those things he knew instinctively: he was to sing of the glories of creation.

Certain things are central to this tribal way of seeing the created world: first, its unity, the sense of a mysterious interrelatedness of all that is, for all are one, rocks and trees and beasts, the living and the dead, all are here and all are now. Then there is a sense that, although the world is a sacred place and full of wonder, it gives a feeling of intimacy, of being a home. You belong, even though the world that can be seen and touched is not as real as the world you are taught to "see" through the rituals and ceremonies, and the oral traditions of myth and folklore.

> The African Bushman [writes Laurens van der Post] had none of that dreadful sense of not belonging, of isolation, of meaninglessness which so devastates the heart of modern man. Wherever he went he felt that he belonged and . . . that he was known.[19]

In such cultures there is nothing that can be called non-religious, no arbitrary division into "holy" and "common," and the land especially, in all its life and variety, is seen as sacred, and each living thing has its own identity and proper place and way of being which must be honoured.

The value of all religious belief, primitive or developed, is that it confirms our intuitive knowledge that the world is given us, that it is sacred and that we must come to terms with its mystery. The Christian belief that it is sacramental, "charged with the grandeur of God" who has made it the sign of his presence, together with some of those insights lost to us but preserved by certain native cultures, could not be more relevant at a time when we are despoiling nature and dangerously polluting our environment: the seas choked with our garbage, the rain forests burning, the ozone layer being depleted at rates that constantly need updating. Some have hunted animals to the point of extinction. We do not lack inventiveness, but we lack restraint; and we have lost the sense of respect for the earth, *and of wonder*. When twenty-five years ago I looked at your mother asleep in her cot I remember worrying about the possibility of nuclear war; today I look at you and tremble at what kind of creation we are leaving you. Please God I am as wrong about the second as I have been so far about the first, and that we shall find some way of meeting the debt we owe to our fragile and wonderful creation, but that will only be so as we come to celebrate, rather than exploit, this amazing earth.

In 1854 Chief Seattle, the Indian chief after whom the city of Seattle is named, delivered a speech to an assembly of tribes preparing to sign away their lands under duress to the white man. "What is man without the beasts?" he asked. "If all the beasts were gone, man would die from a great loneliness of spirit. For whatever happens to the beasts, soon happens to man. All things are connected." He spoke of the white man ravaging the land:

> He treats his mother, the earth, and his brother, the sky, as things to be bought, plundered, sold like sheep or dried beads. His appetite will devour the earth and leave behind only a desert.[20]

St. Francis would have understood that.

Angela Tilby, in *Science and the Soul*, the book she wrote to accompany her television series on "new cosmology, the self and God," writes:

> It is from the moon that we have the astonishing photographs of our living planet, suspended like a blue marble in space. These pictures have become modern icons. They speak to us of the fragile beauty of our existence, of the loneliness and uniqueness of our island planet and the miracle that we are here at all.... If the sight of our island home moves us to religious awe and gratitude, then this is a proper and appropriate response.[21]

To believe in a sacramental world is to believe that spirit speaks through matter, that God penetrates his creation and may be found within it.

> The only news I know, [writes Emily Dickinson]
> Is bulletins all day
> From immortality;
>
> The only shows I see
> Tomorrow and today.
> Perchance eternity.
>
> The only one I meet
> Is God, the only street
> Existence; this traversed
>
> If other news there be
> Or admirabler show,
> I'll tell it you.[22]

Lest you think this account of things is a looking at the world through Christian-tinted glasses, let me end with the strong testimony of someone who does not believe in the

Christian God, but writes with deep insight into what it means to be human: Iris Murdoch. Indeed, her book on metaphysics, though rather more demanding, is almost as diverting as her novels. She pleads that the concept of the holy and the transcendent should not be lost and that we are bound to give true and loving attention to the world. She replaces the traditional concept of God with Plato's concept of the reality of Good. For her this is an essentially religious notion, the actual "objective existence" of the Form of the Good, and she writes:

> The good man perceives the real world, a true and just seeing of people and human institutions, which is also a seeing of the invisible through the visible, the real through the apparent, the spiritual beyond the material.[23]

There remains the question, for those who do believe in God, whether he is to be trusted, and to ask in what other ways we can come to know him. For to say "God" is to say "good," to speak of one who affirms and is concerned for his creation. We live in a tension between the mystery of the transcendent, unknown God and what Angela Tilby calls "the generous enchantment that allures us through the natural world." We need to know whether we can walk through this world as those who, in some amazing way, are not only "fearfully and wonderfully made," but also loved.

But that too, tantalizingly, is another story.

VII

The Meaning of Wonder

Wonder——is not precisely Knowing
And not precisely Knowing not——
A beautiful but bleak condition
He has not lived who has not felt . . .

EMILY DICKINSON[1]

We need nothing but open eyes to be ravished like the
Cherubims.

THOMAS TRAHERNE[2]

I have learned from long experience that there is nothing that
is not marvellous and that the saying of Aristotle is true——that
in every natural phenomenon there is something wonderful,
nay, in truth, many wonders. We are born and placed among
wonders and surrounded by them, so that to whatever object
the eye first turns, the same is wonderful and full of wonders,
if only we would examine it for a while.

JOHN DE DONDIS[3]

The basic command of religion is not "do this!" or "do not do
that!" but simply "look!"

PHILIP TOYNBEE[4]

Belov'd and faithful, teach my soul to wake
In glades deep-ranked with flowers that gleam and
shake,
And flock your paths with wonder . . .

SIEGFRIED SASSOON[5]

I SAID AT THE START that my subject is wonder and I keep on using the word, but I have not yet defined it. Like all words, slippery, imprecise things that they are, it has taken on a variety of subtly different meanings, as a rock attracts lichen. "I wonder . . ." we say, meaning "I am not sure" or "could it be. . . ?"; Churchill could speak of "the boneless wonder" sitting opposite him on the Treasury bench in the House of Commons; and we debase the coinage by passing off a casual "how wonderful" without a second thought as to what we are really saying. But I am using it in the good old Anglo-Saxon sense of the word "wunder," which you find about the year 725 in Beowulf and which means . . . well, that will emerge.

When W. H. Auden gave his Inaugural Lecture[6] in Oxford in 1956 as the new Professor of Poetry he distinguished between what he called Primary and Secondary Imagination. By Primary Imagination he meant that within us which has contact with the sacred in the widest possible sense of that word, and which creates in us the sense of awe and a need to respond. But a need to respond to what? At this stage there is simply the unspecific and intuitive awareness of what might be called the sublime. The function of what Auden calls our Secondary Imagination is to give form to this awareness, to incarnate it, to give it flesh and intelligible form in words and images, in music, shape or colour. The ways in which human minds have responded have inevitably been as diverse as the individual people we are.

Although the underlying themes of my first six letters have been this sense of mystery, of the sublime, of awe and of wonder, let me explore a bit more carefully what these words mean. The mystery is that the created world exists. It is: I am. The mystery is life itself, together with the fact that however much we seek to explore and to penetrate them, the impenetrable shadows remain. Part of the mystery lies in what I have called my transcendence, the fact that I can rise above or go out of myself and feel a sense of awe at what is beyond and other than me, that I can recognize the grandeur of the natural world with its own special and mysterious kind of beauty. This is to have a sense of the sublime, and it is a theme expressed captivatingly in many of the Psalms, and memorably in the book of Job where God commands Job to face the awe-inspiring and startling variety and subtlety of his creation. And they do so in poetry, for that best expresses the voice of wonder.

Goethe reckoned awe to be the highest thing in us and thought we should be content to feel awe in face of the phenomena of the natural world, for that is the limit of our sight. But he knew that for many this is not enough: "they insist on going further like children who peep in a mirror and then turn it round to see what is on the other side." Of course! Wordsworth writes of

> . . . a sense sublime
> Of something far more deeply interfused,
> Whose dwelling is the light of setting suns,
> And the round ocean and the living air,
> And the blue sky, and in the mind of man;
> Emotion and a spirit that impels
> All thinking things, all objects of all thought
> And rolls through all things.[7]

For him, everything in nature speaks of its Original to one who listens

> . . . in the power, the faith,
> Of a baptized imagination.[8]

Yet what is sublime is not related to size: it may be sensed in a pebble on the beach, a flower, a drop of water. So William Blake, who believed that imagination, rather than reason, is the essential part of the intellect, writes of how it is possible

> To see a World in a Grain of Sand,
> And a Heaven in a Wild Flower,
> Hold Infinity in the palm of your hand,
> and Eternity in an hour . . .[9]

and when he does so he is using Auden's Secondary Imagination to set forth a truth that the heart knows but that rational argument can only stammer at. And in Saint-Exupéry's *The Little Prince*, the Little Prince says:

"The men where you live cultivate five thousand roses in one garden—and they do not find what they seek!" "That is true," I said. "And yet what they are seeking may be found in a single rose or a drop of water." "So it can," I answered. And the Little Prince went on: "But the eyes are blind: one must look with the heart."[10]

A sense of the sublime leads to a sense of awe, which is I suppose that combination of wonder and fearfulness you may feel in the presence of what takes your breath away. It is not feeling afraid in the sense of feeling scared, but rather an awe-struck kind of amazement that "the ordinary is rather more extraordinary than the extraordinary . . . it is not the rabbit out of the hat but the rabbit out of the rabbit that is so surprising."[11] "A mouse," said Walt Whitman, "is enough to stagger sextillions of infidels."

> Awe [writes Abraham Heschel] is a way of being in rapport with the mystery of reality. The awe that we sense or ought to sense in the presence of a human being is a moment of intuition for the likeness of God which is concealed in his essence. . . . (It) is an intuition for the creaturely dignity of all things and their preciousness to God; (it is) a sense for the transcendence, for the reference everywhere to Him who is beyond all things . . . (and) it enables us to perceive in the world intimations of the divine.[12]

And awe goes hand-in-hand with wonder. A radical amazement not just at what I see; not just that I see at all, but that I am a wondering being. There are memorials in the Abbey to two of the greatest of the creative scientists, Michael Faraday and Isaac Newton. Faraday wrote:

> Let us consider . . . how wonderfully we stand upon this world. Here it is that we are born, bred and live, and yet we view these things with an almost entire absence of wonder. . . .[13]

and Newton, towards the end of his life, could liken himself to a child who has merely picked up a few pretty shells on an ocean beach. Which brings to mind some words from a poem by Richard Wilbur:

> . . . all that we do
> Is touched with ocean, yet we remain
> On the shore of what we know.[14]

Angela Tilby in her research for *Science and the Soul* found that few of today's scientists who work in particle physics and cosmology give the impression they are dealing with dead, inert matter, but rather that they are viewing with surprise and excitement "a universe that is a place of awe and wonder, and astonishing beauty." David Schramm, a professor in the University of Chicago, told her that whether he was looking at the universe as a whole or at the behaviour of the most elusive sub-atomic particle "there is the same urgency and elegance, a marvellous combination of order and spontaneity."[15]

> For the past eighty years [wrote the cellist Pablo Casals at the age of ninety-three] I have started each day in the same manner . . . I go to the piano, and I play two preludes and fugues of Bach. . . . It is a sort of benediction on the house. But that is not its only meaning. . . . It is a rediscovery of the world in which I have the joy of being a part. It fills me with awareness of the wonder of life, with a feeling of the incredible marvel of being human.[16]

It is when we take things for granted, or get lured by the grasping, manipulating processes of the world, that we lose this sense of wonder and become indifferent to even the most familiar things that lie before our eyes waiting (as it were) to be noticed and affirmed. "There is but one sin," wrote G. K. Chesterton, "to call the green leaf grey." "I have spoken of things which I have not understood," says Job to God when his eyes have been opened, "things too wonderful for me to know." There has always been in Judaism a strong sense of wonder and thanksgiving, and today a practising Jew will thank God three times a day "for Thy miracles which are daily with us, and for Thy continual marvels . . ."; and there exists in the Hebrew prayer book a richly-varied sequence of blessings to be used on every conceivable occasion, everything from seeing trees blossoming for the first time in the year to seeing deformed persons ("Blessed art thou, O Lord our God, King of the universe, who variest the forms of thy creatures").

Now of course I cannot force myself into some permanent state of wonder. How I see the world depends on a hundred different things: on the sort of person I am, my upbringing, my environment, my relationships, the mood I am in, whether the sun is shining or the rain pouring down, whether I have had a good night or a sleepless one, and how life is treating me. What I can do, though it may take a lifetime, is to train myself to see, to notice, to give due attention to what is before my eyes. I can come to understand that there is no object (and certainly no person) not worthy of wonder, and that what makes them so is that each in its or his or her essence is (a) unique; (b) unlikely (are giraffes and flamingoes *likely*? Is a hummingbird? Or Mozart?); (c) "other"; and (d) not mastered, that is to say, not capable of being fully understood, docketed and explained. Again, it is the child's approach to the world that we lose, not because we have resolved its mystery but because we have grown accustomed to its face.

What are the kind of triggers that can open our "doors of Perception," as Blake calls our eyes? Auden had no doubt that the one who best goes on to flesh out our "Primary" awareness is the artist, for it is by the framing of a moment in a painting or a poem, by intensifying our awareness of the shape of things or their colour, or the effect of light on them, or their particularity, that an artist may arouse our wonder.

Just as the native religions have guarded truths about our relationship with the creation that our more cerebral faiths have neglected or forgotten, so the experience of living in a new culture can cause a shift of understanding of the nature both of what is real and what is of value. Barry Lopez tells in his book *Arctic Dreams* of the four years he spent travelling in the Arctic Circle. He sets on the title page words of N. Scott Momaday:

> Once in his life a person ought to concentrate his mind upon the remembered earth. He ought to give himself up to a particular landscape . . . to look at it from as many angles as he can, to wonder upon it . . . to imagine he touches it with his hands at every season and listens to the sounds that are made upon it.[17]

Lopez became obsessed, haunted with the beauty of the Arctic landscape. "I had the same quickness of heart and very intense feelings that human beings have when they fall in love." The book is a kind of poetic reflection on how we see our planet and the mystery of the natural world. He writes of the loss of "the native eye," of the polar bears and the great whales and their "power to elevate human life"; of the mystery of the migration of the snow-geese and their ability to detect electromagnetic fields or to use sound echoes or differences of air pressure as guides; of the awesome nature of the great pale blue and mint-green icebergs, "so beautiful they made you afraid." He comes one evening upon a horned lark sitting on a nest. "She stared back at me resolute as iron." Beside her, golden plovers abandoned their nests, revealing eggs that glowed with a soft, pure light

like the window light of a Vermeer painting. I marvelled at
this intense and concentrated beauty. . . . I took to bowing on
these evening walks, bowing slightly towards the birds. . . .
What, I wondered, had compelled me to do so? . . . I bowed
before the simple evidence of this moment in my life in a tangible place on the earth that was beautiful.[18]

A third common trigger that can open our eyes is suddenly to find yourself in a situation where there is no guarantee
that you have long to live. A young man wrote this prayer from
the battlefield in 1914:

> To have given me self-consciousness for an hour in a world so
> breathless with beauty would have been enough. But thou hast
> preserved it within me for twenty years now and more, thou
> hast crowned it with the joy of this summer of summers. And
> so, come what may, whether life or death, and if death,
> whether bliss unimaginable or nothingness, I thank thee and
> bless thy name.

Not long after he was killed in the trenches.

Ivor Gurney, musician and poet, who also knew the hor-
rors of trench warfare and who spent the last fifteen years of
his life in an asylum, wrote:

> What things I have missed today, I know very well,
> But the seeing of them each new time is miracle.
> Nothing between Bredon and Dursley has
> Any day yesterday's precise unpraised grace.
> The changed light, or curve changed mistily,
> Coppice, now bold cut, yesterday's mystery.
> A sense of mornings, once see, for ever gone,
> Its own for ever: alive, dead, and my possession.[19]

Others, told they have only a short time to live, discover

a quality in the space left to them that previously has passed them by. The knowledge that you are soon to lose the sights and sounds of the world wonderfully concentrates the mind. It was William Blake who said that "the tree which moves some to tears of joy is in the eyes of others only a green thing which stands in the way."[20] Philip Toynbee knew for the last year or two of his life that he had an inoperable cancer. These entries from his *Journals* movingly make my point.

> *12 November 1977* For years all visual beauty has been tangled up with nostalgia. "Tears at the heart of things": poignancy: carried back by a tree to some half-memory of a childhood tree, so freshly seen so long ago. . . . But (today), on this walk, I stopped several times and looked at a single tree as I hadn't done for years. No; as I have never done in my life before. The tree was there and now, in its own immediate and peculiar right: that tree and no other. And I was acutely here and now as I stared at it, unhampered by past or future: freed from the corruption of the ever-intrusive ME. Intense happiness.

> *19 November 1977* Tree-scrutiny . . . I stand apart and look; looking I respect, almost to the point of love. But what I hope to be loving is God; not because he "made" the tree but because he gives me the power to see it with such intensity and clarity.

> *3 December 1977* Walking today, and tree-gazing, I thought with real horror of trying to write about one of these well-studied trees. Why? Because any attempt to describe it would at once prejudice, betray, the tree's superb and individual reality. Words would generalize the tree; decorate it yet blur it.

> *9 March 1978* A bare apple tree in the bright wind. How graceless, that rising and straining; all elbows; a tree that seems to be trying to push itself up against a crushing weight of air. Yet it is as good for scrutiny as the most elegantly sweeping beech. Not beauty but entity is the thing.

> *25 October 1978* St. Luke's Summer. Trees have the power to

startle me more and more.

10 July 1979 I have never seen such elderflowers as these. But that may be because I have paid so little attention to the trees until that surprising walk in the winter of 1977 when I seemed to be looking at a tree for the first time.[21]

Two months before he died, he writes from his sickbed:

Suddenly through the window that I constantly stare through from my bed I see the beautiful pale trunks of beeches faintly shining in the evening sun. How could I have never noticed them before? And what joy they give, even in the middle of these bloody stomach cramps.[22]

A month before he died he writes:

Wet leaves of may and sycamore after a heavy shower, and the sun glittering on them as the wind shakes them. Such things I now look at with renewed intensity and happiness—not because I may not see them for much longer, but because they are of immediate significance: almost direct manifestations of heavenly light.[23]

Remember Abraham Heschel's words in his old age: "I did not ask for success: I asked for wonder." And wonder is giving (and calling) attention to the world in order to praise it.

VIII

The Wonder of You

Men go abroad to wonder at the height of mountains, at the huge waves of the sea, at the long courses of the rivers, at the vast compass of the ocean, at the circular motion of the stars; and they pass by themselves without wondering.

ST. AUGUSTINE[1]

A Stranger here
Strange things doth meet. Strange Treasures log'd in this fair
World appear.
Strange all, and New to me.
But that they mine should be, who nothing was,
That Strangest is of all, yet brough to pass.

THOMAS TRAHERNE[2]

In the absence of any other proof, the thumb alone would convince me of God's existence.

ISAAC NEWTON[3]

How should tasting hearing seeing
breathing any—lifted from the no
of all nothing—human merely being
doubt unimaginable You?

(now the ears of my ears awake and
now the eyes of my eyes are opened)

e. e. cummings[4]

L AST YEAR I HAD to have my portrait painted. Most Deans of Westminster have done so since the first Dean in 1560, although housing all the portraits is tricky and a number end up in unlikely places. It's an eye-opening experience, not least because you come to understand the extraordinary nature of a portrait painter's task: to capture not simply the physical identity of the sitter but his spirit, the inmost essence that makes me *me* and which is expressed (such is our mystery) through the body, through hands and face, through the expression in the eyes and the tilt of the head. And, though the painter has the expertise of his technique and a gift of caring contemplation, he must achieve this with such very ordinary things: sable-haired brushes, powdered earth and linseed oil, and a stretched white canvas.

I have talked about the mystery of me as an embodied spirit or an ensouled body. The words don't matter: what matters is that this being I call "me" is here, now, with my own unique window on the world of which (so it feels) I am the centre. But the wonder does not simply lie in my consciousness of myself, but in the miracle that is this living, breathing body.

I think about the two of you. Each of you began as a cell, following the fertilization of a single egg. Perhaps that cell is the one most astonishing thing on earth. It has the power to divide again and again, so that by the time you are adult your bodies will contain something like fifty trillion different cells, each one programmed to play its own part in keeping you alive and healthy. The cell itself is a kind of sphere with a thin outer membrane containing a smaller denser sphere, the nucleus, suspended in a jelly-like substance. What the electron microscope has done is to show us the extraordinarily high level of organization of cell-life, that when cells are replaced, as all except our nerve cells and brain cells constantly are, some three million genetic bits get replaced with exact precision.

Inside nearly all cells is the nucleus, without which the cell would die, and within the nucleus are the chromosomes, and within the chromosomes the genes (though that is just a word we use to cover the fact that here too is mystery), determining some of our physical and psychological characteristics and handed down from generation to generation. What we call "genes" an Austrian monk named Gregor Mendel, who worked out the idea of inheritance of genetic material during the mid-nineteenth century, called "discrete factors." He realized that each of us inherits two complete sets of genes, one from each parent, and that these do not change during reproduction but are passed on unaltered from parent to offspring. What makes each of us different is that, because each of our parents has two sets of genes, each of us has a 50% chance of getting one or other gene from each parent, or a 25% chance of receiving any particular combination of genes.

Although Mendel worked out the idea of inheritance, he had no idea of how the process works at the chemical level.

That was left to the two British scientists, James Watson and Francis Crick, who made the greatest genetic discovery this century just over thirty years ago. Our genes are stored as deoxyribonucleic acid, known not surprisingly as DNA, which has the remarkable ability to replicate itself. The DNA is so narrow and compacted that all your genes in each of your body's total cells would fit into an ice-cube; yet if unwound and joined together they would stretch from the earth to the sun and back more than four hundred times. Watson and Crick discovered that DNA forms a double spiral, though it is hard to picture it. Deepak Chopra imagines he is standing in an empty room facing a wooden spiral staircase. Suddenly a strange thing happens. It slowly rotates and splits in two, right up the middle, as if a zip fastener had opened it from bottom to top, and the two halves stand apart facing each other.

> Now you notice something that escaped your eye . . . The staircases are surrounded by a swirling cloud of sawdust . . . [which] appears to be formless, but currents and eddies begin to form in it, and then, inexplicably, the cloud gradually rebuilds the half-staircases, adding new steps, banister rails and posts, until you behold before you two complete staircases, identical in every respect to the original.[5]

DNA behaves just like this. Each cell carries the entire instruction book of a hundred thousand genes. Each time you have to make a new cell (and that is millions of times a minute), a molecule of DNA splits itself in half by dividing down the middle, and then out of the swirling cloud of biochemicals it rebuilds itself to form two replicas of the original molecule.

That is astonishing enough, but then you go on to realize that a DNA molecule seems to be just a *thing* made up of other things like hydrogen, carbon and oxygen atoms, which also make up things like blades of grass or lumps of sugar. But DNA is not simply a thing: it is a living memory that resides in a thing, a memory that works forward as well as back, for

> the same speck of DNA deposited in the womb knows how to perform millions of actions that will not be needed for years or even decades to come. Our genes know how to fuse an infant's loosely joined skull bones and at the same time how to compensate for lost calcium in a seventy-year-old femur. It has been estimated that six trillion chemical reactions take place in the body every second. The same speck of DNA controls them all, rarely mistiming a single one.[6]

Michael White, a science correspondent for The Independent on Sunday, uses a different image. He writes:

> Imagine a cell as being a set of huge encyclopaedias. Each volume is equivalent to a chromosome. Each human cell has twenty-three pairs of chromosomes, made up of an incredibly long, tightly-coiled length of DNA So the human "encyclopaedia set" would consist of forty-six volumes. Each volume in this library would be billions of words long. In the same way as each volume of the encyclopaedia deals with a vast number of subjects, each chromosome controls every physical characteristic of the organism. So by this analogy, eye colour would be equivalent to say, Renaissance economic theory; hair type: London double-decker buses in use during the First World War; height: the mating habits of the duck-billed platypus. These individual entries in the encyclopaedia are equivalent to individual genes. . . .[7]

The discovery that all of life, with rare exceptions, is connected by this single, unbelievably efficient chemical messenger is not only one of the great scientific discoveries of our time; it is also a marvelously satisfying, poetic concept, suggesting a unity which speaks equally to the mind and to the heart.

When you were born you each had three hundred and fifty soft bones that will gradually fuse into the two hundred and six we have as adults, each bone alive with active cells, and in these first years of your life all the bones in your body will have been replaced. On the day you took your first hesitant steps, all your senses whirled into action and sent millions of messages to your brain; over a hundred million sense cells in each eye will ensure that you walked towards what attracted you, and sense organs in your ears informed your brain about gravity so that you didn't fall flat on your face. It is with your eyes that you are able to turn the world into your world, and 70% of your sense perceptors are in your eyes, for it is mainly through the eye that we see and make sense of the world. Indeed, the eye is but one aspect of the brain.

There are cells in the eye which are cones and others which are rods, seven million of the first and just over a hundred million of the second. The thin rods only report in black and white, back-up cells useful when the light is poor; the plumper cones, which fire off the message to the brain when a few photons of light cross it, give you an awareness of colour. Different cones specialize in red, blue, and green, and thanks to the cones you can distinguish at least a thousand shades of colour, which will be a huge source of delight to you, all your life. (Is it thirty-two different shades of black that have been discerned in the portraits of Franz Hals? I forget.) Count yourself lucky not to be a toad which, when its mouth is full of worms, closes its eyelids and lowers its eyes as a trap-door in the roof of its mouth, holding the squirming worms down with its very tough eyeballs. Ingenious, but it must be dangerous not to be able to spot your enemy approaching because you are having lunch. Better to be an okapi, which has eyes that can look in different directions simultaneously. Owls, on the other hand, would seem to be colour-blind, possessing no cone cells; some animals see in infra-red; flies, with their compound eyes, see the world curved, like looking through a thick glass paper-weight; and bees can judge the angle at which the light hits their photoreceptors and so locate the position of the sun even on a grey English summer's day.

In the centre of your eye you have a blind spot. In it nerve fibres from the retina converge and transmit the messages it is receiving to the visual cortex in the brain via the optic nerve so that it may decode it. When you look at an object, your two eyes see slightly different images and at first the brain keeps each image separate: only at the very end do they converge so that you see it in three dimensions.

If you look at early ideas of how we see things you find that classical belief was that we are passive observers, taking in the reality and beauty of the world through the eye's pupil, a little hole through which light enters. They had no idea that the world of objects is projected in the back of the eye (actually upside down and sideways reversed), and that the patterns of light and dark on the retina are converted into a code of electrical pulses from the rod and cone receptors which the brain then has to decode. And there are different brain regions for detecting movement and form and colour. Dr. Semir Zeki of University College, London, has shown that there are about sixteen maps in the brain which plot different aspects of the world we see, and that somehow these are brought together by the brain to form a consistent perception of things. But no-one really knows how.

Professor Richard Gregory, who edited the *Encyclopaedia of the Mind*, speaks of the brain as an extremely active receiver and processor. (It has to be: more information is pouring into our eyes every few minutes than is put into a bank of computers for a rocket launch.) First, it acts like a Xerox copier, then more selectively, like a novelist. We see at the back of our brains: we plan in our frontal lobes. It is an immense, almost impenetrable, electro-chemical system that is physically based, and experts are still divided on whether certain illnesses of the brain are best spoken of in physical or psychological terms. Richard Gregory has spent much of his life exploring the brain, yet he can still admit that how we *experience* pain or heat or colour or any sensation from what is a mechanical process is utterly mysterious. For example, in each of us there is a switching mechanism, located in the brain stem, that allows us to shift gear from our left cerebral hemisphere that has to do with our rational speech, analytical thought, and logic and calculation, to our right hemisphere when we are engaged in observing art or listening to music or taking part in anything that stirs our emotions or creative imagination. No wonder it is so exhausting trying to write a *logical* book about belief, mystery and the arts, yet how vital it is that we should bring together these two modes of knowing.

While the eye is the most important part of the brain, everything we experience through our familiar senses of touch, sight, and hearing, is represented to the brain in electric pulses, dots and dashes rather like Morse code. These are the basic units of brain language and the sensation we feel depends on which part of the brain it is to which these pulses go. But we should be wary of assuming that what we see is what there is to see. We may not make the mistake of the ancient philosophers. We know we are not simply passive observers of an objective reality which is replicated in our minds. But measurements have been made of the amount of information the eye can take in at a glance, and it is clear that we hugely over-estimate the amount of information our brains process:

> What we actually see is a very rough picture with a few spots
> in clear detail. What we feel we see is a large picture which is
> everywhere as clear in detail as the one favourite spot on which
> we concentrate our attention. Roughly speaking the area of
> clear perception includes less than 1% of the total visual field.[8]

As you read these lines you are only seeing about two letters in
sharp detail.

In this sense we can never actually see in any given moment all that a photograph or painting reveals, and this will be
relevant when we come to look at how artists help us to see.
Not only do we miss most of what there is to see, not only does
the brain also make use of memory, even guessing as it decodes
the scene for us, but the eye is bound to be selective if the brain
is not to be confused. You focus on what you choose to notice
and it is by observing this and not that and feeding it to the
brain which will then interpret it, that you gradually build up
your own perception of the world and make the world your
own. It was John Ruskin who firmly put down a great physiol-
ogist who stated that sight was "altogether mechanical" by
pointing out the difference between the eye and the telescope:

> Sight is an absolutely spiritual phenomenon; accurately and
> only to be so defined: and the Let there be light! (of Genesis)
> is as much, when you understand it, the ordering of intelli-
> gence as the ordering of vision.[9]

And Socrates insisted that it is more correct to say,

> "eyes are that by means of which we see" than "by which we
> see," as it would surely be a terrible thing if so many powers
> of perception were seated in us like warriors in wooden horses,

and if all these senses did not draw together into some one
form, call it soul or what you will, by which, using these senses
as instruments, we perceive whatever we do perceive.[10]

So: cells, eyes, brains, all of them only explicable up to a point,
and yet we hardly give them a moment's thought. It would be
tiresome to itemize the rest of you . . . to speak of how, when
middle C is struck on the piano the piston of bones in your
inner ear vibrates exactly 256 times a second; that the entire
cycle of blood circling your body takes less than a minute; that
each day you think about 50,000 different thoughts; that when
you flex your hand you are using seventy different muscles ("the
narrowest hinge on my hand," wrote Walt Whitman, "puts to
scorn all machinery"); that you carry on the surface of your
body as many bacteria as there are people on the surface of the
earth. Some things it is better not to know.

> Then there is memory. Nothing is harder to explain, especially
> those visual memories which, if you are anything like me, ram-
> page nightly through your dreams. A physiologist will tell us
> that memory is associated with the hippocampus. "Is memory
> then the hippocampus? Can a surgeon cut it out and present
> it to us as a person's memory? Of course not. It is only what
> has been called the physiological agent of the mystery.[11]

Jacquetta Hawkes has written:

> How this substance, soft like toothpaste, of the nerve cells,
> and little threads of nerve fibre running down between them,
> can hold the impressions of a lifetime . . . and then project
> them . . . like magic lantern-slides showing a girl in a spring
> orchard, a boy riding with his mother in a carriage, is hard
> enough to have baffled the most formidable scientific minds
> of our time . . .[12]

In *Moon Tiger* by Penelope Lively, the 67-year-old Claudia, smelling eucalyptus leaves in post-war Cairo, is overwhelmed by

> wonder that nothing is ever lost, that everything can be retrieved, that a lifetime is not linear but instant. That, inside the head, everything happens at once.[13]

That takes us once again to the heart of the mystery. One day, when you are looking back on your lives, you will find that all the people you have ever been (and we play many parts), all the bodies you have worn, all the faces of people and the look of places you have loved, still live inside your skin; they are still lodged in that part of your brain that is the memory. And a word or a scent or a piece of music can bring them flooding back as vividly as if it was yesterday. What you also discover, of course, is that a knowledge of how the eye works is worthless unless you have explored the experience of seeing; as worthless as possessing a left and right part of your brain if you have allowed one to atrophy at the expense of the other.

For me, facts and figures about this intimate stranger I call my body are impressive up to a point, but as the noughts are added my brain capitulates, and I would sooner leave you with an insight from William Golding's novel, *Darkness Visible* which reminds me of Blake's "to hold infinity in the palm of your hand," and which conveys in one vivid image what it means to see with newly-sighted eyes the wondrous creatures I hope you know yourselves to be. The hero, Sim, meets a man who takes his hand and begins to examine it and read his palm:

> Sim was slightly disconcerted by this . . . but then he began to look into his own palm, pale, crinkled, the volume, as it were, most delicately bound in this rarest or at least most expensive

of all binding material—and then he fell through into an awareness of his own hand that stopped time in its revolution. The palm was exquisitely beautiful, it was made of light. It was precious and preciously inscribed with a sureness and delicacy beyond art and grounded somewhere else in absolute health. In a convulsion unlike anything he had ever known, Sim stared into the gigantic world of his own palm and saw that it was holy.[14]

IX

The Wonder of the World About You

But were it told me—Today—
That I might have the sky
For mine—I tell you that my Heart
Would split, for size of me—

The Meadows—mine—
The Mountains—mine—
All Forests—Stintless Stars—
As much of Noon as I could take
Between my finite eyes—

The Motion of the Dipping Birds—
The Morning's Amber Road—
For Mine—to look at when I light—
The News would strike me dead.

EMILY DICKINSON[1]

Whoever is devoid of the capacity to wonder, whoever remains
unmoved, whoever cannot contemplate or know the deep
shudder of the soul in enchantment, might just as well be dead
for he has already closed his eyes upon life.

ALBERT EINSTEIN[2]

No little Gradgrind had ever seen a face in the moon . . . No
little Gradgrind had ever learnt the silly jingle, Twinkle, twinkle, little star, how I wonder what you are! No little Gradgrind
had ever known wonder on the subject, each little Gradgrind
having at five years old dissected the Great Bear . . .

CHARLES DICKENS[3]

For today let's pause
At my first groping after the First Cause,
Which led me to acknowledge (groping still)
That if what once was called primeval slime
(In current jargon, pre-biotic soup)
Evolved in course of eons to a group
Playing Beethoven, it needed more than time

And chance, it needed a creative will
To foster that emergence, and express
Amoeba as A Minor.

MARTYN SKINNER[4]

VALENTINE: ... The unpredictable and the predetermined unfold together to make everything the way it is. It is how nature creates itself, on every scale, the snowflake and the snowstorm. It makes me so happy. To be at the beginning again, knowing almost nothing. People were talking about the end of physics. Relativity and quantum looked as if they were going to clean out the whole problem between them. A theory of everything. But they only explained the very big and the very small. The universe, the elementary particles. The ordinary-sized stuff which is our lives, the things people write poetry about—clouds—daffodils—waterfalls—and what happens in a cup of coffee when the cream goes in—these things are full of mystery, as mysterious to us as the heavens were to the Greeks.

TOM STOPPARD[5]

L ET'S STICK FOR A while with wonder. Not the wonder I discover in the microscopic world of me, but that more ostentatiously on show in the macroscopic universe. Last night the stars were bright over the mountains. The distance of the nearest fixed star is about 25 million million miles. The Milky Way, which might be thought of as our local neighbourhood, is only one of such assemblages of galaxies (it taking some two million years for light to get from one to the next), and it contains about 300 thousand million stars. But nothing is quite "fixed," and powerful modern telescopes show us that the galaxies beyond the Milky Way are receding away from us in a continuously expanding creation. No longer can we say: Twinkle, twinkle, little star, how I wonder what you are! for we know they shine because they are furnaces of raging gas, mainly hydrogen and helium, held together by gravity but not lasting for ever. A former Astronomer Royal calculated that six specks of dust in Waterloo Station represent the extent to which space is populated with stars. So I might dazzle you by comparing our stellar system to a very small fly—with the sun like a firefly—buzzing away in a very large supermarket; or tell you that there are more stars in these unimaginable galaxies than there are grains of sand on all the beaches in the world.

But once again we are defeated, for our imagination simply cannot conceive of that scale of things; and in fact there is something much nearer home that is much more impressive: the fact of human consciousness, the fact that we are able to probe and cross-examine the universe until it begins to surrender some of its secrets—though not quite, in Kafka's phrase, "rolling in ecstasy at our feet," like some soft and foolish dog. As St. Augustine said, the human mind is of greater worth than the whole inanimate creation, for we can observe the latter, measure it, explore it, wonder at it: it cannot do the same.

Thankfully the days are long gone, except in some of the more perverse academic areas or in certain extreme fundamentalist sects, when science and religion are at loggerheads. They are not competitive, but complementary, disciplines. They add together "how?" and "what?" and "why?" in order to stammer out some answers to the larger mysteries of life, each without the other (as Einstein said) blind and incomplete.

I sit writing on a wooden balcony, of which the floor seems solid. It is 2:45 P.M. I can see the light shaping the mountains, the shadows changing all the time, so that the texture of the hills is never quite the same from one moment to the next. Yet I wonder if any of these apparently obvious, indisputable facts is quite how it seems? Of course science is meant to deal in certainties, in data which anyone anywhere could check and verify. To some extent that is true but, in Annie Dillard's words, "I think science works the way a tight-rope walker works: by not looking at its feet. As soon as it looks at its feet, it realizes it is operating in mid-air."[6] She is not simply saying that we know now that all our ideas of objective reality must be filtered through our extremely fallible perceptions; she is saying that in the past sixty years (perhaps since the then Astronomer Royal, Sir James Jeans, wrote, summarizing a finding in physics, that "the world begins to look more like a great thought than a great machine") modern physics takes us into the world of predictability *and* randomness, order and chance, fixed time *and* relativity, matter that appears solid but is fluid, and light which seems to act sometimes as particles, sometimes as waves.

Let me, an Arts man to my fingertips, plunge briefly and riskily into the cold waters of science, for I am aware that the findings of nuclear physicists have totally transformed the way we see the world, and none have done more by their insight into the building blocks of creation and the mystery of design to awaken a sense of astonished wonder. Take matter. In Christopher Fry's *Venus Observed* the heroine has just arrived from a rough Atlantic crossing and can still feel the lunge of the sea. She asks her host, "Your floor isn't meant to sway?" and gets the answer:

> The floor is battering at your feet like Attila
> With a horde of corybantic atoms,
> And travelling at eighteen miles a second,
> But it cannot be said to sway.[7]

Physicists have come to realize that, contrary to everything our senses tell us, matter and energy have no fixed, concrete existence. Because I hold an orange pen in my hand my mind tells me that if I could smash it into tiny bits I could hold the very smallest bit in my hand too. Yet the elementary particles of matter are not solid or fixed. My pen is actually much more like a flight of birds. When scientists in the nineteenth century first discovered what they called atoms, they might have preferred the metaphor of a bag of peas, for they thought atoms were indivisible, solid as snooker balls (which, of course, aren't). It was Ernest Rutherford who discovered the internal structure of the atom. He found that the positive charge in an atom was concentrated at a point in the atom's centre. He had discovered the nucleus, and in 1919 he split the atom by bombarding it with a radium gun, bullets of radio-active substance shooting out at almost the speed of light. (I guess I am writing this rather more for my sake than yours for, if your education is anything like half decent, you will have learned these facts long before you ever read these words.)

It quickly became clear that there are far more fundamental things than atoms (and a thousand million million atoms could perch on a speck of dust), and that atoms are all in motion. They are all caught up in a ceaseless chase, whether in a liquid like water or in a solid like my pen, or my desk, or the balcony which supports me. I have used the image of a flight of birds because it is as if matter is composed of untold numbers of swarming creatures, swirling with interior activity. Its boundary, this unimaginably tiny particle of matter, consists of a central core (the nucleus) round which other particles circle at the speed of several thousand million million revolutions a second, and they go in a circle because they are attracted electrically to the nucleus rather as the earth is attracted to the sun. This central core is positively charged with particles called protons, and the circling particles, the electrons, are negatively charged. The nucleus, which makes up most of the atom's weight, is nevertheless tiny, the electrons that circle it being no larger than bullets in a battlefield. Most of the atoms consist of space. In fact, to go back to my fly in a supermarket, the six electrons in an atom of carbon, for example, would be like six spiders, with the nucleus as the fly, in a similar space. (Rutherford had fired ten thousand bullets from that radium gun before he hit anything at all.)

So my pen, my table, my balcony, my mountains are mostly holes, empty rooms enclosing the endless dance of the electrons and the nuclei. It has been said that if you could empty the space out of an elephant it would shrink to the size of a mouse—though it would still weigh about the same owing to the weight of all the nuclei.

Now just as *a* and *b* and *c* combine to give us, in their different languages, all the world's literature, so the ninety-two elements combine together to create the infinite variety, profligacy and beauty of the creation. The elements combine, in this atomic dance of the electrons, held together by electricity, in orbits of all shapes and sizes from swelling circles to the narrowest ellipse, and (writes John Stewart Collis)

> neither the imagination, the eye, nor the microscope can help us to do justice to the reality. The notable thing is that though the electrons move round their orbit about seven thousand million times in the millionth of a second, and we should expect endless collisions and hopeless chaos, there is instead the beauty and rest of perfect symmetry.[8]

Now I cannot speak as one who pretends to understand about quantum mechanics and still continue to look my friends in the eye; yet I can sense the excitement physicists have felt in their exploration (for example) into the nature of light. Newtonian physics was bound by the acceptance that nature, beautiful and dynamic as it was, had about it an order, regularity and predictability. Quantum physics is the attempt to grasp the movement and behaviour of objects that can no longer be so described, and the quantum world, concerned as it is with the way atoms and molecules behave, has proved to be far more mysterious and shadowy than we thought. An invisible force, radiation, is sent out from the sun in rays. These rays hit things and light is scattered and heat is felt, yet does the light that bounces off those mountains come as waves or particles? Certainly nothing material is doing the waving. Sometimes the light appears to be waves rather than particles: sometimes the photons, the name given to the quanta of light, appear to be both at the same time, paradoxical as this may be. The waves that make light are varying electric and magnetic fields, intertwined in a dance. Yet light is also a particle. Albert Einstein received the Nobel Prize for proving it. This particle/wave duality lies at the heart of the mystery of the quantum world that is modern physics.

Niels Bohr insisted that the paradox could not be resolved. He said that when we describe a quantum particle it must include both wave and particle properties, even though we cannot know both simultaneously. In 1928 Paul Dirac presented a quantum field theory in terms of a mathematical formula that clarified the wave/particle duality of light without an appeal to paradox. I do not begin to know what that means, but as a result of exploring these mysteries I shall soon dedicate a memorial to Dirac among the other great scientists in the nave of Westminster Abbey with much more enthusiasm than I would have done six months ago.

A Nobel Prize winner, Richard Feynman, who developed the quantum theory of light, was asked if his knowledge of the inner world of science had about it a cold, mechanical feel. He replied that when he looked at nature his sense of wonder was not diminished, but enhanced, by what physics revealed. He still looked at a rose and found it beautiful, but he also found beauty in the dance of sub-atomic particles that made the rose what it was. Kieran Egan, who has written on education in early childhood and of the need to encourage what he calls "the ecstatic response" in children, writes:

> By ecstasy I mean that kind of engagement we see in children's
> responses to good stories and in Einstein's commentaries on
> his work or in (those of many recent scientists . . . (e.g., James
> Watson and Richard Feynman). It is a joy-filled engagement,
> that does not ask the point . . . of the activity; one is wholly
> caught up in it and, while one is engaged, one is enchanted.[9]

But to return for the moment to my flight of birds and
the realization that the science of matter and energy means that
they have no fixed, determinable existence. It is, I read, as if the
bird in each electric field forms a streak of light when they fly
this way and that, but they leave a trail you cannot only see but
touch, so that although the bird disappears from view as soon
as you try and spot it, you can still see where it has been. This
is the basic tenet of quantum reality, the Uncertainty Principle,
which says that elementary particles, although they *seem* to
exist in a definite place, cannot actually be found there. All you
have, as you try to spot your bird, is its trail. Physicists have
learned to call this set of possibilities, this set of measurable
variables that go to make up my solid pen and those solid
mountains, a field: a solid world that consists of vibrations in
space.

So scientists' view of reality shifts and resettles as each
new discovery is made. Einstein discovers that mass and energy
are interchangeable, that mass is locked-up energy, that strange
things happen to energy as objects approach the speed of light,
that an object squashes up as it moves faster and increases in
weight. In some way the energy that impels the object gets
added to its mass, which again makes me question what we
mean by the solidity of matter. And the consistency of time.
Einstein's discovery of relativity, that the faster an object travels

the more time slows down for it, means that a clock at the Equator must go just a little bit more slowly than an identical clock at the North or South Pole, for as the earth spins on its axis the Equator moves faster than the Poles. Since Einstein, science fiction has had a field day.

But what really grabs me and causes me to wonder afresh at the creation is not these half-digested theories of quantum physics. It is what the new cosmology has to tell us of the likely start of it all. Big Bang cosmology is the belief that the universe was born in a single instant some fifteen billion years ago in an unimaginable explosion which occurred simultaneously everywhere, at once filling all space, with every particle of matter racing apart from every other particle; and it seems to become increasingly likely that this is how it was. One model is that space expanded faster than light for a billionth of a second after the Big Bang and then settled down to the expanding universe we see today. Out of the first blazing heat and noxious gases there gradually evolved from the hostile atmosphere of hydrogen, methane, ammonia and water vapour (those lethal gases that still swirl around the planet of Jupiter) the life-supporting chemicals of oxygen, carbon dioxide and nitrogen; and then, after perhaps a thousand million years, the vital green chlorophyll pigments developed that allowed some organisms to create food substance from water and carbon dioxide. By using the energy of sunlight the first plants were produced.

Jacquetta Hawkes ends her memorable account of evolution:

> I cannot help thinking with renewed wonder how this luscious green spring has taken a thousand million years to attain its present singing youth, having been conceived in a dead, hoary world and passed through an old age of flowerless evergreen.[10]

Impressive evidence for the Big Bang theory has come from the discoveries made possible in astronomy and astrophysics and the use of huge new radio telescopes, and the two proven facts of the expanding universe and background radiation would seem to corroborate it. The first means that distant galaxies are receding at some 25,000 miles per second as matter continues to be created and push itself out. The second refers to the scientists' hunch that if there had been an initial explosion it might be possible to trace an echo of the radiation that would have been released by it. Sure enough in 1965 the relic of the initial fireball, the echo of the Big Bang which is background radiation, was first heard as a low and persistent hiss picked up by those trying to communicate with Telstar, the first telecommunications rocket.

Another intriguing theory, which has to do with the seeming wholeness and interconnectedness of different parts of the creation, is that of the physicist David Bohm. He believes that the whole universe was originally implicated, or folded up together, so that there was an infinite potential present, that all the atoms and molecules and organisms were somehow implicit from the start. He would say that what we observe is what has been extricated or unfolded up to this point in our human development. Bede Griffiths, who died last year and was one of the great visionary figures of our time, a Christian priest who sought to combine the wisdom of East and West, writes of the fields of energies that modern physics has shown the universe to be as "a dynamic web of interdependent relationships," in which the whole is present in every part. "The whole cannot be explained in terms of the parts, nor can the parts be understood apart from the whole . . . nor can mind any longer be separated from matter."[11] He is attracted to Bohm's theory that the great explosion of matter and energy we call the Big Bang somehow contained all that later ensued: a gradual explication, over thousands of millions of years, "first of all of the material universe, then of life and then of consciousness," for that too was implicit from the beginning. I like the thought of the first cave dwelling containing within it the blueprint of Chartres Cathedral; the first notes on a shepherd's pipe the blueprint of a score by Haydn; and the idea that the first attempt at human speech contained implicitly the language of *Paradise Lost*.

This links with what I find the most persuasively captivating fact of all: the delicate balance of circumstances that were necessary if life was ever to be developed and maintained. It needs to be exactly the size and the age it is for us to be here. The parameters have to be exactly right if organic life is to exist. Among those parameters are the rate at which the universe expanded. If it had been smaller by a fraction of a million millionth, it would have collapsed. If it had been a millionth greater, it would have expanded too fast for the stars and planets to form. If those forces that hold together the atomic nuclei had been any weaker, the universe would simply have been composed of hydrogen; if stronger, it would have been converted to oxygen.

So the conditions look as if they were built into the fabric of creation from the beginning. "We do not live in any old world," writes John Polkinghorne, scientist and priest, "but rather in one which has been endowed by its Creator with an intrinsic potentiality."[12] And Angela Tilby writes in *Science and the Soul*:

> Every single interaction of every single particle has to lock into place with every other with a precise and intricate delicacy in order to produce exactly this universe. . . . Given the way the universe is, carbon-based intelligent observers have to come

into existence at some stage of its evolution.... We are meant
to be here.... It is as if "the universe knew we were coming."[13]

Remember, on those nights when you look at the stars
and feel totally insignificant in the immensity of it all, that the
number of ways of connecting the hundred million million
synapses in the human brain is greater than the number of
atoms in the universe. "There is a higher level of organization
and richness in a human being," said Professor Ian Barbour of
Carlton College, Minnesota at this year's American Association
of the Advancement of Science meeting, "than in a thousand
lifeless galaxies. It is human beings, after all, who reach out to
understand the cosmic immensity."

Which is where we came in on this Whit Sunday afternoon. My pen, my desk, my balcony, require a kind of dual way
of understanding. They exist, they work, they do not collapse
under me. Those far mountains seem to shift under the mod-
ulating light but remain the same shape. Yet go beyond the molecules to the bonded atoms of which they consist; go within
the atom to its electric field, and what seem solid building-
blocks are found to be nothing of the kind. It is an astonishing
universe.

A chaffinch has appeared below me, loudly demanding
crumbs. So let me end with Thomas Hardy:

These are brand new birds of twelve months' growing,
Which a year ago, or less or twain
No finches were, no nightingales,
  Nor thrushes,
But only particles of grain,
  And earth, and air, and rain.[14]

X

The Spontaneous Wonder of the Child

Most people simply don't know how beautiful the world is and how much splendour is revealed in the smallest things, in a common flower, in a stone, in the bark of a tree or the leaf of a birch. Grown-up people, who have occupations and cares and who worry themselves about mere trifles, gradually lose the eye for these riches, while children, if they are observant and good, quickly notice and love with their whole heart.

RAINER MARIA RILKE[1]

... Unless you become as a little child, or have not ceased to be one, the best that there is to be had will not come your way . . . The lucky ones——most of them some sort of artists, but not by any means all——seem to be always as if they had just come into the world and were going over this remarkable find, in a delectable state of wonder and amazement.

C. E. MONTAGUE[2]

... If you look long enough at anything
It will become extremely interesting;
If you look very long at anything
It will become rich, manifold, fascinating:

If you can look at anything long enough,
You will rejoice at the miracle of love.

You will possess and be blessed by the marvelous blinding radiance of love.
You will be radiance.

DELMORE SCHWARTZ[3]

L AST MONTH WE TOOK you both to a Rare Breeds Farm in Wiltshire and I noticed, Adam, how you "saw" the sheep from a remote Scottish island that live on a diet of seaweed, and the rabbits with ears so long they could have used them as blankets. Unlike me, you really looked; you gave them your whole attention, and when you drove the clapped-out, immovable tractor it was thrilling because it was the real thing, for as yet you make no clear distinction between illusion and reality.

We never see again with quite the wonder and the innocence with which we see as a child, and that doesn't just apply to country children. Uniquely in childhood come those experiences of the world that may sink into the deepest part of our mind in a way that is not possible later in life; and which may then prove the memories on which we draw most pleasurably in old age. Penelope Lively, in her novel *City of the Mind*, writes of Matthew Halland travelling round London with his eight-year-old daughter, Jane,

... seeing, each, a different place. Jane, with the liberation of childhood, without rationality or expectation, sees an anarchic landscape in which anything is possible and many things are provocative. She wrestles with language, scans advertisements, shop-signs, logos on vans and trucks. She pays professional attention to other children, in the way that animals are most sensitive to their own species. She searches out things that tether her to a known world, the hoarding that proclaims her favourite brand of chocolate, Volkswagen cars that are like her father's. Hers is a heliocentric universe, and she is the sun. She is fettered by a child's careless egotism, but freed from adult preconceptions. She does not know what to expect and can therefore assess what she sees in its own terms....

[Matthew] perceived for an instant the perpetual now of childhood, the interminable present from which, eventually, we escape and which we can never retrieve. We cohabit with these mysterious beings who occupy a different time-zone ... [and] whose vision is that of aliens—anarchic, uncorrupt and inconceivable. We talk to them in our language, impose on them our beliefs, and all the while they are in a state of original harmony with the physical world, knowing nothing and seeing everything ... It is children alone who experience immediacy; the rest of us have lost the ability to inhabit the present and spend our time in anticipation and recollection.[4]

Rosemary Sutcliff, the children's writer, who was disabled, describes how one of her earliest memories is of her wheelchair tipping over and depositing her in long grass. Instead of calling for help, she simply lay, observing and recording the close-up miniature world of plants and insects with acute fascination. I am reminded of another of Penelope Lively's books, *Next to Nature, Art*, where a small boy called Jason wanders out "into the anarchic world of the woodland way, bright with sun and leaf...." He follows a speckled butterfly that is wavering around his knees. . . . It settles and Jason, squatting, examines it. Its wings have an intricate pattern of cream spots and its body is powdered with golden fur. Jason perceives that in some way this is marvellous, but the thought does not form itself into words; he simply absorbs the butterfly, amid the humming morning.[5]

In his *Duino Elegies* Rilke writes of this kind of childhood experience:

> . . . we take the very young
> child and force it round, so that it sees
> objects—not the Open which is so
> deep in animals' faces . . .
> . . . Never, not for a single day, do we have
> before us that pure space into which flowers
> endlessly open. Always there is World
> and never Nowhere without the No: that pure
> unseparated element which one breathes
> without desire and endlessly knows. A child
> may wander there for hours, though the timeless
> stillness, may get lost in it and be
> shaken back . . .[6]

Childhood, for most of us, is the secure haven from which we start our unpredictable journeys, a place of permanence where whatever is must be right, for we know no different. The poet Edwin Muir writes in his *Autobiography*:

> Our first childhood is the only time when we exist within immortality, and perhaps all our ideas of immortality are influenced by it. . . . Time does not exist for us. . . . And a child has this picture of human existence peculiar to himself . . . the original vision of the world in which there is a completer harmony of all things with each other than he will ever know again.[7]

No-one has better described this sense of being at one with the world, of a lost innocence, than the Welsh seventeenth-century poet and priest, Thomas Traherne. From his earliest childhood he was transparent to the world about him, and the wonder of those childhood experiences never left him, so that all his life he affirmed the beauty and variety he then knew.

> Certainly Adam in paradise had not more sweet and curious apprehensions of the world than I when I was a child. . . . All appeared new and strange at first, inexpressibly rare and delightful and beautiful. . . . Is it not strange that an infant should be heir of the whole world, and see those mysteries which the books of the learned never unfold? The corn was Orient and immortal wheat which never should be reaped or was ever sown. I thought it stood from everlasting to everlasting. . . . The green trees when I saw them first . . . transported and ravished me . . . they were such strange and wonderful things. . . . Boys and girls tumbling in the street were moving jewels: I knew not that they were born or should die. . . .
>
> The city seemed to stand in Eden or to be built in heaven. The streets were mine, the temple was mine, the people were mine, their clothes and gold and silver were mine, as much as their sparkling eyes, their fair skins and rugged faces. The skies were mine, and so were the sun and moon and stars, and all the world was mine; and I the only spectator and enjoyer of it. So that with much ado I was corrupted, and made to learn the dirty devices of this world, which now I unlearn, and become, as it were, a little child again, that I may enter into the Kingdom of God.[8]

This sense of immediacy as you receive, chiefly through your eye, sights and sounds in what is still a largely unfurnished room is matched by the imaginative ability to visit Treasure Island or Narnia or Wonderland and be wonder-struck by all the delights of those countries of the mind that lie down rabbit holes or on the other side of the wardrobe door. "To starve a child of the spell of the story," writes George Steiner, "or the cantor of the poem, oral or written, is a kind of living burial. . . . If the child is left empty of texts, in the fullest sense of that term," (and he includes pictures and music), "he will suffer an early death of the heart and of the imagination."[9] We are back with the truth that wonder is a prerequisite for any kind of authentic humanness, that wonder is a given that we must nurture or slowly lose. For the fact is that as a child we have the capacity for sustained and continued delight; in our innocence we are open to what the world has to offer and accept what is given in each moment with spontaneous enjoyment and with no thought that it will not last.

In his book, *Visionary and Dreamer*, David Cecil writes of Samuel Palmer's visiting William Blake:

> Life and death, love and hate, good and evil—he perceived these things as directly and freshly as if he had been Adam looking around Eden on the day of his creation. . . . Blake asserted that at the age of four he had seen the face of God looking in at the window of his home.[10]

Blake was not one to sentimentalize childhood: his Songs are of Innocence and Experience, and the latter trace the progress of the human soul as it wanders through the world of experience searching for what it has lost from the time of childhood, having now learned Traherne's "dirty devices of this world." Yet Blake believed it possible to recover the lost images of your childhood, to see again with the eyes of a child, to become vulnerable and trustful as a child is, and aware of your oneness with the world and everyone in it. And one of the most profound and challenging sayings of Jesus of Nazareth, a fire-cracker of a truth, is that it is necessary to become again "as little children" (not childish, but childlike). It is as if we need to be born anew into a fresh awareness of the world and of each other if we are to find our fulfillment together in what he called "the Kingdom of God."

Lucy, in Penelope Lively's *Cleopatra's Sister*, is aware of much to decry in the inner city where she lives,

> but it seemed to her that the place had always this transcendent other quality, that there was always this dimension of unwitting, anarchic wonder—a lovely and mindless alternative universe. She had seen it as a child, she remembered, but differently—now it was newly remarkable, a source not of curiosity but of amazement.[11]

For William Blake this new awareness had to do with finding out what it means to be human, renouncing a self-seeking independence and developing an empathy for all other living things, recognizing the virtues of "Mercy, Pity, Peace and Love." But for him it also, and primarily, had to do with the possibility of seeing once again with the innocent eyes we had as a child; the possibility of rediscovering within ourselves certain gifts we then had, not least the simplicity of vision. Obviously it cannot be the same. That first innocence has gone. Becoming as a little child is not the same as being a little child. But is it possible once again to become "transparent to the world?" For, in Stanley Spencer's words, "We are not given our eyes just to stop us bumping into things."[12]

Before I try to answer this, two small digressions. The first concerns what is sometimes called "the innocent eye," a phrase made popular by the Victorian painter and critic, John Ruskin. It had to do with what we really see when we look at an object and what we infer through our intellect: in other words, the link between eye and brain, and what we take for granted about an object because our mental computer has labeled it "bird" or "tree" so that we no longer see it as it is in this actual here and now, seen from this particular angle and in this particular light. Ruskin was concerned with how an artist conveys a three-dimensional landscape on a flat canvas, and he claimed that what the eye actually sees is flat colours. It is the brain which translates them into the three-dimensional world in which we walk about.

> The whole technical power of painting depends on our recovery of what may be called the *innocence of the eye*: that is to say, of a sort of childish perception of these flat stains of colour, merely as such, without consciousness of what they signify—as a blind man would see them if suddenly gifted with sight.[13]

For example, to a child grass, until it is labeled "green," may look one colour on a dull evening and quite another in bright sunlight. Ruskin believed it was the artist's task to be concerned only with light and colour as they are imaged on the retina, and that the painter should clear the mind of all he or she knows about the object, wipe the slate clean, and regain the "innocent eye" of the child.

But such innocent passivity is not so easily achieved. As Sir Ernst Gombrich writes:

> An artist sees a meadow, not like an innocent child in terms of light and shade, but like a painter in terms of pigments, green and sulfur yellow . . . [and] Ruskin has, without realizing it, amended his own theory of childlike vision. For this mental act rests on knowledge of how colors will affect each other . . . [and] demands a willingness to use a pigment which in isola-

tion still looks unlike the area to be matched in order that it may look like it in the end.[14]

There are many ways of seeing the world, as artists are in the business of proving, and even the painter's eye must focus on what is significant rather than what is insignificant in their field of vision. All a painter can do is to teach new ways of looking: he cannot teach us to "see," and certainly not as we saw as a child. "I don't see clouds and water like that," a woman once said to Turner. "Don't you wish you could, Madam?" he replied.[15]

Ruskin's reference to how the blind would see if they were suddenly to be gifted with sight is interesting, for in fact the eye refuses to accept what the mind does not know. In a recent radio programme, a woman, blind since childhood, spoke of opening her eyes after radical surgery and seeing four brilliant shafts of light, separated by dark valleys. Puzzled, she turned to a nurse, to be told she was looking at her own fingers. A fifty-year-old man who recovered his sight had imagined a quarter moon not as a thin ellipse but like a quarter segment of a circle; he had no sense of height or space and felt he could step straight out of a second floor window to the ground; he was amazed by colours but was over-sensitive to peeling paint or drab walls. He refused to turn the lights on at night. Then there are records of those blind from birth who several decades ago, when eye surgeons first learned to remove cataracts, had their sight restored overnight and were at once plunged into a mystery that overwhelmed them, for they had no idea of form, or size or distance. "When I asked one restored patient to show me how big her mother was," wrote a doctor, "she did not stretch out her hands but set her two index fingers a few inches apart." Some have even asked that the bandages be replaced, and it may take months for them to be able to see properly, to distinguish a sheep from a tree, or fields from clouds. "One man having learned to name an egg, a potato and a cube of sugar," writes Professor J. Z. Young, "could not do it when they were put in a yellow light. The lump of sugar was named when on the table but not when hung in the air on a thread." And there are also instances where the newly-sighted have hardly been able to bear the dazzling beauty of the world until they have come to terms with the glut of visual images and recovered enough serenity not to be overwhelmed.

My second digression concerns the validity of describing what we need to recover as "a child's vision of things." Marghanita Laski, in two studies of what she calls "the Adamic Vision" (of which Traherne's writing is a prime example), writes of this nostalgia for paradise which is often triggered by nature or music and which underlies some of the experiences of which I gave examples in my third letter and which often relate to childhood. She defines an "Adamic" experience as being like a return to something once known, a sense that this is how things once were and ought to be again, resulting in a sense of harmony and renewal. (There are also experiences of desolation and loss. Even Traherne knew moments as a child which were terrifying, when "a certain want and horror fell upon me, beyond imagination . . . from the utmost ends of the earth, fears surrounded me.")

Marghanita Laski thinks this yearning for the lost world of childhood creates in many a desire to transform society into a place of universal brotherhood and peace, and cannot herself interpret such "Adamic longings" in religious terms, (although she admits that it is hard to think of words that describe certain musical experiences that are not religious). But her sharpest sniping is reserved for those who identify childhood with a

state of innocence. She believes that Jesus was startlingly ahead
of his age in saying that little children were of the Kingdom of
heaven, and that until a little over two hundred years ago children were thought of as "imps of Satan" needing to be trained
and brought to heel; that Rousseau changed Western sensibil-
ities in relation to the child, and that Blake and Wordsworth
fully established the romantic view of the child as innocent, loving, "trailing clouds of glory," and knowing nothing of sin.
"Gradually during the 19th century this conception became
fashionable, and by the early 20th century many aspects of it
had become mawkish . . . [a mawkishness which] found its
apotheosis in Barrie's *Peter Pan*, the boy who never grew up."[16]
A. S. Byatt would agree:

> I mistrust . . . theories about . . . the truthful vision of Children.
> . . . Children are just people in process of getting older, vul-
> nerable people learning to be human, and wise children know
> that being men and women is much more interesting and
> complicated that the state in which they are temporarily
> stuck.[17]

Formidable points, well made; good correctives to a falsely romantic view of childhood. There is a real sense in which we
must "put away childish things." Yet I do not believe they inval-
idate the truth that children observe and experience the world
with a transparency and openness that, once lost, diminishes
what it can mean to be human.

> Like my late Unitarian father-in-law [writes John Updike] am
> I now in my amazed, insistent appreciation of the physical
> world, of this planet with its scenery and weather—that pa-
> thetic discovery which the old make that every day and season
> has its beauty and its uses, that even a walk to the mailbox is
> a precious experience, that all species of tree and weed have

their signature and style and the sky is a pageant of clouds. Aging calls us . . . into the lowly simplicities that we thought we had outgrown as children. . . . The act of seeing is itself glorious.[18]

Back, then, to William Blake, who knew that this world "is a world of Imagination and Vision." "As a man is, so he sees," he wrote.[19] Like Plato he uses the symbol of the Cave. (In *The Republic*, Plato uses an image with which to describe the upward journey of the soul to the light of the sun when he speaks of human beings languishing as prisoners in a cave where they ignorantly think that reality consists of the shadows cast by the light of the fire onto the back wall of the cave. Gradually the soul has to be turned round and led up into the light of the sun, gradually becoming accustomed to its bright rays; the sun standing for the idea of the Good, the source of all that is real and of value.) For Blake the Cave is the body, lit by the five windows of the senses. "If the doors of perception were cleansed everything would appear to man as it is, infinite. For man has closed himself up, till he sees all things through narrow chambers of his cavern."[20] He goes on to say, "Unless the eye catch fire The God will not be seen."

Elsewhere he writes: "I question not my Corporeal or Vegetative Eye any more than I would Question a Window concerning a Sight. I look through it and not with it."[21] ("A man that looks on glass," wrote George Herbert, "On it may stay his eye; / Or if he pleaseth, through it pass, / And then the Heav'n espie.")[22]

To his artist friend, George Richmond, Blake once wrote: "I sometimes look at a knot in a piece of wood until I am frightened at it." (That is the awe that leads to wonder.) When the painter Samuel Palmer was taken aged nineteen to meet the elderly Blake, who was lying with a scalded foot looking "like one of the antique patriarchs," the latter told him he began all his landscapes "with fear and trembling." "Oh," said Palmer, "I have enough of fear and trembling." "Then," said Blake, "you'll do." "To walk with Blake in the Country," said Palmer, "is to perceive the soul of beauty through the forms of matter."

If we are to recover this childlike vision, so that sight turns to insight, the true perception of the actuality of things, then what for Blake is the first stage of Innocence that inevitably leads to Experience must move on yet again to the second stage of Innocence. That is not to blot out or deny the experience: it is to transcend it, as artists may; though not only artists, but all who are in touch with the springs of creative imagination—those who achieve a heightened awareness of what lies all about them in an age when many of us are astigmatic, our narrowed vision seeing only the surface of things, or that which lies beyond the end of our noses.

The composer Jonathan Dove describes his experience of writing a dance-liturgy for Salisbury Cathedral:

> To my amazement, after reading once through the text, I found myself at the piano, pouring out music with a completely unfamiliar sense of exhilaration, exaltation and ecstasy. The words, with their powerful images of vast immensity ("And the spirit of God was moving over the face of the waters"), had reached into the child in me, a place untouched by intellect and reason, and released feelings which had for many years found no expression. Once again I was entering into states of being I had been unconsciously seeking but unable to find; I surrendered to wonder, to awe, to joy at the miracle of creation, to rapt contemplation.[23]

But this kind of spontaneity doesn't come easily to us. "Once I drew like Raphael," said Picasso, "but it has taken me a whole lifetime to learn to draw like a child."

> In a sense [writes Donald Nicholl] our whole task in life ... is to recover the vision splendid, to break out of the prison-house of the ego into a second childhood, into childhood transfigured. For whereas the innocence of our first childhood is immature ... unacquainted with sorrow and evil, in our second childhood innocence is transfigured through responsibility and acquaintance with sorrow and evil.[24]

Nicholl contrasts the uninformed, skin-deep spontaneity of a child reacting to an object or an event with the deeper spontaneity of those who respond from the depths of their being, from the heart. You might say of that kind of seeing that it goes hand-in-hand with compassion.

I had thought to add a postscript about what we mean when we speak of beauty. "Beauty" as a postscript: how presumptuous can you get? It needs a letter to itself (a book would be better), but even as I write the words my eye is caught by the alluring quality of the light on the hills; and I would rather walk in it than write about it.

XI

The Meaning of Beauty

Beauty is the real aspect of things when seen aright and with
the eyes of love.

O world, I cannot hold thee close enough!
Thy winds, thy wide grey skies!
Thy mists that roll and rise!
Thy woods, this autumn day, that ache and sag
And all but cry with color! That gaunt crag
To crush! To lift the lean of that black bluff!
World, world, I cannot get thee close enough!

Long have I known a glory in it all,
But never knew like this;
Here such a pattern is
As stretcheth me apart. Lord, I do fear
Thou'st made the world too beautiful this year.
My soul is all but out of me—let fall
No burning leaf; prithee, let no bird call.

EDNA ST. VINCENT MILLAY[2]

THESE LETTERS FORM A very personal book, and nowhere more so than when it comes to beauty. I can only tell you what is beautiful in my eyes. There is no yardstick of beauty common to everyone, and each of us would draw up a different list of what we find beautiful; and yet the deep human instinct to say to each other: "Look at that view, this flower, that face" with the expectation of striking a chord suggests that the pleasure we feel is not entirely subjective.

Last night at about nine o'clock the light had all but gone in the valley below this house, but rays of the dying sun were still touching the thickly-impacted snow that hangs like curtains on the tops of the far mountains and seemed to make them glow from within. The 13,000-ft. Pointe de Zinal was capped by a bright cloud and there was a three-quarter moon. Just now I walked into the next field before sitting down to write to you. The first wild lupines are coming into flower; and I thought how absurd it is to attempt to place natural beauty on a sliding scale of one to ten (one for a thistle, ten for a rose). Is not each natural object beautiful in its unique expression of itself, with a beauty that may be enhanced by the play of light upon it? Can you say that some other view is *more* beautiful than last night's mountains or some other flower *more* beautiful than this morning's lupine? Of course tonight and tomorrow each may have a different kind of beauty or I may not be in the mood to notice them.

When I was a boy, Boots the chemist had what they called their Book Lovers' Library, and you could pick up retired library books for one-and-six (seven and a half pence). I have one beside me that I bought over forty years ago, its distinctive green shield on the cover, a little bit of twisted wire stuck down the spine (I never knew why). It is Eric Newton's *The Meaning of Beauty*, a book partly about why we find beauty in nature but chiefly about what we find beautiful in art. Newton believes that our response to natural beauty is an instinctive recognition of the existence of order, of a law, a determined pattern behind the behaviour of things, what he calls "God's geometry." Although our minds cannot hope to grasp the extraordinary complexity of the pattern of the universe, unless we were able to grasp a portion of it the universe would become a meaningless chaos. "From time to time different aspects of the pattern imprint themselves on the minds of exceptionally sensitive men, and they, in their endeavour to express their delight in what they have discovered, become great artists."[3] As a result, the fragment of life which they have revealed, the aspect of the world they have illuminated, is enthusiastically seized upon by succeeding generations, so that some fragment of life's pattern is isolated, simplified, intensified—"making it lovable, and therefore beautiful." "Beauty," writes Kathleen Raine, "is the real aspect of things when seen aright and with the eyes of love."[4] So the Greek sculptors revealed the beauty of the human body, but Michelangelo saw with different eyes, as did Rubens and Dégas and Henry Moore, and each reveals to us something new so that we say "that, too, is beautiful."

Beauty in the natural world is also a question of recognizing and celebrating order and harmony. The pattern arrived at will often have been dictated by the evolutionary law of development so that each thing may function most effectively, whether it is a butterfly patterned like a leaf to protect it from its enemies, or the double helix spiral of DNA, or the way the light causes every leaf on a tree to form a subtle dance so that each is turned to catch the sun. Beauty in nature is a product of function; but look at the curve of the spiral in a snail's shell, the pattern of a snow crystal or of a leaf, and you are at once in a mathematical world of efficiency, order and harmony. There is a kind of rhythm, a balance that pleases the eye. Yet there is no dull conformity. While an acorn will end up as an oak tree, no one oak tree will be exactly the same as any other. The condition of the soil, the prevailing wind, the amount of sun, the closeness of other trees, will see to that. As a result, the pattern of oak trees becomes much more interesting: their leaves do not quite have a perfect symmetry, their bark, attracting moss or lichens, will vary in texture. An element of chance has entered the scene to disrupt the uniformity, so that whereas a row of telegraph poles is dull, a row of poplars is beautiful enough to be painted by Monet. However often we walk the same path, there will always be something different, always something new to see.

Now there is nothing new in a theory of beauty based on mathematical laws. Plato endorses it and suggests that our appreciation of beauty is ultimately dependent on our recognition of the mathematical behaviour of things creating the sense of order we need if we are to feel secure in the world. Yet what makes an object beautiful is a combination of order and disorder: the fact that the simple geometry of the perfect shape is subtly disrupted. The oak leaf is not quite symmetrical; each larch tree I can see, in its fight for light and air, has ended up with its left side a little different from its right; the tips of each lupine leaf do not quite form a perfect circle. And it is this unexpectedness, this admixture of familiarity and unfamiliarity, that would seem to be the source of their beauty.

When I look along to the mountains, Besso on the left, wrinkled and full of dips and curves that rise to a double peak, the Dent Blanche to the right, its mass balancing that of Besso in quite different ways, and the far-off and snowcapped Pointe de Zinal drawing the eye between and beyond them, I see rock shaped by natural forces, some of it smoothed and moulded by glaciers, and carved into shapes which are beautiful because they are capable of such infinite variety from moment to moment. If all were as smooth and uniform as upturned pudding basins they would be merely dull. So beauty has to do, not just with texture and colour, but with shape.

Last year we went to the National Theatre to see Arthur Miller's play After the Fall. The set was fascinating: much of the stage was taken up by a three-dimensional white spiral, like the inside of a nautilus shell, through which the actors could come and go. The producer, Michael Blakemore, explained in a programme note that it had been based on the spiral that is at the heart of the Golden Mean, known to mathematics as the Logarithmic Spiral. The Golden Mean is an ideal proportion used by the ancient Greeks, an oblong with the proportion 1 to 1.618, thought to be particularly pleasing to the human eye and used by them in the design of buildings. If you draw a vertical line off-centre of the rectangle, creating to one side of it a square and to the other a new and smaller rectangle, the latter will have identical proportions to the first. Then draw a line through the second rectangle to create the same shapes.[5]

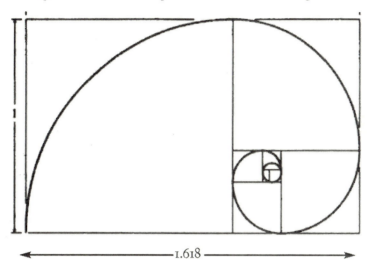

1.618

In theory it is possible to create an infinite number of squares, all diminishing in a spiral to an infinite point. And it is this spiral, rather than the original rectangle, that is at the heart of the Golden Mean. For it is this spiral that is found constantly in nature: in the structure of a sea-shell, in a ram's horn, most obviously perhaps in the curve seen in the cross-section of a breaking wave. It may be a little disguised, as in the petals of a rose or the relation of the ends of the fingers when the up-turned hand is relaxed.

This spiral figures repeatedly in classical architecture. When Michael Blakemore first talked to Arthur Miller about the Golden Mean and the possibility of using the spiral for the set of his play, a play about a man moving through profound doubt to a cautious hope, and about human nature and his own life in particular, Miller told him of a curious construction in an ancient Greek temple of Asclepius, the god of medicine. A flight of steps led down to a cave carefully shaped in the form of a vortex. No-one knows its purpose, but there is a theory that those suffering mental distress were taken to the cave and left there to contemplate the spiral twisting about them. However that may be, as one who is never more at peace than by the breaking waves of the seashore, I find this link of the Golden Mean with its spiral repeated in so many natural shapes an intriguing clue to the perception of beauty.

Simone Weil, a philosophical genius, who was born in Paris in 1909 and who died in 1943, believed that in a world where conventional religious practices touch less and less people

> the beauty of the world is almost the only way by which we can allow God to penetrate us . . . [for] a sense of beauty, although mutilated, distorted and soiled, remains rooted in the heart of man as a powerful incentive. It is present in all the preoccupations of secular life. If it were made true and pure it would sweep all secular life in a body to the feet of God. . . . Moreover, the beauty of the world is the commonest, easiest and most natural way of approach.[6]

"Have you noticed how pebbles on the road are polished and pure after rain?" writes a Master of Zen Buddhism. "And the flowers? No word can describe them. One can only murmur an 'Ah!' of admiration. A Japanese writer has said that we should understand the 'Ah!' of things."[7] So let me end this letter with some words about the "Ah!" of clouds. Not the low rain clouds that have just drifted over to blot out the mountains; nor those high wispy cirrus clouds that pass slowly at some 30,000 feet; but the in-between clouds, the cumulus, those accumulated heaps that sail along through the ocean of air like castles that have cast anchor, these are the ones that so often catch our attention. A cloud happens when too much water gets into the atmosphere, water evaporated by the heat of the sun from land and sea, and when saturation point is reached then the cloud is formed. But why do they not sink to earth, and how can they hold such a distinct and pleasing shape, with the apparent density and sharpness of stone yet with the fragility of air? Nothing in nature is more mysterious than clouds, and nothing (to my eye) as beautiful and full of wonder.

Although awareness of the sky, of the beauty of dawn and sunset, must have been a uniting factor for all strata of society, town and country dwellers alike, there is little written about it until Ruskin produced his chapter "Of the Open Sky" in his *Modern Painters* in 1843. He writes of the sky as speaking universally to the human heart, "soothing it and purifying it from its dross and din"; but the artists who really did justice to the sky in all its moods were Constable and (surpassingly) Turner, whose achievements in light and colour are a classic example of how an artist can open our eyes to a daily and familiar beauty we otherwise fail to see; though with the new danger that we shall pass from looking at a Turner to find new delight in skies to looking at the sky and finding a Turner.

> Yesterday evening Mrs. Arundel insisted on my going to the window and looking at the glorious sky, as she called it. Of course I had to look at it. . . . And what was it? It was simply a very second-rate Turner, a Turner of a bad period, with all the painter's worst faults exaggerated and over-emphasized.[8]

Oscar Wilde's Mrs. Arundel would have approved of Max Beerbohm's Duke of Dorset:

> How nobly the (thunder-clouds) had massed for him. One of them, a particularly large and dark one, might with advantage,

he thought, have been placed a little further to the left. He
made a gesture to that effect. Instantly the cloud rolled into
position. The gods were painfully anxious now to humour him
in trifles.[9]

Scientists may have the power to shape the environment,
and we may have the power to shift the whole delicate balance
of nature in which all phenomena are so interdependent. We
can measure it, describe it, analyse it. What we can never do is
adequately to define why a fleecy cloud or a breaking wave
seems to most people beautiful; and I find the heartfelt words
of the worldly-wise and witty Oscar Wilde, immured within
the thick walls of Reading Gaol, particularly haunting: "I tremble with pleasure," he wrote, "when I think that on the very day
of my leaving prison the laburnum and lilac will be blooming
in the gardens."[10]

XII

The Role of the Artist
in Enabling Us to See

How other future worlds will ripen to God I do not know, but for us art is the way.

RAINER MARIA RILKE[1]

All the languages of art have been developed as an attempt to transform the instantaneous into the permanent. Art supposes that beauty is not an exception——is not, in despite of——but is the basis for an order. . . . Art is an organized response to what nature allows us to glimpse occasionally. . . . The transcendental face of art is always a form of prayer.

JOHN BERGER[2]

Art has only one object——to make matter resplendent with beauty, to create a thing in accordance with the laws of its being, independent of anything else.

JACQUES MARITAIN[3]

The true miracle of the language of art is not that it enables the artist to create the illusion of reality. It is that under the hands of a great master the image becomes translucent. In teaching us to see the visible world afresh, he gives us the illusion of looking into the invisible world of the mind——if only we know, as Philostratus says, how to use our eyes.

E. H. GOMBRICH[4]

The great artistic problem is how to get something of the absolute into the frog-pond.

PICASSO[5]

A COMBINATION OF WRITING ABOUT clouds yesterday morning and reading Tim Winton's rich Australian novel *Cloud Street*—now there's a book about wonder!—led to them descending on us in a demonstrative kind of way so that for a day and a night we have been at cloud level, with a misty white vapour creeping and stealing its way round doors and window frames and blanking out the world.

I spoke in my last letter but one of learning to see with insight, moving into Blake's second state of Innocence, once again giving attention to what is there and seeking to recapture in maturity what children possess quite naturally. Learning to see as painters do. For the great imaginative artists have taken the commonplaces of human experience and distilled them, intensified them, so that we see the familiar transfigured. Often with quite a small vocabulary of visual images they work a miracle.

Most of us have had the experience of looking at paintings by X or Y and saying: "I never saw in that way before; but since I saw with the eye of Cézanne, Constable, Rembrandt,

Michelangelo, the landscape, a tree, a face, a naked body, will never look quite the same again." For me a prime example is the young man who told Blake he began all his landscapes "with fear and trembling," Samuel Palmer. Palmer began to paint just at the time when the Industrial Revolution was drawing labourers from the land into the city slums. His father was a bookseller in Walworth (then on the edge of the country), and as a fragile and asthmatic child he had hardly any formal education. But he used his eyes. And what he saw, he drew. You can go to the University Library in Cambridge and handle his notebooks which are full of drawings of flowers and leaves and corn and trees and cats and faces, all observed with a rare intensity. When he was twenty-three, after Blake's earlier encouragement, Palmer was enabled by a legacy to move out of London with a group of artist friends to Shoreham in Kent and there to write and talk and dream and paint on five shillings a week. There followed the most extraordinary six-year idyll when his painting of the countryside took on a visionary quality. This gift was to desert him later and he became a very proficient but unexciting Victorian artist.

But the Shoreham years are magic. "I must paint the Hills," he wrote, "so as to give us promise that the country beyond them is paradise." And he does: it is as if he lifts a veil between the seen world and the felt. He has that ability of certain artists to reconcile the visible and the invisible. The novelist John Fowles writes that it is the role of the artist "to create worlds as real as, but other than, the world as it is"[6] Palmer does just that. He believed that "earth is but the shadow of heaven," and in those years when his senses were most alive to nature he painted "without caution"; like Blake he could "see a Heaven in a Wild Flower." His small canvases show harvest scenes, landscapes radiant under a great harvest moon, rounded hills, a shepherd with his flock, a mossy thatched roof, a "magic apple tree," a towering bright cloud brimming with light, the smooth bole of a beech tree, a horse chestnut in flower, pear blossom where the paint is literally clotted on the canvas; everywhere lushness, exuberance, excess, a natural harmony, and fruitfulness which to Palmer were a visible expression of God's goodness. His pictures combine a (now rare) pastoral tranquility with an almost hallucinatory brilliance, a sense of the holiness of things, and his art for me works its transfiguring magic on the real, everyday world. His haunting landscapes may not match nature point to point, but they have made a permanent impression on my view of the world.

But let me return to what an artist (that is, for now, a painter) does. The point has been well made that whereas a scientist looks at the world and says, "this is what I have seen," the artist says, "this is what I have loved," his task to put together the kind of shapes and colours that please him. But he does more than simply play with what strikes him as pleasing and worth capturing on canvas: he invests something of himself often at a huge cost (think of Cézanne who, because he was so utterly absorbed in a picture, did not even attend his mother's funeral); he pours himself into the realization of his vision (so that nobody else has before painted, or ever will paint, apples like Cézanne), and his finished product proclaims "this is me." Philip Toynbee writes:

> 4 *December* Piero della Francesca's *Resurrection*. The only representation of Jesus I know which seems to do him justice. Staring at that amazing face and trying to discover its particular quality I came at last upon the word "knowledge." . . . This is the risen Christ because the face reveals a knowledge of something beyond our world. . . . Piero's vision is an astonishing revelation of God working through man. There is an in-

carnation, Piero in the act of painting; we in the act of looking.[7]

How does an artist achieve this kind of "incarnation" of himself in his chosen medium? By paying attention. By the intentness of his looking. By achieving, through disciplining his eyes, that kind of cleansed perception that enables him to see into the life of things, and which is a real act of "in-selfing." It is a looking at the particular through a particular pair of eyes. It is not simply the capacity to copy nature or to conjure up forms and images or to use paint skillfully: it is the capacity to see more than most of us do, or to scan the landscape and select from it those images that will best tell the truth about the way things are.

The artist in his need to concentrate, to contemplate, is not unlike the mystic or anyone who explores contemplative prayer and must learn to still the mind and focus the gaze of both the outer and the inner eye.

> This concentration [writes the artist Francis Hoyland] should be like a bonfire that burns up our "self" (in the sense of the ego) even as it is enabling God to continue with its creation (self in the sense of "soul"). I only know these things as an artist, but they are in strict accord with the teachings of the mystic.[8]

"A painting," writes Gombrich, "bears as much reality to a surveyor's report as a poem to a police report."[9] "When I sit down to make a sketch from nature," said John Constable, "the first thing I try to do is to forget that I have ever seen a picture … so that, by a close observation of nature [I] discover qualities existing in her, which have never been portrayed before, and thus form a style which is original."[10] That attempt to suppress what the brain knows, the attempt to wipe the slate clean, to focus only on what the eye actually sees at any given moment, is part of what it means to give attention, so that for Turner the structure of objects may be ignored in his concern to capture the effects of mist and the dazzle of light. Or an artist like Matisse will ignore what the eye tells him people look like in an attempt to express qualities in them that we might otherwise miss. There is a story of a woman visiting his studio, looking at a portrait and saying: "But surely, the arm of this woman is much too long?" to which Matisse replied, "Madame, you are mistaken. This is not a woman, this is a picture."[11]

If it is the purpose of art to inform us (as well as to entertain us and to give us pleasure) then it will do so by condensing and interpreting the world, directing our attention to particular things, framing and freezing this moment, that face, this effect of light. *The Book of Evidence* is a novel by John Banville about a man who murders a chambermaid. In jail, he writes of how "he has the time and leisure really to get to the heart of things." There is on his cell wall a reproduction of a painting called *Portrait of a Woman with Gloves*:

> I have stood in front of other, perhaps greater paintings, and not been moved as I am moved by this one. When I look at it my heart contracts. There is something in the way the woman regards me, the querulous, mute insistence in her eyes, which I can neither escape nor assuage. I squirm in the grasp of her gaze. She requires of me some great effort, some tremendous feat of scrutiny and attention, of which I do not think I am capable. It is as if she were asking me to let her live.[12]

This or that particular, in nature or in a person, which will probably be the ignored familiar, is not to be forgotten or overlooked: it is to be noticed, and maybe (in the work of a great artist) made to glow with light. "Art," writes Andrew Graham-Dixon, art critic of *The Independent*:

> has always been a form of redemption, a transfiguration of the
> commonplace.... Painting is itself *made* out of ordinary things
> that have been transfigured, the basic matter of earth, or oil
> or ground-up stone. Every painter is a shaman.[13]

It is, then, the painter's primary task to pay respect to the object or landscape or person by observing them with such intensity that what is conveyed to us may transcend their apparently straightforward reality because they have been filtered through the painter's eye and brain. A great artist does this, not necessarily by inventing new forms, but by a kind of distilling and intensifying of what we pass a thousand times and never see, and by rejecting all that is irrelevant he gives the impression of letting us into a new world. When this occurs, as for example with van Gogh's *Sunflowers* or *Yellow Chair*, it is because the artist's attentiveness, his heightened consciousness, has enabled the division between subject and object to be largely transcended. And we take delight at this partial transcendence of the purely material order we can gain from art (or music or books or the theatre). Van Gogh writes from Arles to his brother Theo:

> I want to paint men and women with that something of the
> eternal which the halo used to symbolize, which I seek to con-
> vey by the actual radiance and vibration of my colouring.[14]

In his letters about Cézanne, Rainer Maria Rilke writes of the way the painter gives his absorbed attention to the mystery before him, and of how the resulting work of art equally claims our proper attention too; of how he gave a portrait of

Cézanne's wife his unrelenting attention "and suddenly one has the right eyes," and he saw as he had never seen before.

Rilke would not, I think, have challenged Kathleen Raine's definition of beauty as "the real aspect of things seen aright and with the eyes of love," but he strikes a warning note when he says that he has learned from Cézanne how

> it is necessary . . . to get beyond even love; it comes naturally to you to love each one of these things if you have made them yourself; but if you show it, you make them less well; you judge them instead of saying them. . . . This is how the sentimentalist school of painting came into being. . . . They painted "I love this" instead of "Here it is."[15]

"Here it is." Andrew Harvey was an academic, a Fellow of All Souls, Oxford. As a student he had been drawn back time and again to stand rapt before a Buddhist painting of a butterfly alighting on a flower in the Ashmolean Museum. At the time he was searching for meaning in what he describes as "the bitterness and solitude of my life." He gazes at the butterfly day by day:

> Slowly I realized that what moved me was not merely the dazzling delicate artistry of the work but the attitude of clear joy, of tender, precise and unselfconscious wonder at things, that had created it. That wonder and unself-consciousness were so far from anything I had ever felt . . . that I was amazed at them and frightened at the lacks and absences they exposed in myself.[16]

Later, he travels high up on the Indian border with Tibet and visits a Buddhist monastery. His teacher at the monastery spends many hours with him talking about paintings:

The most beautiful paintings, the greatest poetry, have often sprung from contemplation, from joy, from an instinct of wonder towards all things and a great compassion. If you can see, for a moment, one flower, one face, one dog, as they are in themselves and for themselves, you have begun to be free enough to love.[17]

An artist's task, then, is to open me up to a new and different world, a new way of seeing or touching, and if he or she is to succeed it will take time—both theirs and mine. For little gives up its secret at a glance. Art teaches us to see what the artist wants us to see because he has seen it and is excited by a truth or a beauty newly-revealed; and that truth may be—as in Goya or Francis Bacon or the Isenheim crucifixion in Colmar—ugly and painful; and it may make and remake for us the perceived world. It may modify how I see by enhancing its sense of mystery. Certain things never look quite the same again: trees, for example, after Pissarro or Sisley have painted them; nor do certain fabrics after you have been taught to see by Vermeer; nor do the faces of the old after Rembrandt's late self-portraits:

> You are confronted with yourself. Each year
> The pouches fill, the skin is uglier.
> You give it all unflinchingly. You stare
> Into yourself, beyond. Your brush's care
> Runs with self-knowledge. Here
> Is a humility at one with craft . . .
> . . . You make light drift
> The way you want. Your face is bruised and hurt
> But there is still love left.
>
> Love of the art and others. To the last
> Experiment went on. You stare beyond
> Your age, the times. You also plucked the past

And tempered it. Self-portraits understand,
And old age can divest,

With truthful changes, us of fear of death . . .
. . . To paint's to breathe.
And all the darknesses are dared. You chose
What each must reckon with.[18]

But the creation of a work of art is not entirely one-sided. It demands that I, the observer, should be in some sense a co-creator by the gift of my time and my attention, for only then shall I feel something of the great mystery of the existence of what has been portrayed. When art speaks to us in this way it is not through any act of our willing that it should—other than the readiness to give attention—but rather what Steiner calls

a chemical bonding . . . which seems to lie deeper than do mechanisms of association or remembrance, certainly on the . . . conscious plane. . . . The shock of correspondence (which can be quite undramatic and almost indiscernibly gradual) is one of being possessed by that which one comes to possess.[19]

Perhaps, to use a thought from one of my earlier letters, there is a sense of "homecoming," a kind of recognition. Yet I am reduced to silence if I try to analyse exactly why this or that work of art or piece of music or poem stirs such feelings within me, shifting the boundaries of my sense of what I am and what I know (even if only on my pulse), and what I sense to be of lasting value.

To ask what certain works of art mean, the abstracts of Mark Rothko, for example, which ask only that we should contemplate these great floating rectangles of subtle colour, may be as absurd as the question put to Schumann when he had just played one of his sonatas: "What does it mean?" "It means this," replied Schumann, and played it again. We are admitted to a new, different way of seeing and the perception is itself the meaning. And art which is religious or spiritual (in the broad sense in which I earlier defined those terms and which embraces a great deal of art) may take me into a realm where I am changed by it, however infinitesimally, and become a little more open to a certain truth. The artist has sought to tell the truth about his or her deepest experience of things in a language that felt right for them, and what they have to say can help open me to my own truth.

> Art makes places and opens spaces for reflection [writes Iris Murdoch]. It is a defence against materialism and against pseudo-scientific attitudes to life. . . . The art object conveys, in the most accessible and for many the only available form, the idea of a transcendent perfection.[20]

Nor is looking at pictures an elitist pastime. For all great art both celebrates (and grieves for) what van Gogh called "that something of the eternal" in us, and in the creation. "It is not a substitute for religion," writes that exuberant solitary nun, Sister Wendy Beckett, "but for those who have no other access to God it is a valid means of entering into that numinous dimension that alone makes the 'incomprehensibility' not only bearable but life-giving."[21] This is knowledge for the sake of truth, experience for the sake of what is there to be experienced; it is not knowledge or experience acquired in order to achieve some further end. And this is the value of paintings: it is the way used by a creative and disciplined few who are able to see further and with sharper vision than the rest of us. They are on the same human journey, yet being able to achieve an intensity of experience or an insight into the truth and the value of things, their beauty and their wonder, they reach out across time and space to speak to us, mind to mind, eye to eye, heart to heart. For, as Chesterton knew, "We have forgotten who and what we are, and [art] makes us remember what we have forgotten."

When he saw Picasso's painting of the man with the blue guitar Wallace Stevens wrote this poem:

> They said, "You have a blue guitar,
> You do not play things as they are."
>
> The man replied, "Things as they are
> Are changed upon the blue guitar."
>
> And they said then, "But play, you must,
> A tune beyond us, yet ourselves,
>
> A tune upon the blue guitar
> Of things exactly as they are."[22]

"A tune beyond us, yet ourselves." What every great artist does is to surprise us, to enable us to break with our stock responses and see beyond the familiar; see that things are not "exactly as they are." Later, the man with the blue guitar tells them to

> Throw away the lights, the definitions,
> And say of what you see in the dark
>
> That it is this or it is that.
> But do not use the rotted names.[23]

In Samuel Palmer's paintings from his *Valley of Vision*, it is a combination of his power of imagination and his power of observing, his use of colour and his treatment of light, that takes the familiar and intimate and through the not entirely explicable alchemy of painting makes them extraordinary and strangely affecting. And so it is to colour and to light that I want to turn tomorrow.

XIII

Light and Colour

God said, let there be light, and there was light; and God saw the light was good . . .[1]

Five o'clock. . . . Down by the lily pond Claude [Monet] stood for a moment . . . and allowed his eyes to wander from the remote reflections still visible in the surface of the water to the willow trees almost submerged in the shadow, their tops sunlit. He felt as though the world he knew was drawing away from him, that he could hold neither the shadow nor the light, which had changed to something far more mysterious. The remaining sunlight had detached itself from the shadows, and now it clung to the very texture of things, leaf, flower, grass, had become part of it, even of wood and stone, so that those things which it still lit had become insubstantial, luminous from within. He strolled along the grass verge, saying his habitual goodbye to shrubs and trees now glowing in a final incandescence he had not captured, not yet. He had been wrong to think of light as a veil, playful and shimmering, between him and solid things. That was how a young man saw things, in mid-summer and midday. But now, especially in the early morning and in the evening, he saw it for the illusion it was. He had to look through things now, since nothing is solid, to show how light and those things it illumines are both transubstantial, both tenuous.

EVA FIGES[2]

The prime reality of human life is visual consciousness. It's there all the time and it's absolutely amazingly beautiful. . . .

PATRICK HERON[3]

THE PATTERN OF MY days here is consistent: after break-
fast I write to you for as much of the day as it takes;
and then we walk. But this morning the cloud had
gone, and the world was bathed in such pure light that it proved
irresistible to walk up into the mountains at the head of the
valley, walking for once in that morning light that is quite different from that of early evening. For light is the subject of my
story.

I have written a little already about how the rays of the
sun, travelling ninety-three million miles in four minutes, strike
an object and are scattered or thrown back as luminosity; light-
waves of different frequencies and lengths—the length, that is,
of each crest-distance from that which precedes it. It cannot
penetrate a blind (how else did the latter get its name?), though
it can penetrate glass which is actually full of minute holes. It
is both life-giving, for without sunlight nothing can grow, and
decorative; both should lead us to wonder, but I will confine
myself to the second.

It seems strange that landscape, which changes constantly as the sun moves across the sky, should figure so little in European an until comparatively recently. For Giotto and Michelangelo, says Kenneth Clark, "it was an impertinence." It adds a certain delight to all those Flemish Madonnas and Renaissance portraits when a tiny cameo of fields with oxen ploughing or a turreted castle perched on a hill is glimpsed through a lancet window, but no really serious study of landscape for its own sake took place before the nineteenth century. There was a problem of painting out-of-doors, to say nothing of the difficulty of capturing a fleeting moment, of accurately recording the constantly changing effect of light. Constable and Turner, for example, handled light quite differently, as you can see if you look at a picture like *The Hay Wain* with its sense of an English summer's day at noon, the light gently caressing the pastoral scene, and most of Turner's work post-1819, when he first visited Italy and found a quality of light that was at once fiercer, more brilliant and dramatic than anything he had seen in England. Turner's more emotional response to light led him to explore all possible ways of depicting it, often painting the same place (Venice was ideal) at different times of day and at different seasons: his contemporaries thinking him mad when he had himself bound to a mast during a four-hour storm which nearly sank the ship and terrified the sailors in order to observe the different effects of light.

But Turner was dead by the time of those artists whose thinking and experimenting with the effect of light on landscape was to prove so radical. The sons of a poor tailor from Limoges, a grocer in Le Havre, a storekeeper in the Danish West Indies, a banker in Paris and a rich Englishman—Renoir, Monet, Pissarro, Dégas and Sisley—were to form a loosely-bound group of painters dedicated to painting what they actually saw in front of their eyes rather than what their minds or their artistic predecessors told them they ought to see.

No longer did they feel the need to construct detail by detail, in a photographic sense, the person or object before them. They began to understand that, while the interplay of light falling on objects in the studio had been painted in terms of the gradual transition from light to shade, so that the play of light was achieved by different densities of shading, this was not true in the open air. Here there are harsh contrasts. Here certain parts may appear brilliant, and the shadows not grey or black but carrying reflections of light and colour from nearby objects. So they sought to translate and disentangle the confusion of images, lines and colour which assault the eye: to perceive how things are related to each other: to understand how sunshine, when it bounces off an object, tends to blend its seven prismatic rays of red and orange, yellow and green, blue and indigo and violet into a single uncoloured brilliance of light, and so tones are discoloured in a strong light. They began to look at the apparent, rather than the accepted, colour of things, to trust how their eyes saw them rather than how their brains told them they ought to look. Their aim was nothing less than to capture light and atmosphere in paint. "When the sun lets certain parts of a landscape appear soft," wrote Sisley, "it lifts others into sharp relief. These effects of light, which have an almost material expression in nature, must be rendered in material fashion on the canvas."[4] "I desire," wrote Monet, "to paint the air which surrounds the bridge, the house, the boat: the beauty of the air in which these objects are located, and that is nothing short of impossible."[5] And Pissarro was concerned that the eye should not be fixed on one spot but take in everything, "observing the reflections which the colours produce on their surroundings."[6]

Monet sought to solve the problem of catching the ever-changing light by painting on a houseboat and changing his dozen or so canvases on which he was working as the light changed. The light will change when a cloud obscures the sun or the breeze catches the still surface of the river, and the artist must apply his paint in rapid strokes, caring more for the overall effect than for the detail. That, at least, became the creed of the Impressionists. There were days when Monet would tear a canvas to pieces in a blind rage, others when he threw his paintbox into the sea in desperation at ever achieving his desire to capture what he saw. Georges Clemenceau, a sensitive critic and close friend of Monet, wrote of this idea of the constantly changing nature of the artist's vision:

> Wherever I go I try to grasp the fleeting, to understand the inexpressible mystery of things, and to savour the endlessly changing spectacle of life with a heightened awareness. Life takes place in the setting of a miracle, and man can derive endless joy from contemplating it.[7]

How far Monet succeeded we can judge from his series of paintings of Rouen Cathedral painted all through the day in quite different lights, or his series of poplars or haystacks; in each case, the mass of the stone, the trees, the hay, seems transformed from hour to hour. In the last years of his life, his eyesight failing, he painted his water-lily pond in his garden in Giverny, and Eva Figes, in her short novel, *Light*, beautifully captures the quality of the changing light and the old man's moods as she follows him during the course of a single day.

Cézanne's anguish matched that of Monet. Sometimes he pondered for hours before putting down a certain stroke for, as a contemporary wrote, "For him each stroke must contain the air, the light, the object, the composition, the character, the outline, and the style," in the attempt to restore to each object that exists something of its true radiance. "The landscape thinks itself in me," he wrote. "I am its consciousness."[8]

Artists such as Cézanne, Monet and van Gogh really can shape our understanding of the world, helping us to see with changed eyes. Some of the best letters ever written by an artist are those of van Gogh, not least because of his joy in the mysterious nature and power of colour. Nothing makes the world more beautiful. Ruskin had declared that "of all gifts bestowed upon man, colour is the holiest, the most divine, the most solemn." Scientists may explain it in terms of mathematics, as Newton did when he experimented with a prism and a ray of light in his rooms at Trinity College, Cambridge, measuring the length of the different light-waves, a certain number of which are absorbed by the opaque object they strike, while others are reflected back to our eyes (a daffodil having absorbed all the rays except yellow which it rejects and we receive); but that only deepens the mystery of why the creation should be so enriched, and not be of a uniform shade of grey. And, as the Impressionists showed, things are not of a consistent colour; they depend on shade and sun, the company they keep and the time of day at which they are seen. In certain lights there is a blue tinge to the grass, or shades of green in a woman's face. The sky may be the purest blue at mid-day, but at dawn or sunset rose or green or gold. Eric Newton makes an important distinction between our experience of form and colour. To appreciate form, he suggests, there must be an active exploration by the eye as it observes the scene or an object, "accumulating and correlating images"; to appreciate colour is for the retina passively to accept certain sensations as the light rays of different wavelengths bombard it. "Form has to be read as one reads a book: colour can only be experienced as one experiences a hot bath."[9]

It is no doubt true that, in its strictest sense, beauty in art as in nature is only fully achieved when the fusion between form and colour is perfectly expressed, so that each has an equal impact on the senses. Clearly giving attention to form is the more vigorous activity, and of course it is not a case of "either/or"; and yet, for me, it is the subtlety of colour that first grabs my attention almost every time. Whenever I am stopped in my tracks by some unexpected beauty it will initially be because of a combination of colour and light That is what makes van Gogh's letters so rewarding. "Who will be in figure painting what Claude Monet is in landscape?" he writes in 1888. "The painter of the future will be *a colourist such as has never yet been*."[10] His sense of colour pervades not only his canvases but his letters to his brother Theo. So, in July 1884, he writes:

> Spring is tender, green young corn and pink apple blossoms. Autumn is the contrast of the yellow leaves against the violet tones. Winter is the snow with black silhouettes. But now, if summer is the opposition of blues against an element of orange, in the gold bronze of the corn, one could paint a picture which expressed the mood of the seasons in each of the contrasts of the complementary colours (red and green, blue and orange, yellow and violet, white and black).[11]

In June 1888 he writes:

> I went for a walk by the sea.... It was beautiful. The deep blue sky was flecked with clouds of a blue deeper than the fundamental blue of intense cobalt, and others of a clearer blue, like the blue whiteness of the Milky Way. In the blue depths the stars were sparkling, greenish, yellow, white, rose.... The sea was a very deep ultramarine—the shore a sort of russet as I

saw it, and on the dunes . . . some bushes of Prussian blue . . .[12]

In August of that year he writes

The other day I saw a girl with a coffee-tinted skin. . . . Ash blonde hair, grey eyes, a print bodice of pale rose. . . . This against the emerald leaves of some fig trees. I shall get her to pose in the open air, and her mother too—a gardener's wife— earth-coloured, dressed just then in soiled yellow and faded blue. The girl's coffee-tinted complexion was darker than the rose of her bodice. The mother was stunning, the figure . . . thrown up in strong sunlight against a square of brilliant flowers, snow-white and lemon-yellow. . . . A perfect Vermeer . . .[13]

And in mid-October he describes a sketch of his bedroom, where

. . . colour is to do everything . . . to be suggestive of rest or of sleep in general . . . To look at the picture ought to rest the brain . . .

The walls are pale violet. The floor is of red tiles.

The wood of the bed and chairs is the yellow of fresh butter, the sheet and pillow very light lemon-green.

The coverlet sky-coloured. The window green.

The toilet table orange, the basin blue.

The doors lilac . . .

The frame—as there is no white in the picture—will be white.[14]

You will find if you look, that in the country almost every place has its dominant colour according to the light and time of day. And in towns too. We have a wonderfully observant Texan friend, Betsy Vardaman, who sent a card the other week written at 35,000 feet, flying between Amsterdam (home of the finest van Goghs) and Fort Worth:

Today my colors are grey and white and black [she wrote of Amsterdam]. The skaters (with mufflers of a thousand blues and reds) move as grey beings in a white world. The river is white slate; the sky is dotted with blackbirds which will settle on bare apple branches or chestnuts or poplars in just a minute. And the towns are outlined in white lights. The sheep on the hills are moon-coloured, and the moon convinces me in its fullness it is really a sheep. All things seem quiet, clear and connected. Why can't the world really be this way for everyone?

This morning, as we climbed higher and higher, it was not the magnificence of the dwarfing mountains and tumbling waterfalls, impressive as they were, it was the significance of what was at our feet that claimed the eye. It was the colour and variety of the wild flowers. At first, in the low meadows, the bright yellow of dandelions and vetch, coltsfoot and arnica, the yellowish-green of spurge, the royal blue of gentians, the pink of campion and saxifrage, and the bird's-eye primrose. Higher came the mountain pansies, the tiny heartsease and white violets, forget-me-not and thyme and the just bursting Alpen-rose; and higher still, the purple bee orchids and the Alpine pasque flowers, some a rich buttercup-yellow, others the shade of the crust of that thick Devonshire cream I had as a boy as a wartime treat, and can still taste. And everywhere butterflies, white ones with orange tips to their wings, brown ones with purple "eyes," tiny ones in shades of green and cobalt blue.

And the crazy thing is that nature is so absurdly wasteful, so irrepressible, that most of them will grow and bloom and wither without ever being seen by human eye. It matters to come close and give attention to the tiny and the particular, each created thing in its own small perfection. Each is there to

be noticed in its own light and celebrated for what it is. Because
... because it has something to do with William Blake's "holiness of the minute particular"; and because each could serve to
illustrate the truth for which seven hundred years ago Dame
Julian of Norwich used the tiny hazelnut.

In her desire to show that, once you begin to look for
God, you find him everywhere, and that he is not only the sus-
tainer, but the lover, of all that exists, Dame Julian wrote of how
God

> ... showed me a little thing, the size of a hazelnut, in the palm
> of my hand, and it was as round as a ball. I looked at it with
> my mind's eye and I thought, "What can this be?" And answer
> came, "It is all that is made." I marveled that it could last, for I
> thought it might have crumbled to nothing, it was so small.
> And the answer came into my mind, "It lasts and ever shall
> because God loves it." And all things have their being through
> the love of God.
>
> In this little thing I saw three truths. The first is that God
> made it. The second is that God loves it. The third is that God
> looks after it.[15]

That is why it matters to notice such things; and to wonder at
them.

XIV

Poetry and Music as the
Language of Wonder

For he spoke and it was.[1]

Poetry can do a hundred and one things, delight, sadden, disturb, amuse, instruct—but there is only one thing that all poetry must do; it must praise all it can for being as for happening.

W. H. AUDEN[2]

Pictures cannot be said, but only seen. . . . Poems can only be read. Criticism of pictures or poems is valid only if it extends someone's seeing or reading. . . . The ordinary is inexhaustible and sufficiently surprising and bizarre, when extraordinarily seen. Each poet experiences the ordinary like an Adam, or as if it were a proverb heard for the first time.

GEOFFREY GRIGSON[3]

The artist . . . speaks to our capacity for delight and wonder, to the sense of mystery surrounding our lives: to our sense of pity, and beauty, and pain.

JOSEPH CONRAD[4]

The birds sang in the wet trees
And as I listened to them it was a hundred years from now
And I was dead and someone else was listening.
But I was glad I had recorded for him
The melancholy.

PATRICK KAVANAGH[5]

6 June, Trinity Sunday

THIRTY-FIVE YEARS AGO today I was made a priest. What could be a nicer way of spending this small anniversary away from home than writing to you about the wonder of words as I listen to Mozart's violin sonatas? Few things in my life have given me more consistent pleasure and occasional joy than reading, and (predictably, no doubt, in a proverbially self-absorbed only child) my desert island would have to contain music, a dog and unending shelves of books.

In my second letter I wrote of what George Steiner calls his "wager on transcendence": the belief that, in art or music or literature there is "a space in which giver and receiver are themselves transcended," and I said that to ask "What is art?", "What is poetry?", "What is music?" is one way of asking "What is a human being?" We have a limited number of ways of communicating what we are and what we feel, and yet the variety of human expression within those confines is almost boundless. We have our bodies, than which nothing could be more expressive, even when engaged in the silent language of making love; we have the capacity to think and to create beauty in paint or wood or stone, or to make "out of the sea of sound the life of music"; and we have words. We are back to those twenty-six letters of the alphabet which can be taken and shaped and fashioned to express every conceivable human emotion, from the first bedtime story read to you by your mother—well, to what? Perhaps to what Tolstoy did on 5 January 1872 when he read of a woman, the mistress of a neighbour, who had thrown herself under a train because her lover was neglecting her and planned to marry his children's governess. "You are my murderer," she had written. "If you like, you can see my corpse on the rails at Yasenki." Tolstoy went to view her corpse and tried to imagine what it must be like for a woman to die a senseless death for the sake of love, and out of his creative imagination came *Anna Karenina*. And from those twenty-six letters there have also emerged, again by some strange and wondrous alchemy, Milton's *Lycidas*, Keats's Odes, Donne's love poetry to his mistress and Herbert's love poetry to his God; to say nothing of Shakespeare's unique ability to understand the human soul and all its needs, weaknesses and strengths.

Steiner speaks of the two main functions of language as being to convey that "humane order which we call law," and to communicate "that quick of the human spirit which we call grace. . . . So far, in history, it is language that has been the vessel of human grace and the prime carrier of civilization."[6] By which I take him to mean that what writers have been concerned to capture is all that is deepest and most mysterious within us. And, therefore, least expressible. Only through language can all that spells "person" be expressed: our loneliness and our pain, our innate goodness and equally innate potential to hurt and destroy, our need to love and be loved, our fears and joys, our sense of settling for less than that to which we are called; our mystery and our silent music, the things that we sense but for which we find no words. The poet or novelist who can find the words and images that speak to our human condition in such a way as not just to ratify, but to illuminate and extend our experience and perceptions, is the one who uses language as "the vessel of human grace." For just occasionally they strike a note which resonates deeply in us with an authenticity we cannot wholly analyse or explain. It is as if certain writers, like certain artists, are gifted with a power of spiritual insight that enriches us all.

> What art communicates [writes the novelist Jeanette Winterson] if it's genuine, is something ineffable. Something about ourselves, about the human condition, that is not summed up by the oil painting, or the piece of music, or the poem, but, rather, moves through it. What you say, what you paint, what you can hear, is the means not the end of art; there are so many rooms behind.[7]

In Primo Levi's account of his time as a prisoner in a concentration camp at Auschwitz, he writes of the life-giving quality of poetry at a time when life had become bestial. After a particularly humiliating experience at the hands of a Nazi guard, Levi began to give a fellow-prisoner, a Frenchman, a kind of tutorial on Dante's *Inferno*. Three lines from canto 26 struck each of them in particular:

> Consider the seed from which you spring,
> You were not born to live like beasts,
> But to seek both virtue and knowledge.

Last year, in an interview, that former French prisoner, Jean Samuel, said he still believed in the importance of that moment of shared poetry in allowing them to affirm their humanity and survive.

Artists achieve this enrichment partly through a highly developed ear and eye. A writer is a seer, or a see-er, one who has trained himself or herself to be unusually observant, to watch, to stand (as it were) at a slightly oblique angle to the universe, developing both an ordinary "eye" for the people and events of their daily life, and also an "inner" eye which has to do with imagination, intuition and insight (literally "in-seeing"). They are concerned to explore both the contained world outside them and the limitless world of the imagination they know to be within them. Tolstoy, for example, noticed everything: when his mother died, he writes in *Childhood*, "I was in great distress at that moment but involuntarily noticed every detail," including the fact that the nurse was "very fair, young, and remarkably handsome."

Above all such writers have retained, or rediscovered, that primal sense of wonder at the singularity of people and things: the haunting poignancy of *this* woman's grief; the exact quality of amazed delight of this boy and that girl in their newly-discovered love; the blue of the sky in midsummer; the holiness of *this* human hand. We can read Tolstoy or Lawrence or Dickens or Graham Greene and simply feel more alive, for (like the Impressionists) they make the world that bit more luminous through their precise observation of it. We have seen how a painting isolates and freezes a moment in visual terms: so does a poet, a novelist or a dramatist, with words. A poem invites us to look, puts a frame round a moment which is both ordinary and extraordinary, both common and particular. The poem invites us to notice, to pay attention, to a view, a person, a feeling. You read it, and you may recognize it is true, it is valid for you. For a moment a door is opened and we are invited to see into a familiar, yet more intensely perceived, world. When Seamus

Heaney wants to convey both the ordinary fact and the particular anguish of his mother's death he writes this sonnet:

> When all the others were away at Mass
> I was all hers as we peeled potatoes.
> They broke the silence, let fall one by one
> Like solder weeping off the soldering iron:
> Cold comforts set between us, things to share
> Gleaming in a bucket of cold water.
> And again let fall. Little pleasant splashes
> From each other's work would bring us to our senses.
>
> So while the parish priest at her bedside
> Went hammer and tongs at the prayers for the dying
> And some were responding and some crying
> I remembered her head bent towards my head,
> Her breath in mine, our fluent dipping knives—
> Never closer the whole rest of our lives.[8]

All real poems, all great novels and plays, begin and end in the mystery of who we are and how we relate to each other and the world. It is as if they verify how singular and special we are.

> Most people peed poetry, [writes Geoffrey Grigson] but not much of it: it is a vitamin of which small familiar doses are enough. The poems most people know and enjoy and turn over and over again through their lives are like prayers addressed to the mystery of themselves.[9]

What we sense intuitively about our value and potential is strengthened and affirmed by artists, but chiefly for me by poets, for poetry is above all else the language of wonder.

The best writing I know on the nature and value of poetry comes from Seamus Heaney in his two volumes of lectures and critical writings. Wordsworth had defined poetry as "the spontaneous overflow of powerful feelings." Heaney agrees but adds:

> The overflow is not a reactive response to some stimulus in the world out there. Instead, it is a spun of abundance from a source within and it spills over to irrigate the world beyond the self. . . .[10] Poetry helps us to say in the first recesses of ourselves, in the shyest, pre-social part of our nature, "Yes, I know something like that too. Yes, that's right; thank you for putting words upon it and making it more or less official. . . ."[11] [So a poet has a need to] go beyond himself and to take on the otherness of the world in works that remain his own yet offer rights-of-way to everybody else.[12]

That's finely said; it stresses both the need for a writer to find his or her unique and authentic voice and also their role in enlarging our vision by touching on our common inner landscape. Last night in bed I was reading a novel by Graham Swift, *Ever After*, and I came across this:

> Why should the simplest, tritest words . . . touch us with pure delight? "My true love hath my heart and I have his." Why do the most tired and worn (and bitterest) thoughts—the thoughts we all have thought—return to us, in another's words, like some redeeming balm?

> > Even such is time, which takes in trust
> > Our youth, our joys, and all we have,
> > And pays us but with age and dust;
> > Who in the dark and silent grave
> > When we have wandered all our ways
> > Shuts up the story of our days.[13]

So? We all know this. We have heard this before, and we would rather not dwell, thank you, on the subject. But the words hold us with their poise, their gravity—their beauty.

They catch us up and speak to us in their eloquence and equilibrium, and just for a little moment . . . the obvious is luminous, darkness is matched with light and life is reconciled with death.[14]

The hero of Swift's novel is right: it is often the simplest, tritest words which give us "aural gooseflesh" and speak to us in their indefinable beauty, or move us to pity. When Shakespeare needs language to express the almost unbearable anguish of Lear as at the end he sits with Cordelia in prison he spins his thread from the simplest, most monosyllabic words:

> We two alone will sing like birds i' th' cage:
> When thou dost ask me blessing, I'll kneel down
> And ask of thee forgiveness; so we'll live,
> And pray, and sing, and tell old tales, and laugh
> At gilded butterflies . . .
> And take upon's the mystery of things
> As if we were God's spies; and we'll wear out
> In a wall'd prison packs and sects of great ones
> That ebb and flow by th' moon.[15]

And there is no more touching line in Shakespeare than Lear's as he comes to die with a

Pray you undo this button. Thank you, sir.

(Nor is there a more profound play about perception and blindness. Cordelia knows, and the Fool sees intuitively, what Lear is blind to, and the sighted Gloucester does not see what he perceives once his eyes have been put out.)

I must not be seduced into the theatre, except to record with gratitude that the stage is equally the place where you can have experiences that transcend the ordinary and speak of what

Shakespeare called "the mystery of things." I can never forget the sense of awe (it felt then like sheer terror) that gripped the audience forty-five years ago at Olivier's off-stage howl of anguish in Oedipus when he discovers he has killed his father and married his mother.

Peter Brook, who has worked more theatrical magic than most, speaks of the Holy Theatre, or the Theatre of the Invisible-made-Visible, a place where we may be made to see with new eyes, in which moments are lived more intensely, in which time is arrested or compressed, so that the events are given a depth and significance, "framed" as in a painting or a poem. We may emerge with our sympathies enlarged, our compassion deepened. In the theatre we have the experience *and* (if we keep our ears and eyes open) the meaning too; and we see that two tramps waiting for Godot by a stunted tree take us deep into the anguish of our human loneliness and our longing to be seen, to be noticed. "Tell him . . . tell him you saw me. . . ," says Vladimir to the boy who reports that Godot won't be keeping his appointment with them after all, "and that . . . *that you saw me*."[16] The words are repeated at the end of each act.

How do we explain certain lines and images that lodge like burrs in the mind? The lyric beauty of Philip Larkin's "Cut grass lies frail," for example; or the irresistibly haunting power of Blake's "O rose, thou art sick" and

> Tyger, Tyger, burning bright
> In the forests of the night . . . ;

Keats's

> murmurous haunt of flies on summer eves;

and Walter de la Mare's

> Look thy last on all things lovely;

Auden's

> Altogether elsewhere, vast
> Herds of reindeer move across
> Miles and miles of golden moss,
> Silently and very fast . . . ;[17]

or Houseman's

> Loveliest of trees, the cherry now
> Is hung with bloom along the bough. . . ?

It was Houseman who wrote:

> Experience has taught me, when I am shaving of a morning,
> to keep watch over my thoughts, because, if a line of poetry
> strays into my memory, my skin bristles so that the razor
> ceases to act.[18]

My skin isn't given to bristling, but certainly my spine tingles at the evocative power of the image in these six lines of W. B. Yeats's *Memory*, where the poet uses the mountain grass retaining the form imprinted on it as an emblem of the power of memory, in this case the memory, almost certainly, of the young Maud Gonne.

> One had a lovely face,
> And two or three had charm,
> But charm and face were in vain
> Because the mountain grass

> Cannot but keep the form
> Where the mountain hare has lain.[19]

Certain poems have the feel of magic: the power of sound working its spell to create poetry that Auden compared to the poetry of Ariel—pure enchantment—rather than the poetry of Prospero which makes "wise and true meanings" and relates to our intelligence and our experience.

But we are still left with a host of questions as to

> why there should be the stuff called poetry, to begin with [Graham Swift again] which strikes our hearts at such a magic angle. And why there should be certain things in this random universe which cry out to us with their loveliness. And why it should be poetry that captures them.[20]

I love the Kavanagh lines I set at the head of this letter about being glad to have recorded for the listener (and reader) "a hundred years from now" the melancholy of the birds in the wet trees. Poets through their words can unlock the world for us and make it sing. Heaney records with gratitude that it was his fellow Irishman Patrick Kavanagh who, by writing poems about the potato pits, the stillness and the heat of the sunlit fields, "the inexplicable melancholy of distant work-sounds," the small world of his shared Irish childhood, first made Heaney aware of "the primitive delight of world become word."[21]

He sees Kavanagh as one who sought to retain a "childlike, open-eyed attention to the small and the familiar."[22] For him

> the only true teaching
> Subsists in watching . . .
> To look on is enough

In the business of love.[23]

But it is not so simple. He admits:

> We have tested and tasted too much, lover—
> through a chink too wide there comes in no wonder. . . .[24]

He yearns for

> . . . the newness that was in every stale thing
> When we looked at it as children: the spirit-shocking
> Wonder in a black slanting Ulster hill. . . .[25]

In A Christmas Childhood he writes:

> . . . Now and then
> I can remember something of the gay
> Garden that was childhood's. Again
>
> The tracks of cattle to a drinking place,
> A green stone lying sideways in a ditch
> Or any common sight the transfigured face
> Of a beauty that the world did not touch.[26]

Walking by a canal bank in Dublin he can write:

> O unworn world enrapture me, encapture me in a web
> Of fabulous grass and eternal voices by a beech,
> Feed the gaping need of my senses, give me ad lib
> To pray unselfconsciously with overflowing speech
> For this soul needs to be honoured with a new dress woven
> From green and blue things and arguments that cannot be proven.[27]

For Kavanagh the "moments to see wonders in the grass," the "arguments that cannot be proven," have to do with his constant natural urge to praise all that is given, and equally to see beyond it the holy, the invisible made visible:

> Poetic imagination [writes the Poet Laureate, Ted Hughes] is determined finally by the state of negotiation—in a person or a people—between man and his idea of the Creator. . . . How things are between man and his idea of the Divinity determines everything in his life, the quality and connectedness of every feeling and thought, and the meaning of every action.[28]

If among "the arguments that cannot be proven" should be for you certain convictions about the sacramental nature of the world, a sense of the holy in the ordinary that I have written about earlier, then it may well be artists who, like Hopkins, believe that "the world is charged with the grandeur of God" are those who spell out what you know intuitively, so that in their work you too experience the primitive delight of "world become word." Two twentieth-century writers who have helped me to see are David Jones and Theodore Roethke.

David Jones has something of the prophetic quality of Blake about him. He was both writer and painter, a Roman Catholic who served as a private in the Royal Welch Fusiliers from 1915 and was wounded on the Western Front. Out of his wartime experiences came his great poetic work, *In Parenthesis*, the experience of a young infantryman in the trenches and the attempt to see some signs of how the evil of war may in some way be redeemed. This he followed by *The Anathemata*, a huge, universal work concerned with the whole history (and pre-history) of Britain, a bringing the past into the present. Like all true artists he tells the truth: that is to say, he avoids the dual traps of sentimentality on the one hand or cynicism on the other. He sees both the glory of which we are capable and the distance we have fallen from it with transparent honesty: the nobility as well as the horror and the pain. He is blind neither to the evil of the world, nor to its good. He is a passionate observer of the particular, the concrete, the ephemeral frailty of a flower or a human skull, both in his descriptive poetry and in his paintings, which express his view of the world as sacramental and of infinite value.

"Take practically any page from *In Parenthesis* or *The Anathemata*," writes David Blamires, "and you realize that the loving attention paid to this particular has as its aim a depiction of the universal and the tangible world that points beyond itself to the transcendental."[29] And David Jones could write:

> It is important to know that a beefsteak is neither more nor less "mystical" than a diaphanous cloud. God loves both. [Vegetarians might dissent.] The painter more than any man must know that the green grass on the hill and the fairy ring are both equally real. He must deny nothing, he must integrate everything. But he must deal only with what he loves, and therefore knows, at any given time.[30]

Like Blake, like Dame Julian or Monet or Billy Yellow of the Navajo, David Jones witnesses to the "holiness of the minute particular," the worth of every seemingly ordinary thing.

As does Theodore Roethke, a manic-depressive from Michigan who was a lonely, meditative observer of the beauty and ugliness of the landscape he knew best, and who writes of childhood and love and death. And the need to see the world as holy, and the need to praise it. His poetry has many moments of heightened awareness which come through learning to be still:

> A mind too active is no mind at all;
> The deep eye sees the shimmer on the stone . . .[31]

I teach my eyes to hear, my ears to see . . .[32]

I love because I am
A rapt thing with a name.[33]

I recover my tenderness by long looking.[34]

And here is the final part of a long poem called The Shape of the Fire:

> To have the whole air!
> The light, the full sun
> Coming down on the flowerheads,
> The tendrils turning slowly,
> A slow snail-lifting, liquescent;
> To be by the rose
> Rising slowly out of its bed,
> Still as a child in its first loneliness;
> To see cyclamen veins become clearer in early sunlight,
> And mist lifting out of the brown cat-tails;
> To stare into the after-light, the glitter left on the lake's surface,
> When the sun has fallen behind a wooded island;
> To follow the drops sliding from a lifted oar,
> Held up, while the rower breaths, and the small boat drifts
> quietly shoreward;
> To know that light falls and fills, often without our knowing,
> As an opaque vase fills to the brim from a quick pouring,
> Fills and trembles at the edge yet does not flow over,
> Still holding and feeding the stem of the contained flower.[35]

I link Jones and Roethke because both knew the land-scape of suffering, yet believed (in Roethke's words) that "every-thing that lives is holy." There is nothing escapist in such writers. On the contrary. The pain and anguish of war in the one, the desolation of the depressive in the other, are all too evident; but faced and reckoned with until each comes through into an altered landscape. It is like the deaf Beethoven (to take an extreme example of such transmutation of the material of suffering), soon after the nephew who was like a son to him had attempted suicide, composing the amazing slow movement of the F Major Quartet.

It has been said of Roethke that he had grasped the very essence of the sacramental principle—that nothing may be a sacrament unless everything is, at bottom, sacramental, "and that ours may be considered to be a sacramental universe because, in every aspect and dimension, it is instinct with that which appears to be *for* man rather than *against*—which is none other than Being itself."[36]

At which point my hypocrisy pulls me up short. Perhaps you spotted it before I did. Here am I banging on about giving attention to what is before our eyes, learning to notice and be receptive to what is given moment by moment, and as I write I am listening to music. Listening? No; rather I am using Mozart's sonatas and Haydn's quartets as a kind of calming background noise. Perhaps because, much as I love it, I have never learned the language of music. Yet music, for some, will speak more powerfully than words of that "space in which giver and receiver are themselves transcended." It stands somewhere between matter and spirit, partaking of both. "I didn't stop to wonder about the nature or effects of the music, nor what it meant to my life," writes Bernard Levin as he describes hearing Beethoven's *Egmont* Overture for the first time, "all I wanted to do, as those three amazing chords brought that most thrilling of codas to an end, was to rush out and liberate the Low Countries single-handed."[37]

It can happen that listening to music you are caught up out of yourself in an experience of wonder, exposed to a kind of beauty that cannot be expressed in any other terms. But why these particular sounds, any more than words placed just so on a page or brush strokes placed in this way and not that on a canvas, have a power to move us so profoundly and create in us a rare stillness is something we cannot explain. But nor can we explain it away or deny it. It is not just a succession of feelings: it is knowledge of a deep kind. As J. W. N. Sullivan wrote, "No account of life that denies its supreme importance can be even remotely true." "It may well be," writes George Steiner,

> that man is man, and that man "borders on" limitations of a peculiar and open "otherness" because he can produce and be possessed by music. . . . Music puts our being as men and women in touch with that which transcends the sayable and which outstrips the analysable . . . It has long been, it continues to be, the unwritten theology of those who lack or reject any formal creed.[38]

Music, then, is brimful of meaning but we cannot express it in words. "At the inner core of music," writes Dame Janet Baker, "is the possibility that performing can touch and change the human heart."[39] Hans Küng has recently attempted to define the "traces of transcendence" we find in the music of Mozart. He speaks of his mysterious order, of an ordering of tones and sounds which are "almost superhuman"; of this child-like man who was such a prodigy as never really to be a child; of a music that is "humane in every respect . . . and which constantly makes audible both the light *and* the dark, joy *and* sorrow, life *and* death. . . . But the darkness is always transcended and done away with in the light."[40] In the end Hans Küng is forced back to speak of "the ineffable mystery" that is in the midst of music, adding that for him it is Mozart's music more than any other that reveals how wafer-thin is the boundary between the human and the divine. He claims that

To listen to the adagio of the Clarinet Concerto, for example, is to perceive something wholly other: the sound of an infinite which transcends us and for which "beauty" is no description. . . . To describe such experience and revelation of transcendence, religious language still needs the word God.[41]

In the end, the artist, the poet, the playwright, the novelist, the composer, in answer to T. S. Eliot's taxi driver's question, "What's it all about then?" is saying: "This is what it looks like to me. Let me show you in the most adequate language I know." And the greatest of them is able, mysteriously and wonderfully, to show us not just the essence of a landscape or the inner workings of the human heart, but to show us these things under the aspect of eternity. Whether it is Monet finally triumphing over how the light falls on his water lilies, or Cézanne capturing the elusive subtleties of Mont Saint Victoire, or Shakespeare penetrating into the heart of Lear, each in their own unique way call attention to how things are: they praise the world "for being and for happening."

My contention is that, by watching where they plant their steps, we can do the same.

XV

Entr'acte: Journals and Diaries,
and Kettle's Yard

Then I came back to the cottage with my throat dry thinking
in what a little while I would be in my grave with the whole
world lost to me.

J. M. SYNGE[1]

I was born for seeing
I am employed to watch
I am bound by my oath to this tower,
And I love the world.
I look into the distance
and see, as from nearby,
the moon and the starts,
the forest and the deer.
And in all of them I see
the eternal adornment;
and as the world delights me,
so I delight myself.
Oh, happy eyes,
whatever you have seen,
let it be as it may be,
it has been beautiful!

GOETHE[2]

7 June

THIS LETTER IS A kind of indulgent postscript that I have not been able to resist. It concerns a way of seeing by a peculiarly English group of writers: those who in the past two centuries have left a record in journals and diaries of what they have observed of the world about them. It may appear simple to keep such a journal: to observe the seasons and the changing face of nature. In fact it takes an exceptional power of looking, feeling and responding; and an intuitive sense of what to exclude (which later "nature writing" often fails to do). But there have been a few such writers, miniaturists whom I doubt have been equaled anywhere for their power to convey what it felt like to be in this place at this moment and to observe the world about them with such a perceptive and enviable sense of wonder. A handful were major writers and poets—Hopkins, Blake, Coleridge, Hardy—but to my mind the finest were a nineteenth-century country parson, Francis Kilvert, and a woman living with her brother in the Lakes, Dorothy Wordsworth. In each case I shall confine myself to how they see the natural world in all its diverse moods.

Francis Kilvert began his diary in 1870. He served parishes at Clyro (as curate) and Bredwardine (as rector for too short a time before his death from peritonitis on his return from honeymoon) in the delectable Radnorshire border country of the Wye; and at Langley Burrell in Wiltshire. His almost daily diary gives us a unique picture of a country life that has vanished, creating its atmosphere, sounds and scents, its people and their concerns; and of a good, vulnerable, loving man ("very sleek and glossy and gentle, rather like a nice Newfoundland dog"[3]), who allows us to see him as well as the natural world about him with a particular intimacy.

Kilvert arrived in Clyro in the spring of 1870 aged twenty-four to find it set in a countryside of startling beauty:

9 May 1870 The turtles were trilling softly and deeply in the dingles as I went up the steep orchard. The grass was jeweled with cowslips and orchises. The dingle was lighted here and there with wild cherry, bird cherry, the Welsh name of which being interpreted is "the tree on which the devil hung his mother." The mountains burned blue in the hot afternoon.

16 July 1873 As I walked along the field path I stopped to listen to the rustle and solemn night whisper of the wheat, so different to its voice by day.

16 October 1873 Golden autumn weather and almost a summer day, one of the perfect days of the summertide of sweet St. Luke, still and warm and almost cloudless from the early morning when I walked upon the Common and said my prayers in the fresh morning air, and thanked God for having made the world so beautiful, while a red squirrel rustled seeking mast among the dry yellow leaves under the beeches in the avenue, and the village people crossed the diamond-sparkling common by the several paths, and the sun shone upon the bright tin can of the whistling milk-boy, and the tender morning mist slanted fairy blue across the hollows and deep shadows of the elms. All day long the summer lingered with us and the sun grew hot at noon.

24 September 1874 A day of exceeding and almost unmatched beauty . . . A warm delicious calm and sweet peace brooded breathless over the mellow sunny autumn afternoon and the happy stillness was broken only by the voices of children blackberry-gathering in an adjoining meadow and the sweet solitary singing of a robin. . . . Near the entrance to the village of Kington St. Michael I fell in with a team of red oxen. harnessed coming home from plough with chains rattling and the old ploughman riding the fore ox. . . .

When I returned home at night the good Vicar accompanied me as far as the Plough Inn. The moon was at the full. The night was sweet and quiet. Overhead was the vast fleecy sky in which the moon was riding silently and the stillness was broken only by the occasional pattering of an acorn or a chestnut through the leaves to the ground.

7 October 1874 For some time I have been trying to find the right word for the shimmering glancing twinkling movement of the poplar leaves in the sun and wind. This afternoon I saw the word written on the poplar leaves. It was "dazzle." The dazzle of the poplars.

24 May 1875 As I came down from the hill into the valley across the golden meadows and along the flower-scented hedges a great wave of emotion and happiness stirred and rose up in me. I know not why I was so happy, nor what I was expecting, but I was in a delirium of joy, it was one of the supreme few moments of existence, a deep delicious draught from the strong sweet cup of life.[4]

Richard Hoggart has written of Kilvert: "A sort of love flowed from his finger-ends," and Iris Murdoch speaks of his "transparent artless lucidity." "Why," Kilvert once asked, "why do I keep this voluminous diary? . . . Because life seems to me such a curious and wonderful thing. It is such a luxury to be alive"; and he goes through the world as one who celebrates and gives thanks for it daily.

Dorothy Wordsworth lived with her brother William, first below the Quantocks and then at Grasmere in the Lakes for more than fifty years. In her younger days she was described as a plain, round-faced girl, awkward in movement; later she became melancholic. Yet she is unsurpassed as a lyrical recorder of nature:

> *17 February 1798* A deep snow upon the ground. . . . We walked through the wood into the Coombe to fetch some eggs. The sun shone bright and clear. A deep stillness in the thickest part of the wood, undisturbed except by the occasional dropping of the snow from the holly boughs; no other sound but that of the water, and the slender notes of a redbreast, which sang at intervals on the outskirts of the southern side of the wood. There the bright green moss was bare at the roots of the trees, and the little birds were upon it . . . each tree taken singly was beautiful. The branches of the hollies pendent with their white burden, but still showing their bright red berries, and their glossy green leaves. The bare branches of the oaks thickened by the snow.

> *12 October 1800* We pulled apples after dinner, a large basket full. We walked before tea by Bainriggs to observe the many-coloured foliage. The oaks dark green with some yellow leaves, the birches generally still green, some near the water yellowish, the sycamore crimson and crimson-tufted, the mountain ash a deep orange, the common ash lemon colour, but many ashes still fresh in their summer green.

> *31 October 1800* A very fine moonlight night—The moon shone like herrings in the water.[5]

Like Kilvert, the spirit in which she writes is one of spontaneous thankfulness.

Coleridge often stayed with the Wordsworths in Grasmere. He explored the world on foot and wrote down his immediate impressions at great length in his notebooks, even at the unlikeliest moments: "I went to the window to empty my urine-pot, and wondered at the simple grandeur of the view . . . ," which he then describes. He can write of the November sky, full of "black clouds, two or three dim untwinkling stars like full stops on damp paper . . ."; "oak leaves a sober silver grey on their backs; the long bracken, unreapt, wet and rotting, strait dangling, from the mossy green hillocks like unkempt red brown hair"; "the trout leaping in the sunshine spreads on the bottom of the river concentric circles of light"; "the huge enormous mountains all bare and iron-red—and on them a forest of cloud-shadows, all motionless . . . Mem. beautiful shadow of the Fern upon the lichened stone which it overcanopied"; "In this whole bason . . . but one field is sunny—that with a white cottage—The grass yellow-green, so bright—the white cottage sparkles like a diamond in the surrounding gloom"; "Aspens— one a lovely light yellow—the other red, or rather poppy-color'd"; "The full moon glided on behind a black cloud. And what then? And who cared?"

Here is a brief seasonal taster, for which I am much indebted to Geoffrey Grigson's lovely anthology, *The English Year.*[6]

Winter: "The landscape had turned from a painting to an engraving: the birds that love worms fall back upon berries . . ."(Thomas Hardy); "Ice bares, boys slide . . . Most owls seem to hoot exactly in B flat . . ." (Gilbert White); "The blue mountains were silver-ribbed with snow and looked like a dead giant lying in state . . . Home by the upper road crazy with face ache

. . . After dinner and four glasses of port I felt better" (Kilvert); "What a lovely thing a bit of fine, sharp, chrystallized, broken snow is, held up against the blue sky catching the sun—talk of diamonds!" (John Ruskin, whose Diaries, notes Geoffrey Grigson, "mixed egoism and petulance [when the weather is not what he wants] with clear perception.")

Spring: "Green woodpecker laughs at all the world. Storm-cocks sing . . . Swifts squeak much." (Gilbert White); "Blade leaves of some bulbous plant, perhaps a small iris, were like delicate little swords, so hagged with frost" (Hopkins); "I found cowslips and the first bluebells and the young ferns uncurling their crozier heads" (Kilvert); "Walnut showing leaf. Sycamore and horse-chestnut nearly cover'd. I observed a snail on his journey at full speed and I marked by my watch as he went thirteen inches in three minutes, which was the utmost he could do without stopping to wind or rest" (John Clare).

Summer: "The jasmine is so sweet that I am obliged to quit my chamber" (Gilbert White); ". . . No sunshine, except for a quarter of an hour on the roses, leaving Thame. All wet with rain they were and infinitely lovely" (Ruskin); "The mountains and the valley were flowing golden in the evening sunlight. Above Pen y llan a crowd of purple thistles stood in fatal and mischievous splendour among the waving oaks" (Kilvert); "Elms at end of twilight are very interesting: against the sky they made crisp scattered pinches of soot" (Hopkins).

Autumn: "The first frost of autumn. Outdoor folk look reflective. The scarlet runners are dishevelled; geraniums wounded in the leaf, open-air cucumber leaves have collapsed like green umbrellas with all the stays broken" (Thomas Hardy); "Hedge-sparrow begins its winter note" (Gilbert White).

* * *

KETTLE'S YARD

I guess my love for those who so acutely observe the changing of the seasons is a mixture of the sense of loss that you feel if you live in the noise and pollution of a great city, and the recognition that this "wondering eye" which is so central to any sense of the numinous, so quickly becomes atrophied when you are no longer in touch with the natural pattern of the year, the rise and fall of the sap, the annual blossoming and dying, death and rebirth; and St. James's Park, for all its willows and pelicans, is a poor substitute.

Before I leave the artists and writers whose contemplative gaze helps us to notice what we might otherwise miss and who can teach us to see into the life of things, I want to describe a house which has been created by a man who was a natural contemplative with an equal love for natural objects and works of art. Kettle's Yard stands just off Northampton Street in Cambridge, a house full of light and space. It was the home of Jim Ede, friend and patron of many artists, including David Jones and the sculptor, Gaudier-Brzeska. He brought together pictures, sculpture, pottery, glass, furniture, plates, and stones picked up on the beach, and his genius was to place them in a room so that the visiting light revolving daily in that space would create a constantly-changing play in their relationship to each other.

After his wife died, Jim Ede left Cambridge but gave Kettle's Yard to the University as an open house for anyone to visit each afternoon of the year, leaving everything—the pictures on the walls, the books on the shelves—exactly as it was. In terms of the arts, the ambience is of the 1920s: the walls are white, the wood scrubbed, the floors of brick or planks of wood; but the secret of the pleasure you feel is twofold: the relatedness of everything to everything else, and the creation of proper spaces in which to see each work, each stone, each flower, in its own right.

It was central to Jim Ede's outlook that a room is already furnished by the light that enters it, that the shape of each plate or piece of sculpture is "caressed by the still light in the same loving way." "It is salutary," he writes, "that in a world rocked by greed, misunderstanding and fear . . . it is still possible and justifiable to find important the exact placing of two pebbles."[7]

Jim Ede wanted above all for Kettle's Yard to be a still and calming place, full of surprising moments when the light catches the grain of a wooden floor, the curve of a dish or the texture of stone. He writes:

> I often think that such a fleeting moment . . . is even more important than the paintings and sculpture, for it is this which brings inspiration to the artist. On the other side, were it not for the vision of the artist revealing such beauty, we might never see it. It is I suppose this natural interaction and interrelation which is at the root of life's joy.[8]

Lest you should think that the creator of Kettle's Yard was some kind of rarified aesthete, I should add that when he left Cambridge in his eighties and moved to Edinburgh, he spent his days visiting a hospital, looking to see which patients had no visitors, and (if they wished) spending time with them. There, surely, is the true integration of the two sides of the human spirit.

XVI

Rilke and the Giving of Attention

We are the bees of the invisible.

RAINER MARIA RILKE[1]

Whereas material goods are diminished by sharing, the spiritual treasuries of knowledge and of beauty, of poetry, music and the rest, by being shared are not diminished but increased.

KATHLEEN RAINE[2]

8 June: A.M.

THE STRANGEST THING HAPPENED on Saturday. We had to drive down to Sierre at the head of the valley, a small town filled with roses and surrounded by vineyards, that stands on the Rhone, to buy provisions. Months ago, when I was thinking around the subjects of these letters, I knew that the poet Rainer Maria Rilke would demand attention. I knew that he had experienced a terrible state of creative paralysis when he had half completed his finest work, the *Duino Elegies*, and that he was stuck, a poet at the height of his powers, able to write nothing of real value for almost ten years. I knew that a friend had rented a house for him, the Château de Muzot, and that here, suddenly, the inner music began again, and in an extraordinary creative spurt, in less than a month, he finished the Elegies and then, within a week, wrote the entire cycle of *Sonnets to Orpheus*, fifty-five sonnets. I had read his triumphant letter which tells of his sense of joy at their completion: "I went out into the cold moonlight and stroked the little tower of Muzot as if it were a large animal——the ancient walls that granted this to me." But where (indeed, in what country) the Château de Muzot might be I had absolutely no idea.

It was lunch-time. We drove out of Sierre seeking shade in which to have a picnic, turning this way and that in the one-way streets and frequent cul-de-sacs. At last we got above the town and stopped beside a vineyard, above which stood a small medieval château. "Boulevard R. M. Rilke" it said on the road sign; the château was called Muzot. It was the house rented for Rilke in 1922 in that "incomparable landscape" that he loved, framed by mountains "filled with little eminences ... that afford the eye a continual play of most bewitching modulation, like a game of chess with hills."[3] Here was the little tower he stroked in gratitude for having found the place where his inner and outer worlds came together so fruitfully. W. H. Auden reminds us of that lonely vigil in the tower of Muzot in his sonnet sequence, *Sonnets from China:*

> Let us remember all who looked deserted:
> Tonight in China let me think of one
>
> Who through ten years of drought and silence waited,
> Until in Muzot all his being spoke,
> And everything was given once for all:
>
> Awed, grateful, tired, content to die, completed,
> He went out in the winter night to stroke
> That tower as one pets an animal.[4]

But why is Rilke so relevant to my theme? Poor Rilke: born in 1875 into a suffocatingly genteel household, his father a railroad clerk, his mother a cold, complex, socially ambitious woman, a fervent Roman Catholic who left her husband when Rilke was nine and who had longed for a daughter. For the first five years of his life she sometimes dressed him as a girl, called

him Sophie, and treated him as if he were a doll. She damaged
him greatly. In his idiosyncratic version of the story of the
Prodigal Son, the young man leaves home because he cannot
bear to be loved by those who would confine him and make
him conform to their image of him.

All his life Rilke felt inadequate, thinking himself not
equal to the poet's task. He was convinced that "the life we live
is not life," and the *Duino Elegies* are a passionate argument
against our acceptance of a shallowness in living and a blindness
in perceiving. With his acute sensitivity he knows about that
emptiness we can feel within ourselves, the hunger for the reality that beckons yet escapes us, and he set about finding a way,
in art and poetry, to transform the emptiness of human longing
into something fruitful. He imagines the artist as a polished
surface like a mirror who, by not wanting anything of the world
and learning to see it with a disinterested intensity, makes it
real. He writes of how things (a piece of wood, a stone, an ancient sculpture) are not simply objects: they are objects seen,
understood and loved by human beings, and so capable of being
transformed. It is the role of the artist so to transform them:

> ... when the traveler returns from the mountain-slopes into
>   the valley,
> he brings, not a handful of earth, unsayable to others, but
>   instead
> some word he has gained, some pure word, the yellow and
>   blue
> gentian. Perhaps we are here in order to say: house, bridge,
>   fountain, gate, pitcher, fruit-tree, window. ...
> But to say them, you must understand,
> oh to say them more intensely than the Things themselves
>   ever dreamed of existing. ...[5]

The turning point for Rilke came when he was studying an archaic torso and realized that it was

> still suffused with brilliance from inside

and more alive than himself. The poem ends: *You must change your life.*[6] Any poem, novel, painting, piece of music worth meeting says the same. It questions us. It seeks to change our understanding of reality, of how each thing is in itself. It seeks to change, marginally or dramatically, the way we see.

Rilke always had an extraordinary eye for almost anything he really looked at: children, dogs, the quality of light on a tree or a mountain, a work of art; and he looked at them so that he might take them inside himself and so transform them. He looked with the same rapt attention as the artist whom he feels to be a kindred spirit, Cézanne, and quotes his friend, the painter, Mathilde Vollmöller, who said of Cézanne that he sat in front of nature "like a dog, just looking." Rilke wrote a number of letters on what he learned from Cézanne about giving attention, when "suddenly one has the right eyes":

> One lives so badly, because one always comes into the present distracted. I believe that the only time I lived without distraction were the ten days after my daughter's birth, when I found reality as indescribable, down to its smallest detail, as it surely always is.[7]

Rilke came to believe that in a life that had been changed we are "doing justice only where we praise."

But now, in the Château de Muzot he came to understand that the task of poetry was the creation and affirmation of the world. The pure activity of being consciously alive is sufficient; but each must learn, as it were, how not to be a stranger to our

own inner landscape out of which we view the world about us.
To be is to sing, but in order to sing we first have to see:

> For a long time he attained it in looking.
> Stars would fall to their knees
> beneath his compelling vision . . .
>
> Towers he would gaze at so
> that they were terrified:
> building them up again, suddenly in an instant!
> But how often the landscape,
> overburdened by day,
> came to rest in his silent awareness, at nightfall.
>
> Animals trusted him, stepped
> into his open look, grazing,
> and the imprisoned lions
> stared in as if into an incomprehensible freedom;
> birds, as it felt them, flew headlong
> through it; and flowers, as enormous
> as they are to children, gazed back
> into it, on and on.
>
> And the rumour that there was someone
> who knew how to look,
> stirred those less
> visible creatures. . . .[8]

In a letter, Rilke wrote of his line "For a time he attained it in looking":

> I love in-seeing. Can you imagine with me how glorious it is
> to in-see a dog, for example, as you pass it—by in-see I don't
> mean to look through, which is only a kind of gymnastic that
> lets you immediately come out again on the other side of the
> dog, regarding it merely, so to speak, as a window upon the
> human world lying behind it: not that; what I mean is to let
> yourself precisely into the dog's centre, the point from which

it begins to be a dog, the place in it where God, as it were, would have sat down for a moment when the dog was finished, in order to watch it during its first embarrassments and inspirations and to nod that it was good, that nothing was lacking, that it couldn't have been better made.[9]

"To be here is magnificent," wrote Rilke when he had won through to this new vision of things and the *Duino Elegies* and the Sonnets celebrate the fact.

> Don't you know yet? Fling the emptiness out of your arms
> into the spaces we breathe; perhaps the birds
> will feel the expanded air with more passionate flying . . .[10]

> . . . Listen, my heart, as only
> saints have listened: until the gigantic call lifted them
> off the ground; yet they kept on, impossibly,
> kneeling and didn't notice at all:
> so complete was their listening . . .[11]

> . . . Children, one earthly thing
> truly experienced, even once, is enough for a lifetime . . .
> Truly being here is glorious . . .[12]

> But because truly being here is so much;
> because everything here
> apparently needs us, this fleeting world, which in some
> strange way
> keeps calling to us. Us, the most fleeting of all.
> Once for each thing. Just once; no more. And we too,
> just once. And never again. But to have been
> this once, completely, even if only once:
> to have been at one with the earth, seems beyond undoing.
> And so we keep pressing on, trying to achieve it,
> trying to hold it firmly in our simple hands,
> in our overcrowded gaze, in our speechless heart . . .

> . . . O Earth: invisible!
> What, if not transformation, is your urgent command?
> Earth, my dearest, I will. Oh believe me, you no longer
> need your springtime to win me over—one of them,
> ah, even one, is already too much for my blood . . .[13]

Rilke wrote a tiny poem about a rose for the epitaph which is on his grave. Ironically, it was when he went into his garden at Muzot to pick a bunch of roses for a visitor that he pricked his finger on a rose-thorn. The wound festered and revealed an advanced state of leukemia. Two months later he was dead. Growing in the garden at Muzot today are an abundance of roses. When we left the place where at last

> all his powers spoke,
> And everything was given once for all . . .[14]

I took with me a single rosebud from a scarlet rose bush that was trailing through the garden fence, and I remembered Rilke with gratitude; though still a little dizzy to discover that, with the whole of Europe to choose from, we had found ourselves in his backyard.

XVII

Hopkins and the "Inscape" of Things

Trout finned as trout, peach moulded into peach . . .
To know their station and be right for ever . . .

W. H. AUDEN[1]

Each mortal thing does one thing and the same:
. . . myself it speaks and spells,
Crying What I do is me: for that I came . . .

GERARD MANLEY HOPKINS[2]

Jenkin seemed to be able to enjoy everything: even ugliness. I learned from him that we should attempt total surrender to whatever atmosphere was offering itself at the moment; in a squalid town to seek out those very places where its squalor rose to grimness and almost grandeur, on a dismal day to find the most dismal and dripping wood, on a windy day to seek the windiest ridge. There was no Betjemanic irony about it; only a serious, yet gleeful, determination to rub one's nose in the very quiddity of each thing, to rejoice in its being (so magnificently) what it was.

C. S. LEWIS[3]

But imagine, among the mud and the mastodons
God sighing and yearning with tremendous creative
    yearning, in that dark green mess
Oh, for some other beauty, some other beauty
That blossomed at last, red geranium, and mignonette

D. H. LAWRENCE[4]

IN 1868 GERARD MANLEY HOPKINS became a Jesuit, burnt his verses and "resolved to write no more . . . unless it were by the wish of my superiors." Seven years later, in the year in which Rilke was born, he broke his silence with *The Wreck of the Deutschland.*

From an early age Hopkins had a keen eye and a great love of nature. At Oxford he had known and walked with Walter Pater who helped him to look with intensity at the "movement of light in the grass and among leaves . . ." and at minute particulars. Yet he gave up writing poetry when he joined the Society of Jesus out of a fear that his love of the material creation implied a neglect of the Creator. He needed a philosophical framework that would show him that a love of the world and a love of God are not mutually exclusive (which he knew instinctively), and he found one in the work of a medieval Franciscan theologian, Duns Scotus.

Scotus taught that the material world was in itself a symbol of God, that when the Bible speaks of God as the Logos (the Word) who *names* his creation into being, it is implying that all created things are in some sense linked in being derived from the universal Logos, and that what connects them to God is to be found in their "thisness" ("haecceitas" in Duns Scotus, what Auden calls their "eachness," and Lewis their "quiddity"); in other words, that which makes each thing distinctively itself, with its own distinctive "taste." Scotus believed that behind the unique nature of each particular thing (an oak tree, say) we can perceive a common nature (treeness), behind which is the Creator.

For Hopkins, the discovery of the teaching of Duns Scotus came as a revelation. It matched his belief in a sacramental universe and it showed him how the senses, chiefly the giving to an object your intense visual attention, were connected to faith. To Scotus's term "thisness" he gave the name inscape, by which he meant the absolute selfhood of an object, and he began by defining "inscape" in the place he knew it best: in himself.

"That taste of myself, of I and me, above and in all things, which is more distinctive than the taste of ale or alum, more distinctive than the smell of walnut-leaf or camphor, and is incommunicable by any means to another man."[5] It is what is radiated back to you when you look hard enough at an object, or seek to understand a person by giving time to them: a unique meaning, because each person and thing is a different manifestation of its kind.

Such "inscape," such unique inner meaning, is not dependent upon being recognized: it is intrinsically there, whether we take time to notice it or not. It is not found entirely by analysis, but by a balance between attention and receptiveness, and it requires the use of all our senses. Hopkins' journals are extraordinary records of an observing eye. He constantly seeks the form and shape of what he sees: sunsets or clouds or a snake gliding through a hedge; a squirrel, a plant, a leaf; he will draw a dead rat floating down a river, or seek to mesmerize a duck. His Jesuit colleagues would be amazed to see him hanging over a frozen pond to observe trapped bubbles in the ice. "What you look hard at," he said, "seems to look hard at you." "I saw the inscape freshly," he wrote in his Journal, "as if my eye were still growing." In May 1870 he writes:

> I do not think I have ever seen anything more beautiful than the bluebell. . . . Its inscape is mixed of strength and grace, like an ash tree. The head is strongly drawn over backwards and arched down like a cutwater drawing itself back to the line of the keel. The lines of the bell strike and overlie this, rayed but not symmetrically, some lie parallel. They look steely against the paper, the shades lying between the bells and behind the cockled petal-ends and nursing up the position of their distinctness, the petal-ends themselves being delicately lit.[6]

And on April 8, 1873 he writes:

> The ash tree growing in the corner of the garden was felled. . . . I heard the sound and looking out and seeing it maimed there came at that moment a great pang and I wished to die and not to see the inscapes of the world destroyed any more.[7]

For Hopkins, beauty lay in the recognition of the uniqueness of everything he saw. But not just beauty. For if you can look at things with a wondering attention they will reveal something both of themselves and their Creator and *become a means of praise*. It is not simply that we *may* give attention: we are obliged by our very humanness to do so.

> What is fickle, freckled (who knows how?)
> With swift, slow; sweet, sour; adazzle, dim;

> He fathers-forth whose beauty is past change:
> Praise him.[8]

Every particular object has for Hopkins a transcendent significance: "All things . . . are charged with love, are charged with God and if we know how to touch them give off sparks and make fire, yield drops and flow, ring, and tell of him," he said in one of his sermons. And he used two other words that can be puzzling: "instress" and "selving." "Instress" simply means the effect on the beholder of the "inscape" of the bluebell or the ash tree or the running stream. You see the "thisness" of each and you break out in the "instress" of praise and delight—rather as Thomas Traherne did when he saw the corn as "orient and immortal wheat"; or Barry Lopez when he bowed to the horned lark; or the Polish poet Czeslaw Milosz who stood as a child in a blacksmith's shop and remembers:

> . . . At the entrance, my bare feet on the dirt floor,
> Here, gusts of heat; at my back, white clouds.
> I stare and stare. It seem I was called for this:
> To glorify things just because they are.[9]

So Hopkins can write:

> I kiss my hand . . .
>   . . . to the dappled-with-damson-west;
> Since, though he is under the world's splendor and wonder
> His mystery must be instressed, stressed;
> For I greet him the days I meet him and bless when I
> understand.[10]

What of "selving?" By this he means that something is, it exists, and at the same time it is distinctive, its own individual self. And the poem which for me contains the very heart of

Hopkins' perception of the world, and expresses in a few lines what Rilke meant by "in-seeing" (and I guess what Blake meant by "seeing through the eye") and what Hopkins means by "inscape," is the sonnet *As Kingfishers Catch Fire*. It contains these lines:

> Each mortal thing does one thing and the same:
> deals out that being indoors each one dwells:
> selves—goes itself: myself it speaks and spells
> Crying What I do is me: for that I came. . . .[11]

By being itself, by revealing its particular "inscape," each creature and object we see can give us brief glimpses of the Creator.

In her autobiography, *Farewell Happy Fields*, Kathleen Raine writes of a cock pheasant seen in early childhood and never forgotten.

> So perfectly himself was he, with his golden eyes and his gold-brown train; he was himself to the least feather of his feathered breast. . . . The fear that I felt at the otherness of his life was part delight in his beauty, part awe in the presence of his touch-me-not, his "I am that I am." Every creature has a measure of power peculiar to itself and to its kind; I was in the presence of his bird-kind, his pheasant-kind, and the proud life that informed that feathered dress, that jeweled head and harsh beak; that deliberate gait; the absoluteness of his being there before me. I beheld and worshiped.[12]

Sylvia Plath echoes that sense of wonder at a pheasant's inscape.

> You said you would kill it this morning.
> Do not kill it. It startles me still,
> The jut of that odd, dark head, pacing

Through the uncut grass on the elm's hill.
It is something to own a pheasant,
Or just to be visited at all.

I am not mystical: it isn't
As if I thought it had a spirit.
It is simply in its element.

That gives it a kingliness, a right.
The print of its big foot last winter,
The tail-track, on the snow in our court—

The wonder of it, in that pallor,
Through crosshatch of sparrow and starling.
Is it its rareness, then? It is rare.

But a dozen would be worth having,
A hundred, on that hill—green and red,
Crossing and recrossing: a fine thing!

It is such a good shape, so vivid.
It's a little cornucopia.
It unclaps, brown as a leaf, and loud,

Settles in the elm, and is easy.
It was sunning in the narcissi.
I trespass stupidly. Let be, let be.[13]

"Let be." I find there an echo of Hamlet's words to Horatio when, finally, he moves beyond the need for revenge and says of the danger inherent in his duel with Laertes:

> . . . there's a special providence in the fall of a sparrow.
> If it be now, 'tis not to come; if it be not to come, it
> will be now;
> if it be not now, yet it will come. The readiness is all.
> Let be.[14]

The words are an acceptance of what is given—the readiness to be open to the "kingliness" of the visiting pheasant; whatever the next moment will bring—a true openness to the moment that is now and all it contains.

Do you remember Philip Toynbee learning to look at trees?

> 13 *November* I can now repeat the tree experience at will. It is in no way pantheistic . . . no feeling the tree and I are One. . . . Quite the contrary: a sharp awareness of the tree's individual identity. . . . I hope never to lose that vision of the tree's "inscape": its very potent self and presence. If anything the tree might become so intensely, blazingly real that my God-given vision would have seen heaven in the tree. And the tree would be more a tree than ever: through the transfiguring eye. It's surely a false mysticism . . . which turns against the physical world instead of transfiguring it.[15]

"I have often felt," wrote Hopkins, "when I have felt how fast the inscape holds a thing, that nothing is so pregnant and straightforward to the truth as simple yes and is."[16] It is, writes Sam Keen,

> when we cease making materialistic claims over objects and persons . . . and allow them to be what they are in their own right, that we touch the inviolable strangeness which is their sacredness. . . . Wonder adds nothing to our knowledge about an object. It is rather that the object comes into focus and is respected and relished in its otherness.[17]

Rilke would have understood what Hopkins is saying (though his poetry could not have been known to him), the long, contemplative, loving gaze that draws from each small particular its own mysterious life. I wonder what either would have made of Annie Dillard's account of the "thisness" of a weasel?

> The sun had just set. I was relaxed on the tree trunk, en-
> sconced in the lap of lichen, watching the lily pads at my feet
> tremble and pass dreamingly over the thrusting path of a carp.
> A yellow bird appeared to my right and flew behind me. It
> caught my eyes; I swiveled round—and the next instant, in-
> explicably, I was looking down at a weasel, who was looking
> up at me.
>
> Weasel! I had never seen one wild before. He was ten inches
> long, thin as a curve, a muscled ribbon, brown as fruitwood,
> soft-furred, alert. His face was fierce, small and pointed as a
> lizard's; he would have made a good arrowhead. There was
> just a dot of chin, maybe two brown hairs' worth, and then the
> pure white fur began that spread down his underside. He had
> two black eyes I didn't see, any more than you see a window.
>
> The weasel was stunned into stillness as he was emerging
> from beneath an enormous shaggy wild rose bush four feet
> away. I was stunned to stillness twisted backward on the tree
> trunk. Our eyes locked.... Our look was as if two lovers, or
> deadly enemies, met unexpectedly on an overgrown path when
> each had been thinking of something else: a clearing blow to
> the gut.... It felled the forest, moved the fields, and drained
> the ponds; the world dismantled and tumbled into that black
> hole of eyes.
>
> He disappeared.... I think I blinked, I think I retrieved my
> brain from the weasel's brain, and tried to memorize what I
> was seeing, and the weasel felt the yank of separation ... and
> vanished under the wild rose.... I tell you I have been in that
> weasel's brain for sixty seconds, and he was in mine....[18]

A bit over the top? Perhaps; but it makes you wonder.

XVII

People and Objects:
Their Singular Peculiarity

To be fully extended according to one's own nature and capacities—that's the only thing that matters. And the beauty of it is that since every human soul is unique the light that it sees and the light that it shines have never been seen or shone before.

PHILIP TOYNBEE[1]

No creature was ever loved too much, but some in a wrong way, and all in too short a measure.

THOMAS TRAHERNE[2]

I SPOKE IN ONE OF my earlier letters of human experiences of pain and suffering which reveal something of our mysterious transcendence through the way we can face and overcome them. Brian Keenan's astonishing account of his five-year ordeal as a hostage, *An Evil Cradling*, is a classic description of the power of the human spirit to transcend one of the most cruel forms of torture: isolation, the cutting off of almost all sensual perception, and a fear of what the next day may bring. In his book there is a magical moment when, after an interminable time of sitting in the dark, he is brought a bowl of fruit containing some small oranges.

> My eyes are almost burned by what I see. The fruit, the colours, mesmerize me in a quiet rapture that spins through my head. . . . I lift an orange into the flat filthy palm of my hand and feel and smell and lick it. The colour orange, the colour, the colour, my God the colour orange. Before me is a feast of colour. I feel myself begin to dance, slowly, I am intoxicated by colour. . . . Such wonder, such absolute wonder in such insignificant fruit.

> I cannot, I will not eat this fruit. I sit in quiet joy, so completely beyond the meaning of joy. My soul finds its own completeness in that bowl of colour . . . I want to bow before it, loving that blazing, roaring, orange colour. . . . It is there in that tiny bowl, the world recreated in that tiny bowl . . . I focus all of my attention on that bowl of fruit. . . . I cannot hold the ecstasy of the moment and its passionate intensity. . . .
>
> I am filled with a sense of love.[3]

What has been implicit in all I have been concerned to show you is this one truth: that to see anything *truly*, as it is in all its singular particularity, is to see it with the eyes of love. Once you recognize of everything that exists that it is unique, that

> . . . myself it speaks and spells
> Crying What I do is me: for that I came

then it is restored to its proper status and worth. It is the irreplaceable otherness of things that claims our attention: "Such wonder, such absolute wonder in such an insignificant fruit."

Of course Brian Keenan was seeing it when for weeks his senses had been starved of light and colour, but the principle holds. The tree as tree is an embodied image of its Creator and the more you learn to see it and the mystery of its growth and annual blossoming, the more it speaks of what is holy. David Jones's treatment of flowers, writes David Blamires, reflects "a momentary balance that can be disturbed almost by a breath of air, but which, in the moment of its apprehension, shares in eternity."[4] The bird that woke me this morning with its endlessly repetitive song was no doubt saying, "I am a chaffinch, I am a chaffinch" with tedious delight. Thomas Merton once said that the Shakers used wood in such a way as to make beds and chairs that revealed the "logos," the innermost principle of their being. For Billy Yellow of the Navajo, each living thing has an identity, a proper place and a way to be, that must be daily affirmed. It is there, given, before our eyes and under our noses, waiting for us to notice and to celebrate it.

"To see what is in front of one's nose needs a constant struggle,"[5] wrote George Orwell; yet artists achieve it by seeking to discover the inner identity, the essential "thisness" of a person or a thing, in that mysterious, contemplative give and take between the see-er and the seen. But giving attention is not the prerogative of artists: they simply point the way. What I need to understand is that no-one else has ever, can ever, look out of my eyes and see things exactly as I do. My genetic make-up, my characteristics, my experience and my potential mean that I have my own unique story and my own unique way of seeing; and if I am to see with love what is given me to enjoy then what is out there has to be recognized and named before it can become alive and take root in me. Like God giving the creatures an identity by naming them, I must (as it were) name each thing for myself by my initial and repeated attentiveness to it if I am to relate to the mystery of the created universe of which I am a part. A friend describes how sometimes, by learning how to see the landscape, he makes each part of it exist for him in a way they have not before:

> I let myself be drawn into it, become a part of it. I then will with love each thing to be by naming it. I start with the big things: the downs, the sky, the green space of the fields. I then add the trees, each with its own glistening beauty. Then, with joy, some birds and a young calf with its mother. . . . Things are not just objects before us; they are what they are through the love and word that gives them being and meaning. . . .

There is a Zen Buddhist saying that we begin by thinking that rivers are merely rivers and mountains merely mountains, and go on to think (once we explore the mysterious nature of matter) that rivers are not rivers and mountains not mountains; but that the person who is enlightened, the one who sees into the heart of things, achieves the deep understanding of what it means for rivers to be really rivers and mountains really mountains. There is another Zen Buddhist saying: "There, where your eye alights, experience": and A. S. Byatt inscribes her most recent novel, *The Matisse Stories*, which is a celebration of colour, "For Peter, who taught me to look at things slowly."

Sadly, there is no guarantee that contemplating mountains or learning to love orchids and snails will lead to contemplating people and learning to love them. Yet this is infinitely more important and, when the chips are down, this is what we are here to do.

A few nights ago, quite late, we turned on the monochrome one-channel television. There had just started an hour-long documentary, culled from contemporary wartime film from Germany, Russia, and other nations, about the Nazi attempt to exterminate the Jews during the Holocaust. It contained previously unshown sequences from the prison-camps, both during the War and when they were liberated. I have never forgotten the horror of the news-films which I saw aged fifteen; and once again I was silenced and ashamed by the unimaginable bestiality of which human beings are capable. That attempt at the genocide of a whole race can never be forgotten and the fact that it was attempted witnesses to a destructive potential in human beings that diminishes us all. Perhaps the most distressing images of the Gulf War and the ongoing conflict in Bosnia-Herzegovina—because they have been of individuals and we can only understand suffering in such direct, personal terms—are that of the skull of the Iraqi soldier incinerated at the driving wheel of his truck, and the charred remains of a child's hand (Sim's "holy hand") emerging from the ruin of a house in a Muslim village after a Croatian vengeance attack.

My letters may have seemed remote from the reality of that daily horror, for is not the life of a single child worth more than a thousand sparrows, a hundred works of art, a whole library of books? Of course: but if you are blind to the worth of the one you will not see the worth of the other. This is the point exactly. Once wonder goes; once mystery is dismissed; once the holy and the numinous count for nothing; then human life becomes cheap and it is possible with a single bullet to shatter that most miraculous thing, a human skull, with scarcely a second thought. Wonder and compassion go hand-in-hand. Seeing is a radical activity. It affects everything. It is Rilke's "you must change your life."

Yet if the Holocaust (the resonances of which echo today in policies of "ethnic cleansing") is a startling reminder of our latent inhumanity, our failure to see the face the skull once wore or the mystery which the child's hand once contained, there is also within us an almost limitless potential for the quality that goes with restored sight: compassion. And the beginning, the middle and the end of that most lovely of qualities is a question of how we see. How you see me: how I see you.

There is in each of us Vladimir's cry to the boy concerning Godot: "Tell him . . . that you saw me": a hungering need to be seen, noticed and so given value. This is not some childish craving for attention. It is the only way I have to become *myself*. From my first moment of consciousness I needed that relationship with my mother, that instinctive sense of being noticed, given attention, and all that I am now has been shaped, indeed created, by a thousand successive relationships. It is how we are made: we thrive on love. It isn't only babies who languish and grow sick if they are starved of it. I am affirmed when you, by your noticing, by your giving attention, affirm me; for egos are lonely, and egotism a lonely way of being, and our spirits are fed by what we freely give each other. Sister Wendy Beckett writes of one who sat for her portrait: "She asks for no tenderness, she asks for recognition."

However old or wise we grow, the child we once were is always part of us and, in one way or another, every human being (far less confident than we appear, most of us) cries out or acts out—or, often, disastrously, stifles—their need to be known, forgiven, affirmed and encouraged. Martin Luther has a lovely phrase about Jesus: "Christ's proper work is to declare the grace of God, to console and to enliven." And the importance of recognizing and giving attention to each other is because we cannot be fully human or fully alive unless we are in some way giving and receiving the kind of attention that is a form of love. Martin Buber, who made such a clear distinction between what he called an "I–it" and an "I–thou" relationship (treating what is before your eyes simply as a thing or giving yourself to it, to him, to her, in a real exchange) writes:

> Egos appear by setting themselves apart from other egos. Persons appear by entering into relation to other persons. . . .[6a] Each soul stands in the splendour of its own existence. In each man there is something precious that is in no other man. Therefore one should honour each . . . for that which is hidden within him, which only he and no one of his companions possesses.[6b]

We talk of society and the individual, but Buber's words suggest that the concept of society is meaningless unless each of its members knows what it means to say "I am"; but that equally you cannot discover what it really means to say "I" unless you have also learned to join with others in saying "we." I would go much further and claim that it is in the discovery of other persons, it is in the recognition of their uniqueness by seeing them with love, that we become aware of God as the mystery in and between us, holding us and uniting us at the very centre of our being.

But for the present let me stick with this costly human insight: that it is in learning to see each other, without preconceptions, without envy and without expectations, but with attentiveness, that we fulfill what it means to be human. For we may then discover yet another mysterious paradox: that we are both other and the same, that I can accept that you are your own distinctive self and allow you to be so, and yet understand that our lives touch and connect at many points. We both need love and feel pain; we both know times of joy and grief. We must each fashion our own distinctive story but we share the same human journey; and unless there is peace and freedom for you, there can be no real peace or freedom for me. Given that truth as the ground on which we meet, I am not concerned whether you are a Christian, a Buddhist, a humanist or a Jew; male or female, black or white, rich or poor. For I am required as a human being to be attentive to your singularity and your God-given potential and to try to see you (as I believe God does) with love. Morality is always ultimately about the value we put on each other—and on ourselves—and what is demanded of each of us, if we are not to trivialize what we are, is a profound respect in the face of each other's mystery.

> The substance of love of our neighbour [wrote Simone Weil]
> is [attentiveness]. It is an attentive way of looking.... The soul

empties itself of itself in order to receive in itself the being that
it is looking at, just as he is, in all his truth.[7]

Take faces. You'll see a lot today. Each one is the only one
of its kind in the universe. Nor will any of those faces remain
quite the same from moment to moment. The face is the most
exposed part of the body, yet try and describe it and the meaning and the mystery of it slip through your fingers. Frederick
Franck, an American writer and artist, attended the Second
Vatican Council in Rome.

> Once you . start drawing a face you realize how extraordinary
> it is—a sheer miracle. I often drew Cardinal Ottaviani. He
> fascinated me. I saw him as a Grand Inquisitor. He was old
> and half-blind. One eye was glassy, the other drooped. He had
> a confusing multiplicity of chins. As I continued drawing him
> I began to see him differently. Where I had only seen arrogant
> rigidity and decrepitude, I saw the human being—until I re-
> alized that I was seeing him with a kind of love.[8]

There are echoes there of Brother Roger, Prior of Taizé,
who writes in his book *Festival*:

> There are only beautiful faces, be they sad or radiant. My life
> is discerning in others what is ravishing them, what rejoices
> them; it lies in communicating with the suffering and the joy
> of people. Ever since I was a youth, my desire has been never
> to condemn. For me the essential, in the presence of some
> other person, has always been to understand him fully. When
> I manage to understand somebody, that is already a festival.[9]

That kind of compassionate regard was beautifully described sixteen hundred years ago by one of the Desert Fathers
when he wrote:

It is right for a person to take up the burden for those who are near to him, whatsoever it may be and, so to speak, put his own soul in the place of that of his neighbour, and to become, if it were possible, a double man; and he must suffer and weep and mourn for him as if he himself had put on the actual body of his neighbour.[10]

As you know, I have been concerned in all these letters to make no assumptions that you will grow up to share my Christian faith, but to write so far as I can of what it means to be human. But I have now reached the point where both logic and my own integrity demand that I explain why I have to go further: why for me the central reality, the truth by which all other truths must be judged, the love against which all other love has to be tested, is the God whom some call "Christlike"; and to do so by starting, once again, with the only reality I know with absolute certainty: me.

XIX

Giving Attention and so Learning to Love

. . . and they were full of eyes within.[1]

You are to love your neighbour as yourself.[2]

Say to yourself, "I am loved by God more than I can either conceive or understand." Let this fill all your soul . . . and never
leave you. You will soon see that this is the way to find God.

HENRI DE TOURVILLE[3]

Religion resides in our eyes rather than in our minds.
We see; then we love.

ALUN LEWIS[4]

10 June

Each mortal thing does one thing and the same: . . .
selves—goes itself: *myself* it speaks and spells
Crying What I do is me: for that I came.

SHE ASKS FOR NO tenderness: she asks for recognition."
The test of whether I am looking at myself or another
person *with* my eyes or *through* them, with eyes that scan
the surface or eyes that give attention, is whether I am prepared
to take time to search for the self beneath the mask. "Mask" is
not the word: it suggests something we don or remove with
ease, like a fancy dress, and we are far more complex than that.
Of course we wear our protective disguises, but the self of
which we are conscious is but the tip of the iceberg, the rest
lying buried deep in our unconscious, though like the iceberg
capable of inflicting powerful damage.

This is not about some kind of potentially embarrassing
mutual analysis: it is about honesty, the honest acceptance of
ourselves and each other as we are, rather than as we should
like to appear or as we should like others to be. To believe that

you or anyone else is not complicated, often neglectful and self-ish, sometimes envious, unloving, angry and full of self-pity, is to reveal a serious form of blindness. But it is equally blinkered not to know that you and everyone else have the capacity to be creative, thoughtful, courageous and self-sacrificing, funny, loving, and compassionate. The recognition that is allied to love lies in accepting myself as I am, and you as you are, rather than fastening upon myself the image I should like to have, or upon you the image I should like you to have. Any genuine encounter of loving and being loved turns on my readiness to acknowledge your unique, though frequently exasperating, self. And my own.

Love is a dangerous, many-faceted word. I'm not speaking of an emotional feeling, but rather of a going out of yourself, the giving that is called "agapē", not the passion of "eros"; a *giving* of your time and your attention to that which you recognize to have value. That covers many aspects of love, but where it relates to persons it means the ability to recognize their value and the attempt to meet their need.

Much of my time is spent with individuals who have never really been able to love themselves, who feel unloved, unspecial, and of little value. Some have never been on the receiving end of being loved for their own sake, even as a child. Many see God in threatening, judgmental terms. Many have damaged feelings and feed on guilt. There is only one truth I know that takes on such feelings at sufficient depth, that challenges them on their own terms and neutralizes the poison. It is the truth that dawned on those who met and spent time with Jesus of Nazareth: who watched him as he encountered damaged people, sinful and perplexed people, and told them they were loved. Told them God even cared about the death of a sparrow. In the most perceptive of all the gospels, that of John, the message is plain: we may journey through the world as those who are valued and loved. Despite what we are. Despite all life's unpredictable and sometimes cruel nature. We are not to doubt that we are loved.

You will meet many people who have been so starved of love for their own sake that it is a foreign concept. It may be that they recognize with their mind the validity of this truth, but it is quite another thing to believe that it is true of you and accept it in your heart. Often people will test you repeatedly to show they are as unlovable as they believe themselves to be. Holding to what you know is the truth about them in the face of constant aggravation, simply continuing to *be there*, is sometimes intolerably hard, but only such a keeping faith with what you know to be their value (because it's yours too) may in the end be the only evidence they have that they may after all be worth loving. But, in order to do this, you need to have learned and learned and learned again to see yourself with love.

I said much earlier that you might define a religious attitude to life as that which accepts the mystery (and the wonder) of existence; I would now want to add that it is also one which gives proper attention to persons and things, because they are lovable and because there is no other way of learning to love them. Yet the starting-point has to be with the person you know best of all. You cannot—it is implicit in Jesus's command—love your neighbour unless you first love yourself. The truth is that God delights in me because I am me. He sees me as I am, and he invites me to explore my potential as a lover and so become what I could be.

There is a brief, marvelous essay by St. Bernard of Clairvaux called *On the Love of God* (St. Bernard's lily grows here in the Alpine pastures in one particular place: it is a slender, white perennial). In it he distinguishes four different degrees of love, each one more advanced than the rest: love of self for self, ("for whoever hated his own self?"); love of God for what he gives us; love of God for what he is; and, finally, love of yourself and your neighbour *for God's sake*—a state of loving which St. Bernard doesn't believe to be attainable in this life. So even when we have finally achieved unity with God the highest kind of love still includes "love of *self* for God's sake."[5] Thomas Merton has an interesting comment on that:

> This is the high point of St. Bernard's Christian humanism. It shows that the fulfillment of our destiny is not merely to be lost in God, as the traditional figures of speech would have it, like "a drop of water in a barrel of wine or like iron in the fire" but found in God *in all our individual and personal reality*, tasting our eternal happiness not only in the fact that we have attained to the possession of his infinite goodness, but above all in the fact that we see his will done in us [my italics].[6]

So the key to understanding our value is not just in seeing that we are capable of transcending ourselves by giving attention to other persons and things in the process of learning to love them; or of creating, as artists do, beauty and order out of chaos. It is the realization that each one of us is quite literally irreplaceable:

> Each mortal thing does one thing and the same: . . .
> . . . *myself* it speaks and spells
> Crying What I do is me: for that I came.

I have my own special identity that can never be replicated, not in a million years. Not even two snowflakes are ever quite the same. And this recognition of my true worth is something entirely different from selfishness, that turned-in-upon-myselfness of the egocentric. It is precisely the opposite. Only in beginning to recognize my unique worth shall I be able to recognize yours, for the truth is that unless we know ourselves to be lovable we are powerless to love.

When we fall in love, or share in a deep friendship, what each values is just this uniqueness, this otherness that is both similar and complementary yet distinct. The lover's "I love you because you are you" puts its finger on it. What I am claiming is that this is what God says to each one, and what makes each of us unique and irreplaceable is not that we are unusually gifted in some way. It lies rather (and here is the heart of it) in that personal, intimate relationship with God which is mine and mine alone. In some amazing sense I matter to God because nothing and no-one else in his whole creation can reflect his love back to him in exactly the same way. Helen Oppenheimer writes:

> Everyone can agree that Michelangelo is irreplaceable, but when God says of a drunken tramp, "but I loved that one. I did not want him lost," God's other children must try to see the point. We should see it, after all, if the tramp's mother said it. What belief in a heavenly Father requires is the exercise of imagination to see each other's irreplaceability as well as our own.[7]

W. B. Yeats was walking one day over a bit of marshy ground in Ireland when he felt

> all of a sudden, and only for a second, an emotion which I said to myself was the root of Christian mysticism. There had swept over me a sense of weakness, of dependence on a great personal Being somewhere far off yet near at hand. . . . That night I awoke lying on my back hearing a voice . . . saying, "No human soul is like any other human soul, and therefore the love of God for any human soul is infinite, for no other soul

can satisfy the same need in God."[8]

This, then, is ultimately what makes you and me and every other living soul a person who is not to be casually overlooked, dismissed, or abused. In Arthur Miller's play, *Death of a Salesman*, Willy Loman is an unattractive, unsuccessful traveling salesman. At the age of sixty, after long years of work, struggling to pay the mortgage, improving his home, growing apart from his two sons, he despairs at the apparent purposelessness of his life. His wife, to whom he has been unfaithful yet who can see him with clear and loving eyes, says:

> He is not the finest character that ever lived. But he is a human being, and a terrible thing is happening to him. So attention must be paid. He is not to be allowed to fall into his grave like an old dog. Attention, attention must finally be paid to such a person.[9]

I hadn't originally meant to write this particular letter. I had meant to move from writing of the most difficult human quality to explain away—compassion—to the God whom I believe to be its source; but too many of the walking wounded came knocking at the doors of my memory, among them many who had not understood that compassion, like charity, begins at home. It is a kind of blasphemy to view ourselves with so little compassion when God views us with so much. It is a refusal to accept this gift of myself, my own frail but unique mystery, to which "attention must be paid."

But it also requires a kind of quantum leap in our understanding of the nature of God.

XX

The Christlikeness of God

[God's] changelessness means that he cannot cease to be what he is, but it does not preclude his doing some new thing to express what he is.

JOHN V. TAYLOR[1]

There comes a moment in the play [Brecht's *Mother Courage*] where the soldiers carry in the dead body of a man they suspect to be the son of Mother Courage, though they aren't sure. She must be forced to identify him. I saw Helen Weigel act the scene, though acting is a paltry word for the miracle of her incarnation. As the body of her son was laid before her, she merely shook her head in mute denial . . . and as the body was carried off she looked the other way and tore her mouth wide open. The sound that came out was raw and terrible beyond any description I could give of it. But in fact there was no sound. Nothing. The sound was total silence. It was a silence which screamed and screamed through the whole theatre.

GEORGE STEINER[2]

The bird on the branch, the lily in the meadow, the stag in the forest, the fish in the sea, the countless joyful creatures sing, God is Love. But beneath all these sopranos, as it were a sustained bass pan, is the *De profundis* of the Sacrificed, God is Love.

SOREN KIERKEGAARD[3]

WAY BACK IN MY sixth letter I wrote of what I understood by the paradox of the transcendence and immanence of God: of the need to hold together concepts of God beyond and God within. I spoke of the God who is beyond our understanding being able to transcend himself. I have just been writing of how we transcend ourselves with every act of self-giving love, that love which may be defined as the willingness to give yourself away. Just so, I believe, God transcends himself by giving himself in an act of love within his creation. He does so in order to identify himself with his creatures and allow us to glimpse what lies at the creation's heart. We call it the Incarnation.

Now this is not some profound book of apologetics: these are very personal letters about the nature of wonder, in this case the wonder of God "doing some new thing to express what he is." Whole libraries are filled with attempts to explain this mystery, and much blood has been spilled (God forgive us) in its defence. It is a truth that has shaped countless lives, inspired great music and art, changed the civilized world. It has been misrepresented, challenged and derided. All I can tell you is that I know nothing else that comes near to making sense of my daily experience of living in the world, of both its delight and its pain. Nothing else that begins to answer some of the questions or helps in meeting the darkness that most people experience at some time in their lives.

"There is no end to the writing of books, and much study is wearisome," I read this morning as part of the first lesson for morning prayer, and it rang a warning bell. For the best part of a month I have written to you almost daily. I have tried not to dissemble but to tell you the truth as I see it or as I find it expressed in the words of others. It has proved both stimulating and costly: costly in terms of time and concentration, but costly too at times because it has involved moments of personal exposure—the kind of vulnerability that Englishmen usually avoid. If I were to end these letters by saying, "I give you my word," it could mean either or both of two things: that you can trust me; and that I have tried to convey some inner truth that is personal and important to me and share it with you in the only way I can. In words. Such words (if they are not to be some kind of banal pulpit-talk or theological jargon that neither of us really believes or understands) must have come from the heart and be consistent with my life. In other words: this book is a small act of love, framed in words which I hope may link with life as you know it. Whether you accept it as such is up to you.

The story the New Testament tells is, of course, a love story. Its claim is that because God loves and values his creation "the Word is made flesh." The implications may be mind-blowing, but the principle is no different from my desire to "give you my word" (the essence of what it is to be me) because I love you; no different from what we have seen artists and writers attempting to do; no different in having to be expressed in words and images that will connect with what you understand and experience. It is not enough simply to accept the reality of the transcendent God but go no further. You have to accept that self-disclosure is no less of the very essence of his being than his hiddenness; and you then have to ask what possibility there is for him to communicate what lies at his centre (language falters here) other than in our language. Just as I can use words like love or beauty or pain with some confidence that you will understand them, so it is possible for God to communicate with us because there is within us something that belongs to the same order of being, what the Bible calls being made in "the image" (or the likeness) of God. And like speaks to like.

I cannot "prove" this in any scientific Q.E.D. sense. But I know without a shadow of doubt when at those moments I experience that unselfish form of love we call compassion either in myself or in others that I touch something which is as deeply rooted, as primary, in human nature as selfishness and, I believe, is the more authentic and will ultimately prove the more powerful. Wherever compassion shows itself, even for a moment, it is like the sun breaking through to light up an object, and if it is not a sign of our "Godlikeness" it is quite simply inexplicable.

But come back to the thought of the creative artist. St. Augustine somewhere comments on those words of St. John, "the Word was made flesh": "the Word is, in a way, the art of the almighty and wise God." The Word—Jesus Christ—is God's supreme work of art: if you like, his self-portrait. Think of how an artist uses the only available means—canvas, paint, stone, wood—to convey a truth through form and colour. Every work of art is a form of incarnation: the spirit of the artist uniting with matter. It is an attempt to find images that will tell us something true, something of lasting value, about a person, a landscape or an object. It starts with the invisible: an idea, a way of seeing, which is then enfleshed in something you can see and touch. In his mind's eye Michelangelo sees the completed perfection of a human body in the rough stone and chisels away until it emerges. And, as we have seen, the mark of the greatest artists, novelists, poets, and composers is to reduce us to a kind of silent wonder in face of some aspect of beauty or truth about the human condition which we had not noticed or understood; a kind of truth that seems to impinge on us from that which is outside and beyond us and yet speaks directly to our hearts. I may stand in front of Rembrandt's portrait of his son Titus, and understand truths about the unique value of this boy to his father, but also truths about human vulnerability and the transient nature of beauty that will be as true for your great-great-grandchildren as they are for me. Yet miraculously these truths are embodied in a square of canvas and some dried paint: a word made flesh.

Now if Rembrandt or van Gogh, creating round the heads of his portraits such an effect of light "as to suggest the divine potential in every human being," feel compelled to communicate what lies within them in this way, God's yearning to communicate something of himself to his creatures must be unimaginably greater; especially if the inmost nature, the true and authentic voice of God, is not revealed in the power of the whirlwind but in acts of suffering, self-giving love. What we could never have guessed, however rich in beauty the world may be, however troubled we are by our questing, mysterious spirits, is now revealed—fleshed out—in a particular life and death. In a wordless, newborn child and in the man that child became.

Those who tell that story present us with compelling images, as a painter or poet would, images that seem to point beyond themselves to the very heart of reality. They tell of the blind seeing, the deaf hearing, the outcast welcomed, the guilty being set free, the hungry fed; of a shared meal, a traitor's kiss in a garden and a friend's denial before cockcrow; a night of torture, a nailing to a cross and an empty garden tomb; of men and women living in the spirit of the man who, alone of all our race, "looked full at the ineffable mystery and told us he was Father."[4] The one they knew as Jesus possessed a sense of contagious freedom and now, with increasing confidence, those who followed him found that they had been set free to live in what they could only describe as "a new creation."

You can question it: you can dismiss it. But you cannot avoid the bedrock of their belief: this man, whom we watched and listened to and grew to love we now know to be God's way of giving us, in a most costly act of love, the essence of himself; bone of our bone, flesh of our flesh. Christ "the image of the invisible God."

Now of course the Christ whose story is told in the gospels is not God in all the wonder of his unimaginable power. He is the "image," the "icon" of the transcendent God whose very transcendence lies in his self-giving. Jesus Christ is not God pretending to be man. He is fully human in every sense, capable of being abused, ignored, tortured and killed, yet one who was so possessed by, and open to, the spirit of God that it is no longer possible to define God as other than Christlike. In his struggle to put this mystery into words St. John writes: "No one has ever seen God; but . . . he who is closest to the Father's heart, he has made him known";[5] and he sums up what he has come to believe by recording Jesus as saying: "Whoever has seen me has seen the Father."[6]

So God's self-portrait turns out to be at once more ordinary and more extraordinary than anyone had dreamed. As ordinary as the man in the village carpenter's shop. As extraordinary as every human being is shown by this man potentially to be; and Christianity, at its authentic best, is the story of those who take God at his word (and at his Word): the Word made flesh, the human face of God, the truth expressed in the only terms in which we can understand it, as a costly act of love. God in the person of Christ is also saying: "Trust me. You are mine and I love you. I give you my word. All is well."

* * *

11 June: P.M.

I could stop there; but I would only have told half the story. For I claimed that I knew of no truth that comes so close to answering the questions and meeting the darkness that most of us experience at times. And even if the darkness keeps its distance from us, there is an evil that is daily all too evident. The genocide and the cancer cell. The terrorist bomb and the "black dog" of depression. The experience of sickness or pain or bereavement can make even our most transfigured moments seem no more than a self-deluding, selfish indulgence, powerless to affect the depth of anguish we may feel in the face of darkness. Then we resort to language that Flaubert likened to "a cracked kettle on which we beat out tunes for bears to dance to, when all the time we are longing to move the stars to pity."[7] Which is why even the most rewarding experiences of natural religion are ultimately impotent. And why I look to the God disclosed in Christ.

Listen to and respect those who cannot bring themselves to believe in God, especially those who cannot reconcile the pain they feel, or the hurt they have been done, with a God whose nature is love. But never give any credence to those who say they believe, yet would remove God from his world. The Christian faith only retains its credibility when it is centred on the one they called "Emmanuel" because that means "God is with us." God does not provide answers to our questions concerning suffering and the existence of evil. What he does (what else *could* Love do?) is to enter into the questions. He enters into the pain, the dirt and the danger, and takes the kind of body that when it is flogged, suffers, and when nails are thrust through it and it is hung up on a roughly-hewn cross, dies. As Dietrich Bonhoeffer wrote from his Nazi prison-cell, "only a suffering God can help."

A couple of years ago, at Baylor University in Texas, I had to address two thousand undergraduates in the theatre they use for a weekly chapel forum. I struggled to speak about the God in whom I have come to believe (though not as arrogantly as the students' paper later claimed: "Abbey reverend summarizes God's character"); but as I left the building I found chalked on the curb, along with messages about tennis tournaments and Wayne loving Darlene, words which put the case far more succinctly than I had: "Jesus wept. Is your God man enough to cry?" Someone understood.

It isn't just a God whose nature is love who has to be reconciled to human suffering, it is a God whose nature is *suffering* love. For that is, by definition, what love is. As I have said, it is a going out of yourself for the sake of another, as in compassion (from the Latin *cum* + *passio*, meaning "I suffer with, or alongside"): that sometimes fatal imaginative capacity for knowing what it is like to live inside someone else's skin, "and suffer, and weep and mourn for him as if he himself had put on the actual body of his neighbor." There is a feeble, powerless understanding of religion that sees it as no more than a moral code, and which is no understanding at all of the life-changing nature of believing in the God who would have us know that when we suffer he suffers in and with us. The cry of desolation of Jesus on the cross, his sense of forsakenness, is the ultimate paradox of the God so totally at one with his creation that he too knows in Christ that moment when the whole of your world contracts into a single. blinding experience of pain: pain of body, mind and spirit. God at one with all who for whatever reason feel they are forsaken. Here is mystery indeed.

Christians talk of the Passion (the suffering) of Jesus: it might equally be called the compassion of God. There is no virtue in believing in an enfeebled Christianity that does not put that truth at its centre, as the New Testament certainly does, for what St. Paul or St. John claim is that it is the crucified Jesus who is the most definitive picture of God the world has seen. Here is the "Beyond" in our midst with a vengeance. Here, if anywhere, is a cause for wonder.

I find it hard, in these final letters, to draw the parameters of what I want to say. I am chary of saying too much, leaving you a bit punch-drunk; but I am scared of saying too little, leaving you perplexed. So let me add two more things.

The first I can state very simply, though it is a most profound truth. It is the fact that the readiness to forgive and be forgiven is the most powerful weapon in the whole armory of love. At the Cross, which I more and more believe was the "still centre of the turning world" where all masks are finally stripped away (*this* is what we do to each other daily and to the God within us: *this* is God's response), Jesus asks his Father to forgive those who are nailing him there. That is not only the key to how what seems wholly evil may be turned to good, how the poison of hatred or resentment may be halted in its destructive course and neutralized. It is also a startling insight into the nature of God who uses the Cross to assure us that, do what we may, we are loved and forgiven, and that we only have to turn to him to know it is true.

In Peter Shaffer's most recent play, *The Gift of the Gorgon*, Helen is trying to persuade her playwright husband that the terrorism of the I.R.A. must not be avenged, that there is no limit to forgiveness. He tells her that blood calls for blood, a life for a life, as in the ancient Greek drama. Any talk of "forgiveness" is a sign of weakness. Helen replies:

> Surely, surely we've learnt one thing over the ages? The dead have to be *resisted*! When they call for blood, we have to be deaf! . . . We have to be bigger than they were, or what's the point? You go on about passion, Edward. But have you never realized there are many, many kinds?—Including a passion to kill our own passion when it's wrong. I'm not just being clever. The truest, hardest, most adult passion isn't stamping and geeing ourselves up. It's refusing to be led by rage when we most want to be. That means every time a bomb goes off, yes, and every time a baby is killed, and every other filthy thing that makes you sick with fury. Stubbornly continuing to say No to blood. All right, the Greeks wouldn't have understood this, but they were savages, finally. The whole of their country ran with blood. . . . They had Gods to take the big view *for* them. Athena could come down suddenly and stop the boys fighting, like a schoolmistress in a playground. We haven't got *anyone* to do that. We're the boys and the mistress, *both*—that's the impossible and wonderful thing about *us*! No other being in the universe can change itself by conscious will: it is *our privilege alone*. To take out inch by inch this spear in our sides that goads us on and on to bloodshed—and still make sure it doesn't take our guts with it.[8]

The second truth about the Incarnation is that the presence of Jesus in history didn't just reveal the nature of God once. It revealed the presence of God as he has always been and always will be. I like an image used in a novel by Helen Waddell, that of a fallen tree sawn through the middle, all the rings in the wood exposed. She speaks of how the dark rings which we only see where it is cut across go up and down the whole length of the tree, and likens the exposed part to the life and death of Christ: "the bit of God that we saw."[9] But it continues. Because God is not confined to time but is eternally himself and unchanging, he always was and always will be Christlike. If a mother feels the anguish of her son dying of AIDS, then the God in whose likeness both are made must in some unknowable way suffer that anguish too. Love knows no other language.

As a man, I am bound to test that claim at my centre: to link head-knowledge (which only takes me so far) with heart-knowledge (which seems to take me further). As a priest, I have had to sit with the dying, try to console the bereaved, spend untold hours encouraging the unloved, and listening to the hurt and the lonely. I have also known what it means to be diminished by a long, debilitating illness, when I found it difficult to think or even to pray. All I know is that, for me, the only words that helped had to do with Christ crucified—or, rather, with the Easter Christ who still bears in his hands and side the marks of the nails and spear. The only words that I sense have helped others have had to do with this concept of a suffering God, whose love for each of us cannot be altered or diminished, and of whom I can say with the Psalmist:

> If I reach up to heaven thou art there;
> if I go down to hell thou art there also.[10]

It is often said that the older we get the less intellectual baggage we need to cling to, and the more stubbornly we hold to a few transforming truths—I guess those whose truth has been borne out by our experience and whose validity it would be as foolish to deny as to deny that grass is green and whisky intoxicating. There have been enough times when I have found that "here and there in the world and now and then in ourselves is a New Creation, usually hidden, but sometimes manifest and certainly manifest in Jesus who is called the Christ."[11] I have scented a different reality that has to do with God, a destination I can only glimpse in this life, both like yet unlike my profoundest human experiences; though self-giving love when I spot it in others is, I guess, the best clue I'll get.

When I began I spoke a little of the insights of that formidable body of witnesses whom we call the Christian mystics. If you were to summarize their particular vision, you would have to say it is of the Oneness of God; of the timeless nature of what is real and of lasting value; of the self, the ego, known to our senses but not to be confused with the true deep Self; and of a Love lying beneath the creation and enfolding all that exists. I hope you may have glimpsed in these letters something of that interrelated vision as a constant, underlying motif.

XXI

"Come and See"

You have eyes: can you not see?[1]

If your eye is sound, your whole body will be full of light.[2]

LAST NIGHT I BEGAN to wonder if the final words of yesterday's letter had not been a bit too easy, a bit glib; if I hadn't fallen into the preacher's trick (so easy with no-one to challenge or tease out your words) of being so unspecific about why such seemingly unlikely truths shape my life, as to vanish in a puff of theological smoke.

I have had no sudden conversion, no moment when the earth moved and the scales fell from my eyes. When the Damascus Road brigade make their bids for such blinding (or rather, unblinding) experiences, holding no such dazzling trumps in my hand, I have to pass. God has never shown himself in such a knockdown kind of way as to leave no room for doubt; and, as a naturally somewhat guarded soul, what attracts me is this very reticence: he invites and he waits, he never commands. As Love would, of course, leaving room for faith rather than certainty and affirming my freedom. The ways to God are as varied as human beings (and sometimes as crazily idiosyncratic), and when I worked amongst students, where some had clear and decisive conversion experiences with a strong emphasis on accepting Jesus as their personal friend and saviour, I sometimes felt judged and dismissed because I could not with integrity use that son of language. I hope that by the end of this letter I shall have gone a little way towards explaining why.

I would not be what I am, or writing these letters to you, if I did not believe with all my heart (on my better days, anyway) that God is my Creator and that he is Christlike: that is to say, that his name and nature are Love. My faith begins and ends with God revealing himself in human terms and all that the Incarnation implies. But although it begins with, and indeed centres on, Jesus of Nazareth, it does not end with him. I am drawn to him as I am drawn to no other man who has ever lived, but he is no longer just a man. This belief in the Christlike God, exploring, questioning, sometimes doubting it, and re-defining, seeing new aspects, new meanings, hopefully with a deepening insight and perception, is the business of a lifetime. In a sense it has never not been part of me, though my understanding has changed so much: less childish certainly, but still not as childlike as it should be in terms of trust and love.

I guess my journey is not unusual and is echoed by that of those who first saw him. For once again it is a question of learning how to see. If you could only use one verb to describe the very heart of what Jesus is and says and does it would have to be that verb. He asks the first two men whose curiosity is aroused by him to "come and see" where he is staying and they spend the day there. They in turn, drawn to follow this man, invite others to "come and see"; and the first link in the chain of disciples is forged. He claims to have come "to open the eyes of the blind"; to enable people to see. They notice how he sees God's love for his creation, each flower, each sparrow; how he pictures God at the heart of such ordinary scenes as a farmer sowing his land or children playing in the marketplace. He draws their attention to the mystery, the "beyond" in their midst, yet keeps them firmly rooted in their everyday lives. They listen as he tells stories which allow people to see the reality of God and his fatherly love in terms of a shepherd searching for a straying lamb, a father longing for his son's return home, a woman overjoyed at finding her lost pension. They watch as he challenges the priorities of the lawyers and religious leaders who claim to see: he accuses them of blindness, of lacking any true understanding or vision.

They watch in particular his dealings with individuals: they notice how he sees into the heart, not superficially; each is the focus of his loving attention. He meets the rich young man and "looks steadily at him and loves him." He meets a Samaritan woman at a well and, seeing her need, draws her attention to the God who is to be found within her. When much later (with an insight they never achieved while he lived) those who write his story choose which few incidents to record, two of the most significant stories they tell are of two men, both born blind, both of whom are healed. When the first is questioned by the authorities as to how this healing was achieved, he replies with moving simplicity: "I do not know. . . . All I know is this: I was blind and now I see."[3] The other incident is in itself a kind of parable about the degrees of perception needed before we can claim to see each other with changed eyes. Jesus takes a blind man by the hand, puts spittle on his eyes, lays his hands on him and asks "Can you see anything?" "I see people," he replies, "they look like trees, but they are walking about."[4] Trees: not necessarily just "green things that stand in the way" for (as Blake said and as Philip Toynbee found) they can "move you to tears of joy"; nevertheless *things*, objects without feelings. Then Jesus lays his hands again on his eyes and he sees clearly. "Do you not yet understand?" Jesus asks his followers. "You have

eyes; can you not see?" "Whereas trees have roots," writes George Steiner, "men have legs and are each other's guests."[5]

What Jesus is demanding of them is that shift of focus: a new childlike yet mature innocence of perception that sees beneath the surface, a seeing that goes from without to within. "If your eye is sound," he tells them, "your whole body will be full of light." Those first disciples, who being closest to him had the best chance of achieving this kind of enlightenment, failed to do so when they looked at him. They saw further than the crowds or the religious authorities or Pilate. But as John (the most visionary of the gospel writers, the one with the best "inward eye") looks back from the far side of Easter, he reveals that only after that final week that culminated in the Cross and in the extraordinary days that followed did they really begin to see who this man might be and what he was trying to show them. In his words: "The Word became flesh . . . and we saw his glory . . . full of grace and truth."[6]

"Glory" isn't a word with which we are very familiar. I like how Frederick Buechner puts it:

> Glory is to God what style is to an artist. A painting by Vermeer, a sonnet by Donne, a Mozart aria—each is so rich with the style of the one who made it . . . that . . . it couldn't have been made by anyone else. . . . The style of an artist brings you as close to the sound of his voice and the light in his eye as it is possible to get this side of actually shaking hands with him.
> . . .
> In the words of Psalm 19, "The heavens declare the glory of God." It is the same thing. . . . Not just sunsets and starry nights but dust storms, rain forests, garter snakes, the human face, are all unmistakably the work of a single hand. . . . To behold God's glory, to sense his style, is the closest you can get this side of Paradise, just as to read *King Lear* is the closest you can get to Shakespeare.[7]

Well, yes; but (as Buechner would be the first to say) it isn't just the heavens or a human face that are telling the glory of God. It is a very particular human face, for (in St. Paul's words) we can now encounter "the glory of God in the face if Jesus Christ."[8] And if you were to ask St. John, "Where chiefly did you see that glory?" I think he would either have replied, "When he was hanging on the cross," or, more probably, "When he left the supper table, wrapped a towel about his waist, and began (despite our startled protests) to wash our dusty feet." For that stands the notion of glory—and the concept of God—on its head. It is to enter a foolish, topsy-turvy world, where the first are last and the last first, where value lies in being, not in achieving, where the just law of "an eye for an eye" is countermanded by the radical action of forgiveness, and where greatness lies in the compassionate, often humdrum, service of others.

Yet what they saw in the end, what the professional persecutor-turned-missionary Paul saw after he had so dramatically regained his sight (in both senses), what John saw once his eyes had been opened, was that they had to see beyond the figure of Jesus to God himself. When he said, "Whoever has seen me has seen the Father," the point Jesus is making is not about himself but about the Father. "You want to see the glory and the love of God—in so far as human eyes can do so?" asks John. "Then look on this man whom we have seen with our own eyes."

But they only saw this truth in retrospect. So keen is John to make us understand the change in them that he uses three different verbs all meaning "to see" when he tells the story of finding the tomb empty on Easter morning, the grave clothes still wrapped but the body gone. John outruns Peter and gets there first. He "peers in" and sees (a verb simply meaning to use your physical eyes) the linen wrappings lying there; Peter goes into the tomb and sees (a verb meaning looking with an eye to detail) the napkin that had been round Jesus's head "rolled up in a place by itself." Then John goes in, and "he saw and believed," and here the verb means to see with discernment and insight: the penny drops and you see what you have never seen before.

Yet it is not quite so simple. For it is one thing to have known Jesus, watched him, lived through the devastating final days of losing him, followed by the wonder of daring to say once again to each other "we have seen the Lord," knowing it could not be true, yet knowing that it was; it is one thing for them to see all that and to understand that the world would never be the same again; it is quite another for us to do so. Yet they didn't see, not at first. John writes of Jesus telling them that only when "the Spirit is given" will they fully understand the truth, and Paul was to write that "no one can say Jesus is Lord except under the influence of the Holy Spirit."[9]

When I say, as I do daily, "I believe in the Holy Spirit," what do I mean? I mean that Jesus's life is patently one that was transparent to the God who is also Spirit; it was all of a piece, contagious in its freedom. Jesus was the only truly Spirit-filled human being. You can say that his purpose was to create relationships, to establish a community, that would reflect the love of God and be a foretaste of the Kingdom of God. To claim, as the first Christians did, "Jesus is Lord" is to say that he defines what life in the Spirit is like; that he is the one around whom the Spirit-filled community is to be gathered.

Let me put this in another way. If I am to see God and the world, myself and my neighbour, as Jesus Christ saw them I need to be open to his spirit. This is not as strange as it may seem. We are embodied spirits and we relate to each other both at a physical and a spiritual level; we influence deeply those we love and are as deeply influenced by those who love us. Those who were inspired by Jesus (and the word literally means to have spirit breathed into you: "And he breathed on them, saying 'Receive the Holy Spirit'"[10]), were so persuaded by his vision of what life might be, by what they had seen of his glory (his "style") of living and dying, by what he had enabled them to see of God and by what he had shown them of the meaning of true personhood, that they wanted to live in his spirit. That had been God's desire from the beginning of time and the whole Bible leads to this point where through Christ eyes are finally opened.

There are some words of John Taylor in *The Go-Between God* which many years ago helped open my eyes to this truth:

> The Holy Spirit is the invisible third party who stands between me and the other, making us mutually aware. Supremely and primarily he opens my eyes to Christ. But he also opens my eyes to the brother (and sister) in Christ, or the fellow man, or the point of need, or the heartbreaking brutality and the equally heartbreaking beauty of the world. He is the giver of that vision without which people perish. We commonly speak about the Holy Spirit as the source of power. But in fact he enables us not by making us supernaturally strong but by opening our eyes.[11]

So much that I have been writing about is contained in those words: the Spirit within us opening our eyes to the creation and its creatures, its beauty and its pain; inspiring writers and artists; enabling us to look at ourselves and each other with compassion and give proper attention to the mystery each one of us is; looking to the only one of our race who saw clearly into the heart of God and in his freedom and trust spelled out for us the meaning of "the love that moves the sun and the other stars."[12]

But notice what the Spirit does. He doesn't simply open my eyes to the significance of Jesus of Nazareth, who is now a part of history: he opens my eyes to the indwelling Christ. The experience of God is of one who is Christlike and whose nature the human Jesus allowed me to grasp; but in learning to call Jesus "Lord," those first disciples were acknowledging one who is now beyond time and no longer limited by space, now encountered as a life-giving Spirit. Once Jesus had left them his followers had to look for him elsewhere and in a new form. They found him again (and only they could know the truth of this) within the communities that started to form in his name: by looking into each other's faces, listening to each other's words, hearing words of forgiveness from one another's lips, receiving the broken and shared bread at one another's hands. They believed he was alive in their midst, teaching them through the Holy Spirit, feeding them with the living bread. This, too, is a mystery, hard (like all mysteries) to explain in words which tend to buckle under the weight of such a reality. But the New Testament is full of it. It is implicit in Jesus's own promise: "I am with you always"; in his comparing the relationship of his followers with himself to that of a vine and its branches, "I in you and you in me."

How can we be certain those are the exact words of Jesus? We can't. They may or may not be. They are put into his mouth by John, whose task it was to interpret all he had seen and heard in the light of his continuing experience, but what we can know beyond any shadow of a doubt is that he wrote after a lifetime's knowledge of what Christ had come to mean for him and his fellow-Christians as he learned to see under the guidance of the Spirit. So Paul can write, time and again, that we are "in Christ"; that we are like cells in the body of Christ; that "I live, yet not I, but Christ lives in me."[13]; and he prays for his fellow Christians "that through faith Christ may dwell in your hearts in love."[14] And those who read his words would have known him to be writing of a mystery they found true in their daily lives.

When I quoted Hopkins' sonnet about each thing crying

> . . . what I do is me: for that I came

I did not go on to the sonnet's end. This speaks of how, in finding his or her true self as a child of God, each person

> Acts in God's eyes what in God's eyes he is—
> Christ—for Christ plays in ten thousand places,
> Lovely in limbs, and lovely in eyes not his
> To the Father through the features of men's faces.[15]

That is the most important opening of our eyes by the Spirit: when Christ is encountered as we relate to each other, and that will be so wherever within our small communities (those places where we meet with others in any significant way) we create love, show compassion, work for justice, or help reconcile those who are divided; grant forgiveness or ask for it; or stand for truth. The Church, in so far as it is the Body of Christ, the place where the Word is read and the bread broken, should be the place where these things happen, where the spirit of Christ is self-evident. Quite often it is so, but by no means always. And certainly not exclusively. Mother Teresa describes the loving care her Sisters of Charity give to all in need—Muslims, Hindus, Christians, the labels are irrelevant for all are human—as "serving Jesus under the distressing disguise of the poorest of the poor," and she does so in the light of Jesus's own reported words that the Christ (who when he washed his disciples' feet so starkly revealed where love's priority lies) is most predictably to be found in the hungry and thirsty, the naked, the sick and those in prison, and—we are bound to add—the refugee.

Paul once wrote: "I pray that your inward eyes may be enlightened, so that you may know what is the hope to which he calls you . . . and how vast are the resources of his power to those who have faith."[16] I am reminded of Rilke's "You must change your life." I can't claim to have done so; and my inward eyes don't always function too well. But I hope I have said enough to explain a little why I opted all those years ago to be a follower of Christ.

Only up to a point is it about looking back; chiefly it is about looking within and without: of relating to a God whom Jesus has shown to be Christlike and who is to be found in unlikely people and unlikely places. It is about how the way what he said and what he did resonate in that deepest and most private part of me the Bible calls "the heart," and recognizing the contemporary power and relevance of his words and actions. For me, now, Christ is like an omnipresent icon, speaking of God and pointing to God; for the sole purpose of a painted icon is to lead us through a contemplation of the visible to the mystery of the invisible.

Those who have dared to speak of the end of it all, the ultimate purpose for which we were born, do so in terms of a growth in love and a growth in seeing: the kind of seeing that is more than seeing "puzzling reflections in a mirror" but is a seeing God "face to face." St. Augustine says of heaven, "We shall rest and we shall see, we shall see and we shall love, we shall love and we shall praise, in the end which is no end."[17]

We can speculate as philosophers do . . . but speculating isn't the sort of seeing that I have in mind. Half-an-hour ago, after a day of storm clouds obscuring the mountains, the sun suddenly broke through and momentarily lit up a nearby field that is a carpet of wild flowers as if a sudden searchlight had been switched on to bring it dramatically to life. It made me think of R. S. Thomas' poem which says in fourteen lines what is perhaps the most important thing of all.

> I have seen the sun break through
> to illuminate a small field
> for a while, and gone my way
> and forgotten it. But that was the pearl
> of great price, the one field that had
> the treasure in it. I realize now
> that I must give all that I have
> to possess it. Life is not hurrying
>
> on to a receding future, nor hankering after
> an imagined past. It is the turning
> aside like Moses to the miracle
> of the lit bush, to a brightness
> that seemed as transitory as your youth
> once, but is the eternity that awaits you.[18]

The truth God had revealed to Thomas, he writes elsewhere, "if that is the right way to describe the knowledge—half hope, half intuition—by which I live," was that "alongside us, made invisible by the thinnest of veils, is the heaven we seek .. . it is within us, as Jesus said. That is why there is no need to go anywhere from here."[19] We are therefore

> . . . to hold the position
> Assigned to us, long as time

Lasts, somewhere half-way
Up between earth and heaven.[20]

Part of being human is to experience moments of true perception about those things that touch you so intimately that suddenly you *see*. What you see (or read or hear) at such moments has a ring of truth about it, not just of a general kind but as something that takes on a dimension and depth for you so that it becomes *your* truth. It seems to be making a claim on you. Such moments don't come often. Hold on to them. Cherish them until they become so much a part of you as to be second nature. For there is only one persistent

demand made upon us by the Spirit. It is that we are receptive. That we keep our eyes open, our minds unclosed. It is, in short, that we retain all our lives our sense of wonder.

XXII

Prayer as Giving Attention to God

God is both other than I am and also the same. For God is apprehended as the source from which I continually flow, and the source cannot be separated from that which continually flows from it. . . . In my deep communion with the mystery of another person and in the mystery of my own being, what I find is God.

H. A. WILLIAMS[1]

The condition of all valid seeing and hearing . . . lies in a self-forgetting attentiveness, a profound concentration, a self-merging which operates a real communion between the seer and the seen—in a word, in contemplation.

EVELYN UNDERHILL[2]

Our whole business in this life is to restore to health the eye of the heart whereby God may be seen.

ST. AUGUSTINE[3]

When in Shakespeare's Tempest, Ferdinand first sees Miranda, there bursts from his whole being the cry "O, you wonder!" and our praying should have some of that utterly delighted perception in it.

ALAN ECCLESTONE[4]

Stand still in your own space.[5]

A FEW LETTERS BACK, WHEN I was seeking to pinpoint where our true value as individuals lies, I said it is not because we are attractive, gifted, or nice to know. My value lies in the fact that I am my unique self, that no-one else who has ever lived, or who ever will, can be in exactly my relationship with God, or reflect his love back to him in exactly the same way. Just as no-one else can be to me what you are, nor can anyone else be to you what I am. For ultimately that's what life is about: it's about learning to stand in your own space and discerning in its unfathomable depths a power greater than yourself who invites your attention; and not simply your attention but your love. And it is that kind of giving attention that we call prayer.

I wrote, at the start, of my own transcendence, the sense I have of that within me which is the very ground of my existence and yet somehow "other" than me; of finding God beyond and within; and of how this changes everything that being a *person* means. Archbishop Anthony Bloom writes of the world of *things*, which, while as mysterious as sub-atomic physics shows them to be, have "density, weight and volume, but no depth. We can always penetrate to the heart of things . . ." (an apple, a stone), but we cannot penetrate to the depth of the human heart, for

> that is rooted in the immensity of God himself. . . . It is only when we have understood the difference between a presence that asserts itself and a presence we have to seek because we sense it in our hearts . . . that we can begin our search in the knowledge that we are blind, blinded by the visible which prevents us grasping the invisible.[6]

There is in each of us a Self that lies deeper than our conscious ego, that still point of your being where you are most truly you, so that the journey of prayer is largely a journey inwards. Not that prayer is self-analysis. Quite the reverse: it is a way of becoming detached, of escaping at least momentarily from the constant clamour of self. It is the way we begin to shift the centre of living from self-consciousness to self-surrender. "Nothing in all creation," writes Meister Eckhart, "is so like God as stillness." Prayer is about learning how to become still, open and receptive to the now, the present moment in which alone God is to be found. It is a kind of observing, a way of seeing.

Eckhart was certain that if we seek God in the external world we shall find him nowhere; if we seek him within, we shall begin to find him everywhere. So giving attention to God is really just a way of accepting what it means to be a person, or more simply, what it means to *be*.

> We are citizens of two worlds [writes Hugh Lavery]. The temporal is the world of work and worry, the world that is too much with us. But we have other experiences, brief ecstasies . . . still moments when we enter a kingdom. Then we cease to

do. We simply are. Being silences and subdues doing and the temporal melts into the eternal.[7]

Learning not to do, even learning not to be anything but just to be, takes a lifetime. (Probably rather more.) Praying is the toughest discipline there is, and the most worthwhile. "Prayer," writes Iris Murdoch, "is properly not petition, but an attention to God which is a form of love."[8] Of course praying as "seeing," as attending, as achieving stillness, is not exclusively Christian. Zen is a way of enlightenment, a way of so giving an object your full attention that you begin to see into its essence. Zen, in contrast to Zen Buddhism, is a Buddhist sect said to originate from a sixth-century Indian monk who apparently meditated for nine years with such persistence that his arms and legs fell off. It lays emphasis on the small details of ordinary life and the natural world. It is a form of contemplation (seeing) with the inward eye rather than meditation, which involves the mind. Zen painting seeks to simplify the "thereness" of an object, Hopkins' "inscape," with a few telling strokes, like a Japanese haiku poem. In Zen, you do not seek to blot out the world, but to become completely detached from it, no longer clinging to things but learning both to understand them and let them go. It seeks to grasp the unity of the visible and the invisible. "Zen teaches nothing," wrote Thomas Merton, "but it enables us to wake up and become aware. It does not teach, it points."[9]

In a play by Peter Shaffer, *Five Finger Exercise*, an undergraduate is trying to explain to his father why an Indian friend is the person he most admires in Cambridge. What is striking about him is that

> He's completely still. I don't mean he doesn't move. I mean that deep down inside him there is a sort of happy stillness that

makes all our family rows and raised voices seem like a kind of blasphemy.[10]

St. John of the Cross, a sixteenth-century Spanish mystic, said that the heart of prayer is giving "loving attention to God"; and certainly the starting point of prayer is to realize that it is not about words (or not much of the time): it's about listening. It is about becoming still, remaining still, waiting, not being afraid of silence. If you are going to watch birds with any kind of seriousness you have to be prepared to wait and watch with great patience and remain still (as we did two days ago, in the silent woods, until we gradually became aware of a faint, high-pitched tinny sound and watched as the goldcrests and a tree-creeper explored the nearby fir trees for insects); if you are going to let a painting speak to you, you have to respect its silence and its stillness. It has demanded an intensely concentrated act of seeing on the pan of the artist and it isn't going to give up its secret at a hurried glance. Birds, paintings, music, books, people: we have to learn to go at their pace and tune to their wavelength. What we receive is related to what we give. Giving attention to God is no different, though much harder. For we are so used to *doing* that learning to *be* is like learning a foreign language. And we mustn't expect to feel much. Feelings are not what count. What counts is simply being there. In Eliot's words from *East Coker*:

> I said to my soul, be still, and wait without hope
> For hope would be hope for the wrong thing; wait without love
> For love would be love of the wrong thing; there is yet faith
> But the faith and the hope and the love are all in the waiting.
> Wait without thought, for you are not ready for thought.
> So the darkness shall be the light and the stillness the dancing.[11]

Giving "loving attention to God": that sounds fine until you try it, when you find your mind is giving attention to everything else. What can help? Evelyn Underhill wrote a classic book on prayer and mysticism, and wrote of two kinds of illumination: what she calls "the illumination of the self," by which she means the growth of my inner intuitive sense of the presence of God which allows me to see myself (and therefore everyone else) in a new way; and "the illuminated vision of the world," the growing ability "to see God in nature and to obtain a radiant consciousness of the 'otherness' of natural things. . . . Most people, moved by emotion or beauty, have known flashes of rudimentary vision of this kind." 11 Which is partly what these letters have been all about, and we are back with those who by their heightened perception—of beauty, the transcendent, the sacramental, the extraordinariness of the ordinary—help us to see. For prayer too is seeing, noticing, not just the unusual, but quite ordinary things and people in our everyday lives and, like the artist Stanley Spencer, "learning to say thank you" for them. "Prayer," wrote Father John of Kronstadt, a nineteenth-century Orthodox priest who served the naval base at St. Petersburg and is recognized by the Orthodox as a saint, "prayer is a state of continual gratitude."

Now this is not a book about prayer. It's a series of letters about wonder, of which giving attention in order to see is an implicit part. So let me rein myself in and limit myself to some practical advice; plus an insight which I have found profoundly important.

The first concerns your body. You can't be still if you are uncomfortable. Eastern faiths such as Zen Buddhism and Yoga have taught us the importance of the body for achieving a proper state of relaxation. Kneeling upright, or crouched in a kind of shampoo position, doesn't help. Some like to pray standing. Others sit upright, the back and the neck straight, hands resting in the lap. I use a prayer stool that fits neatly over your ankles as you kneel, and on which you can sit in comfort for quite long periods. Only when the body is at ease is the mind at ease.

How you breathe is also important. Stillness is achieved by the stilling of our agitated restless minds and bodies. Most of us breathe much too shallowly most of the time, engaging only the upper part of the lungs. So it's good to begin by very gently giving attention to our breathing for a few moments, until we are breathing in and out in a smooth unbroken rhythm and our body is calm and centred.

My second point concerns the best way towards simple contemplation. Some like to pray with their eyes open, focused on an object; others with their eyes closed. Evelyn Underhill's advice is to take an object—a candle, a leaf, a stone, a flower, your own hand—and look at it with close attention, allowing the distractions to drop away, focusing simply and wholly on what is before you. She writes:

> Do not think, but as it were pour out your personality towards it: let your soul be in your eyes. Almost at once . . . you will perceive about you a strange and deepening quietness; a slowing down of our feverish mental time. Next, you will become aware of a heightened significance, an intensified existence of the thing at which you look. As you, with all your consciousness, lean out towards it, an answering current will meet yours. It seems as though the barrier between its life and your own, between subject and object, has melted away. You are merged with it, in an act of true communion: and you know the secret of its being deeply and unforgettably, yet in a way which you can never hope to express.[13]

Or you can take a crucifix, seeking to let the truth of God's love and forgiveness, symbolized by this small object, re-assure and affirm you at the deepest level of your being.

Or you can take a word or a simple phrase. (I am concerned here only with simple contemplative prayer, not with meditation, which has to do with using the mind and the imagination.) Because our mind is so full of thoughts and sensations the quiet repetition of a word or a familiar phrase is one of the simplest and most effective ways of practicing the presence of God. Words like "Abba," the word Jesus used to address the Father; or the words "Come, Lord Jesus," or the Psalmist's "Be still, and know that I am God." There is the Jesus Prayer which has been said for centuries and is one of the greatest treasures of the Orthodox Church, the words, "Lord Jesus Christ, Son of God, have mercy on me, a sinner." The Orthodox have always taught that the Jesus Prayer sums up the whole of the Gospel. It is repeated, quietly and slowly, over and over again as a way of bringing us to be in God's presence with no other thought than the wonder of God being who he is and us being who we are. Other words that I love to use are from that verse from the hymn known as St. Patrick's Breastplate which begins, "Christ be with me, Christ within me," and ends "Christ in mouth of friend and stranger." To say such words slowly, repeatedly, means that they gradually become part of you and may then well up from within you quire outside your formal times of prayer.

But perhaps best of all is to take the Lord's Prayer. It does not really matter if occasionally you get no further than the opening two words, provided your understanding of the words "Our" and "Father" is a fraction deeper as a result. Edwin Muir writes in his autobiography:

Last night, going to bed alone, I suddenly found myself . . .
reciting the Lord's Prayer in a loud, emphatic voice, with deep
urgency and profound disturbed emotion. While I went on I
grew more composed . . . and [gradually] my soul grew still;
every word had a strange fullness of meaning which astonished and delighted me . . . meaning after meaning sprang from
it, overcoming me again with joyful surprise; and I realized
that this simple petition was always universal and always inexhaustible, and day by day sanctified human life.[14]

And Simone Weil once wrote:

The Our Father contains all possible petitions . . . it is impossible to say it once through, giving the fullest possible attention
to every word without a change, infinitesimal perhaps but real,
taking place in the soul.[15]

Simone Weil also points out that there is all the difference
in the world between real attention, which has to do with waiting, emptying your mind, expectant and receptive, and a kind
of misdirected muscular effort:

If one says to one's pupils: "Now you must pay attention," one
sees them contracting their brows, holding their breath, stiff-
ening their muscles. If after two minutes they are asked what
they have been paying attention to, they cannot reply. They
have been concentrating on nothing. They have not been paying attention. They have been contracting their muscles.[16]

Now for the insight. It is one of those simple yet profound
truths that, once expressed, is so obvious. Jean-Pierre de Caus-
sade was an obscure eighteenth-century French priest who
wrote anonymously a book called *Self Abandonment to Divine
Providence*, and the heart of it lies in the phrase by which it is
best known: "the sacrament of the present moment." He begins

with the New Testament assertion that God's nature is un-changeable love, that he loves us at every moment of our lives and "can no more stop loving us than the sun can stop radiating heat." It follows, he says, that if God's love comes to us at every single moment then he is with us in the moment that is now. If we don't find God in the actual world around us, and in our-selves at this moment, then we can't expect to find him in our so-called "spiritual" times of prayer. Therefore it is to this mo-ment, and to this moment alone in all its singular *nowness*, that we should give our attention, so "that every moment of our lives" becomes "a sort of communion with the divine love." But we don't. Rilke wrote:

> Who has twisted us round like this, so that
> no matter what we do, we are in the posture
> of someone going away? Just as, upon
> the farthest hill, which shows him his whole valley
> one last time, he turns, stops, lingers—
> so we live here, forever taking leave.[17]

Forever looking back, remembering, perhaps wishing we could go back to some happiness, reliving some past glory or some bygone love, perhaps nursing a grudge, letting in the slow poison of resentment, or perhaps regretting a lost opportunity that can never recur; or words better left unsaid and actions better left undone. Or looking forward, either, if you are young, ambitiously and with hope; or, as you grow older, with anxiety, even a kind of dread. It is human and understandable, yet it is daft; for I cannot change the past and the future lies out of my hands.

Yet, far from being a kind of fatalism, living each moment as it comes is the only way to live with hope. It is not the cynical attitude of "eat, drink and be merry, for tomorrow we die." It is a grateful receiving and giving attention to what is before my eyes, with all the insight of which I have tried to speak, a giving myself fully to this present moment because *it is* and because *I am*. I have never seen this day, all it contains, before and I shall never see it again, nor will I ever again be exactly this self I am now. It is quite literally the only way we can know God, in the here and now and by living this moment fully. It is also, of course, the only hope we have of ever changing how we are, with the possibility of redeeming the past or affecting the future. "*This* is the day that the Lord has made," says the Psalmist, "let us rejoice and be glad in it."[18]

I love Kierkegaard's answer to the question he asks himself of how Jesus could act without anxiety when he knew of his imminent arrest:

> It was because he had eternity with him in the day that is called today: hence the next day had no power over him, it had no existence for him.[19]

If I am even to begin to live like this (and the kind of prayer I have spoken of is the most effective way of learning it), then two things are necessary. First, that I really do come to know at gut level that I do walk through the world as one who is loved, whatever may be happening to me, and that every moment, even the worst, can be used by God. And, secondly, that I learn to give attention to each moment as it comes—this person to be seen (repeat, seen), that tricky letter to be written, this humdrum task to be done, these letters to be written to you; and that is difficult, and most of the time we forget. But that, and that alone, is how we are called to be. Not what we are called to *do*, but how we are called to *be*. Attention givers. For that, when you think of it, is not a bad definition of love.

During the Second World War, a German widow hid some Jewish refugees in her home. When her friends found out they became alarmed. "You are risking your life," they said. "I know," she replied. "Then why do you persist in this foolishness?" "Because," she said, "the time is now, and I am here."[20]

* * *

Postscript: This is a bit of a cheat, for I'm adding it many months later having just watched the playwright Dennis Potter giving his last television interview, faced as he is with terminal cancer. Speaking of his approaching death he said:

> We forget that life can only be defined in the present tense: it is, and it is now . . . and that nowness has become so vivid to me that . . . I'm almost serene. I can celebrate life. Below my window . . . the blossom is out in full. It's a plum tree; and instead of saying, "Oh, that's nice blossom," looking at it through the window it is the whitest, frothiest, blossomest blossom there ever could be. And I can see it; and things are both more trivial than they ever were and more important than they ever were, and the difference between the trivial and the important doesn't seem to matter, but the nowness of everything is absolutely wondrous. . . .[21]

XXIII

Living the Eucharist

That singular command,
I do not understand,
Bless what there is for being,
Which has to be obeyed, for
What else am I for,
Agreeing or disagreeing?

W. H. AUDEN[1]

Our thanksgiving is always made through Jesus Christ who
made the whole creation eucharistic in assuming our humanity
and giving its praise a human voice.

A CARTHUSIAN[2]

. . . to apprehend
the point of intersection of the timeless
with time, is an occupation of the saint.

T. S. ELIOT[3]

"Eternity" is there,
We say, as of a Station.
Meanwhile he is so near,
He joins me in my Ramble——
Divides abode with me——
No Friend have I that so persists
As this Eternity.

EMILY DICKINSON[4]

AUDEN'S "BLESS WHAT THERE is for being" in the poem
I've just quoted brings me back to my beginning: me,
here, now. In a world that was created to be praised.
Aware of a God who is now or nowhere. I'll go along with
mind-blowing theories of the Big Bang, but not with the
thought of a God who, unimaginable aeons ago with an
unimaginable burst of energy, decides to start things off and
then remove himself. What the Big Bang, or any other theory
of creation, implies in terms of God is that he holds it now in
all the wonder of its creative being; that unless his creative and
sustaining power is at work at this moment then everything
would collapse into non-being.

Annie Dillard's book *Pilgrim at Tinker Creek* is an account
of the woods, streams and fields of the Shenandoah Valley in
Virginia. A naturalist who seeks to observe the "minute particulars" in the constantly changing life of her valley, her book celebrates the world about her. She sees Tinker Creek as

an active mystery, fresh every minute. [It contains] the mystery of the continuous creation and all that providence implies; the uncertainty of vision, the horror of the fixed, the disillusion of the present, the intricacy of beauty, the pressure of fecundity, the elusiveness of the free, and the flawed nature of perfection. The mountains are a passive mystery, the oldest of all. Theirs is the one simple mystery of creation from nothing, of matter itself, anything at all, the given.[5]

She describes many wonders: such as the free fall of a mockingbird, unfurling its wings a split second before hitting the ground, and the beauty and grace performed all around us all the time. "The least we can do," she says, "is try to be there."

What Annie Dillard does is to try to claim what is given, moment by attentive moment, never ignoring the pain of nature red in tooth and claw but seeking to live each moment to the full by giving attention to the natural world and celebrating it. She writes at the end of a description of watching life in a pond:

This is how you spend this afternoon.... *Spend* the afternoon [for] you can't take it with you.... Like Billy Bray I go my way, and my left foot says "glory," and my right foot says "amen": in and out of Tinker Creek, upstream and down, exultant, in a daze, dancing, to the twin silver trumpets of praise.[6]

(Billy Bray, described by William James as "an excellent little illiterate English evangelist" of the early nineteenth century, said: "I can't help praising the Lord. As I go along the street, I lift up one foot, and it seems to say, 'Glory'; and I lift up the other, and it seems to say, 'Amen'; and so they keep up like that all the time I am walking.")

Two of the strangest things have happened in the past few moments as I try to get my mind around Auden's phrase about blessing what there is for being: the woodpecker, who has been silent since the end of May, arrives with a breathtaking non-chalance and displays his scarlet and white belly on a tree eight feet from my window; and a few moments later the whole house sways and shakes for a few seconds in an earth tremor. Sheer coincidence, of course; but you have to admire the timing.

There is a sharp distinction between thinking that God made nature for our benefit (to exploit it or place its wild animals in cages and stare at them), and believing that the world is created by God as the place where we are to exercise all our human powers of creativity, imagination and endurance, and learn those two most crucial things: what it means to trust and what it means to love. Our role in the world that is given us is to wonder at it, to explore it, and to restore to it and to our own lives their true meaning. In one of his poems the French writer Charles Péguy put these words into the mouth of God: "If there were no Frenchmen, some things I do would not be seen."[7] If there were no Christians, there would still be a wealth of religious activity, profound insights into the transcendence of God and the nature of human beings. But I believe that the deepest insight of all would be lost. And that lies in what you may think a surprising place. It lies in what Christians do when they come together for the Eucharist.

Eucharistia is a Greek word meaning "thankfulness," first used of the sacrament by Ignatius in the early second century. To understand the Eucharist you have to understand our place in the creation. If I say we are placed on this earth to live "eucharistically" I want to leave that thought hanging unexplained for a while, for its sense will emerge.

The Bible sets out to show that we were intended to receive the creation as we receive our lives, thankfully, as a gift, holding them on trust, offering them daily back to God from whom everything comes. The form that offering is to take is thanksgiving, which doesn't just mean Stanley Spencer's "learning to say thank you," but also implies a way of being and a frame of mind that is trusting rather than anxious, grateful rather than grudging, compassionate rather than judgmental, and outgoing rather than selfish. But this is not how we are. Human nature is strangely perverse, and we tend to see the world as an end in itself, using and abusing it as we wish and regarding each other with a guarded, often critical eye.

God is not so easily diverted. He has created us for himself and he knows "our hearts are restless until they rest in him." And so the Word becomes flesh in order that our eyes may be opened to truth. "You have eyes: can you not see?" At the very end of his life Jesus did two things that, more than any other, lodged in the minds of his friends. The first, the washing of their feet, spoke as no other action could, of the plain, unromantic, down-to-earthness of the love God both shows and asks for. The second has proved even more meaningful in the two millennia that have passed since Jesus first took bread and wine and did with them four deeply significant things.

He took bread into his hands; thanked God for it; broke it; shared it. And he said: "This is my body, my blood. This is me." (The English words "This is my body" are linguistically impossible, both in Hebrew and Aramaic. They mean: "this is me—this is what I am like.") He is showing them the profoundly simple pattern of this one totally good human life: a life taken and lived in complete openness to the Father and so *offered*. A life lived *thankfully* at every point by one who saw God's hand in everything. A life spent in the costly love of others and finally *broken* on the Cross. A life totally shared.

Those four actions of offering, thanking, breaking and sharing, together show the pattern of what self-giving love means, and are the only definition of God we need to know. And if we "see" this final demonstration of what he has come to show, then if we accept Christ's authority in our lives we are committed to trying to make that pattern our own. It may be so wrapped up that it is hard to discern, but strip away the often excess fat of prayers and readings and address and you have in these four actions the living heart of our central act of worship.

"What do you mean?" they asked Schumann. "I mean this," he answered; and played the piece again. "What do you mean?" they asked Jesus. "I mean this," he replied; and he took the bread, gave thanks, broke, and shared it. And that piece has been played in every conceivable setting and in every known language ever since.

That is what I mean by learning to live eucharistically, learning to set our whole lives, in times of unhappiness as well as when times are good, within this context of thanksgiving. For in doing so, we are not just acting for ourselves; we are helping to restore, however infinitesimally, the whole creation to its proper relationship with God. By taking the bread and wine which represent God's gifts worked upon by human hands and giving thanks for them, we are setting our lives in their true relation to God, and we are properly restoring matter to what God intends it to be——our means of contact with him. We are saying that life is to be celebrated, given thanks for "at all times and in all places"; that it is to be a movement of love and adoration towards God. In this way, whether in the Eucharist that will have been celebrated this morning in St. Faith's Chapel in the Abbey, or the Mass we attended yesterday in the little Alpine village church at Ayer, or in a thousand places even as I write these words, the world is being helped to recover its true value and meaning. And I know of no other instrument by which this may be, and is so consistently being, achieved. This is why the Mass, the Eucharist, the Holy Communion, the Lord's Supper properly stands at the heart of so much Christian worship. It encapsulates the very essence of the Christian way of life.

But it does more. For it is as the bread and wine which represent our lives and our work are offered; it is as we give thanks for everything we value in them and for all that God has shown us; it is above all as we share with others, known and unknown, the bread that has been broken, that we are identifying ourselves with the way of self-giving love. It is as if we are saying to God in return: "This is my body: take me." And it is as we accept Christ's pattern as our pattern that his Spirit is present within us and among us as surely as the bread is placed in our hands. There are some words attributed to St. Augustine which perfectly express this truth:

> You are the body of Christ: that is to say, in you and through you the work of the Incarnation must go forward. You are meant to incarnate in your lives the theme of your adoration—you are to be taken, consecrated, broken and distributed, that you may be the means of grace and vehicles of the Eternal Charity.[8]

That is a little of what I mean by living eucharistically, living in this Christlike pattern. It is for me a wonderful carpetbag of a truth, which implies seeing and being and a costly kind of loving, and forgiving and reconciling, and all in the context of thanking. Bishop Stephen Bayne, onetime Ecumenical Officer for the Anglican Communion, has written:

> Eucharistic people take their lives and break them, and give them, in daily fulfillment of what Our Lord did and does. No

need to ask what school of thought you follow or how you speculate about the manner of these things. He took his life in his own hands—this is freedom. He broke it—this is obedience. He gave it—this is love. And he still does these simple acts at every altar and in every heart that will have it so; and time and eternity meet.[9]

Yet that's not quite all. For the final insight, the mind-shifting word that really does change your perception, is the word "remembrance." "Do this in remembrance of me." In Greek the word is *anamnesis*, but it does not mean what we mean by "remember." It means "to bring out of the past into the present." No doubt that's what "remembering" something always is: a re-membering, a putting together again in your mind of something you had discarded. In the French theatre the word for a performance is *représentation*, an occasion when something is re-*presented*, something that was and now is. There is a sense in which a drama abolishes time. It takes yesterday's action and makes it live again: it makes it present. As a result, if the audience can so identify with the actors as to be taken out of themselves they may be changed a little by what they have seen. Painters, poets, composers, may enable us to transcend time, at least partially, by representing (making present) certain things, places, moods, so as to let us enter into them afresh and live them now.

What the Eucharist does is of a different order. It is both in time and beyond it. It looks back to the past, to this man doing these actions; it looks to the future and sees people coming together to share bread (with all that means in a grossly unjust world), open to God and to each other, as a tiny foretaste of how things might be. But chiefly it looks to the God revealed in Christ who is to be met now or not at all, here or nowhere.

Blake wrote of "holding Eternity in an hour," and T.S.

Eliot writes of apprehending

> the point of intersection of the timeless
> with time . . .

and of the Incarnation as

> a moment in time, but time was made through that moment:
> for without the meaning there is no time, and that moment
> of time gave the meaning.[10]

When Jesus speaks of a new quality of life for those whose eyes are opened and who when they look at him see the Father, he calls it "eternal." It is not measured in terms of our linear time which comes to a shuddering halt with our last breath. It is measured as we measure our deepest relationships; only this relationship with God is binding and goes even deeper, and our covenant with him is not simply for this life but for eternity. "People who dwell in God," wrote Meister Eckhart, "dwell in the eternal Now," and for him it is only in the present moment that the world of time touches the world of eternity. He defines eternity as "the possession of all time, past, present, and to come, in full plenitude, in one single moment, here and now."[11] It is as if eternity lies at the heart of each moment, giving it significance. Frederick Buechner writes that, inhabitants of time that we are, we nevertheless stand

> . . . with one foot in eternity. "God inhabiteth eternity," but
> eternity stands with one foot in time. The part of time in
> which he stands most particularly is Christ, and thus in Christ
> we catch a glimpse of what eternity is all about, what God is
> all about, and what we ourselves are all about too.[12]

What I am struggling to say is that in the sacrament of the Eucharist we are bringing into the present everything that speaks of what God once did in Jesus Christ: the Incarnation, the suffering and the Cross, the presence of Christ after his Resurrection, the giving of the Holy Spirit, because they are not trapped like flies in the aspic of time. It is Helen Waddell's tree cut across, the dark rings present at every point in the tree. They have to do with what is eternal, with the Christlike God as he was once known and is for ever seeking to be, and as he is present to us under the forms of bread and wine.

Quakers do not make use of the sacrament of the Eucharist because they believe the whole world is sacramental. It's a healthy nudge that, a reminder that, as Gandhi said, "If you don't find God in the very next person you meet it is a waste of time looking for him further."

Yes, I know. And yet, . . . For me this is the place, and these are the truths, to which I return again and again. I need something tangible, the reality of bread and wine. I need to be fed. I need to hear the familiar words. And despite all those days when I feel nothing, go through the motions, wonder what the point is, I know that the invitation to "do this" is the one command of Christ I can't refuse if I am to remain true to those few insights whose validity I cannot deny and by which I would want my life to be shaped.

XXIV

Postscript

At the back of our brains, so to speak, there is a forgotten blaze or burst of astonishment at our own existence. The object of the artistic and spiritual life is to dig for this sunrise of wonder.

G. K. CHESTERTON[1]

I HAVE PACKED UP MY books and dismissed all those witnesses who for the past month have been crowding into this small room, jostling for attention, scratching at the door and tapping on the window. "No more room," I have said time and again, "the place is already swimming in quotations." Now, as our time here comes to an end and we prepare to leave this valley, where the only sound is that of birds and the periodic crack of the loosened winter snow as it tumbles down the mountains, for the polluted city where the most frequent sounds are those of wailing police sirens and the periodic thud of a terrorist bomb, I want to add a postscript.

I recognize that some could dismiss my choice of theme as an indulgent irrelevance in the dark times in which we live. I think such a view would be profoundly wrong. P. J. Kavanagh, who seems to be one of two stragglers still lurking behind the curtains, writes:

> We live in times that are particularly conscious of the hellish nature of the world. We should be aware of suffering, torture,

injustice. There are, however, times when our preoccupation with these things, and skepticism about the idea of "beauty," would seem to imply that our forefathers lived in kindergartens and sucked their thumbs, whereas we alone have found the courage to open our eyes and look at the world. . . .[2]

It may seem as if poetry, the creative arts and the world of the imagination, are useless in the face of so much that is evil and destructive; as Seamus Heaney has said, "no lyric has ever stopped a tank."[3] No; but there are lyrics, paintings, buildings, music, that have stopped a person dead in their tracks, amazed at the work of the human mind and hand and eye; seeing beauty, experiencing momentary wonder that they had never noticed, and enlarging their understanding of what it means to be a person. Zbigniew Herbert or Vaclav Havel in Eastern Europe when the Communists were in power, Irina Ratushinskaya and Osip Mandelstam and Solzhenitsyn in Stalin's Russia, Brian Keenan and his fellow hostages in captivity in the Lebanon—reveal human spirits that are imprisoned but not contained, confined but not held captive. There is an incident recorded by the Polish poet, Czeslaw Milosz. He spent most of the War in Nazi-occupied Warsaw, a poet whose work is filled with childlike wonder at the beauty of the earth now forced to record the terrible anguish of the Ghetto. Crossing a field under heavy gunfire in 1944, just as the Warsaw uprising began, he refused to let go of the one book he held under his arm—T. S. Eliot's *Collected Poems*—"because I needed it and because it belonged to the Warsaw Library." Such people, sometimes in solitude and with no guarantee of recognition, have been true to their vision of what is human and stake out for us the parameters of the human spirit.

For me, as I have explained, the ultimate act of seeing is

that partial but authentic vision of God I see in Jesus Christ and the Kingdom of which he speaks. Its language of love is universal; its goal, holiness and community; its building blocks, justice and freedom, compassion, forgiveness and mercy. But if my chief concern has been with what is human that is because there is another area of vision, which I term religious, and which is expressed in the quite common transcendent experiences of life as well as in literature and theatre, music and art.

I have claimed that the capacity to see and to wonder, by giving proper attention to the mystery of people and things in the process of learning to love them, is what it means to be human. Without it we shall have no vision of what it means to live either as stewards of this astonishing creation or as fellow-members of the human race. When the writer Michael Ignatieff joined *The Observer*, he set out his credentials in his first weekly column. He argued that creativeness, especially a desire to create what is beautiful, is not the sole preserve of artists but "an intrinsic feature of all human activity," that what matters about individuals, "what makes each of us different and valuable beyond price, is that each of us, however blindly, however badly, is the artist of our lives"; and he points to the fact that those who had kindled the hunger that has led to revolutionary change in Eastern Europe have been the poets and the playwrights. He goes on:

> You need pity to have any passion in politics, but you need wonder too, simple wonder at the artistry of the most ordinary life. And once you rekindle your wonder at human beings, you rekindle your anger.

Ignatieff writes of how we seem to prefer to pay to watch an actor poignantly miming a homeless man on the stage of the

National Theatre than to pay to house the actual homeless man who lives under its arches. The man's claim

> is that he has as much right to be the artist of his life as the actor does. . . . Insisting that we are all incorrigible artists helps me to grasp the [wonder of] the human quality which makes me concerned in other people's lives . . . and define the kind of society I would like to live in; one which tried . . . to help each individual to think of their life as something they could create rather than simply endure. Judged by that light, we have a long way to go.[4]

"You need pity . . . but you need wonder too." My final concern is that you should understand that those who write books, or a bulky handful of letters, write because of what they lack, not because of what they have. I have written of what I long for, not what I possess; of how I should like to be, not of what I am. Nor am I so unrealistic as to think that life allows time for much in the way of gazing. Yet the truth remains that among all those shouting their wares in the marketplace there are those who have turned aside and noticed that the horse chestnut in spring is not just "a green thing that stands in the way," and that "whereas trees have roots, men have legs and are each other's guests"; and it matters that we notice too.

Now I shall go out and look once more at the wild lupines, gather some firewood and light a fire, open a bottle of wine, listen to some Mozart, and, having written to you almost nonstop for a solid month, heave the most enormous, elephantine sigh of relief.

If you turn the page, you will find a final poem. It's by Richard Wilbur and it is for your grandmother, Alison, who more than anyone else helps me to see.

One wading a Fall meadow finds on all sides
The Queen Anne's Lace lying like lilies
On water; it glides
So from the walker; it turns
Dry grass to a lake, as the slightest shade of you
Valleys my mind in fabulous blue Lucernes.

The beautiful changes as a forest is changed
By a chameleon's tuning his skin to it;
As a mantis, arranged
On a green leaf, grows
Into it, makes the leaf leafier, and proves
Any greenness is deeper than anyone knows.

Your hands hold roses always in a way that says
They are not only yours; the beautiful changes
In such kind ways,
Wishing ever to sunder
Things and things' selves fir a second finding, to lose
For a moment all that it touches back to wonder.[5]

Acknowledgements

The author and publisher acknowledge with thanks permission to reproduce copyright material as listed below:

Elizabeth Barnett, literary executor, for "God's World" (1913, 1941) by Edna St. Vincent Millay from *Collected Poems* (HarperCollins).

Carcanet Press for the poems "Proustian Moments" and "Rembrandt's Late Self-Portraits" from *Collected Poems* by Elizabeth Jennings and extracts from Poetry Notebook by Geoffrey Grigson.

Chatto & Windus, London, for the extract from *The White Bird* by John Berger.

Ecco Press for the poem "Blacksmith's Shop" © 1991 Czeslaw Milosz Royalties, Inc., from *Provinces* by Czeslaw Milosz.

The Estate of Miss Ruth Pitter for the extracts from *Collected Poems* (1968) by Ruth Pitter.

Faber and Faber, London, for the extract from "Testimony" from *Collected Poems* (1947) by Siegfried Sassoon.

Faber and Faber, London and New York, for the extract from *Arcadia* by Tom Stoppard.

Faber and Faber, London, and Doubleday, New York, for extracts from "Infirmity," "What Can I Tell My Bones?," "Her Becoming," and "The Shape of Fire" from *Collected Poems* by Theodore Roethke.

Faber and Faber, London, and Farrar, Straus & Giroux, New York, for extracts from "Clearances" from *The Haw Lantern* by Seamus Heaney.

Faber and Faber, London, and Harcourt Brace Jovanovich, Orlando, for extracts from "The Rock" and "East Coker" from *Collected Poems 1909–1962* by T.S. Eliot; and "For Dudley" and "The Beautiful Changes" from *New and Collected Poems* by Richard Wilbur.

Faber and Faber, London, and Harper, New York, for the extract from "Black Rook in Rainy Weather" from *Collected Poems* by Sylvia Plath.

Faber and Faber, London, and Alfred A. Knopf, New York, for extracts from *The Death of Tragedy* by George Steiner and *The Man with the Blue Guitar* by Wallace Stevens.

Faber and Faber, London, and New Directions for extracts from "Field Mouse" from *Collected Shorter Poems* by Ezra Pound.

Faber and Faber, London, and Random House, New York, for extracts from "The Age of Anxiety," "The Fall of Rome," "Sonnets in China," and "Precious Five" from *Collected Shorter Poems* by W.H. Auden.

Éditions Gallimard, Paris, for extracts from *The Tidings Brought to Mary* (1912) by Paul Claudel.

Hamish Hamilton, and Rogers, Coleridge & White for the quotation from *Light* (1983) by Eva Figes.

HarperCollinsPublishers, London, for the extracts from *Part of a Journey* and *End of a Journey* by Philip Toynbee; *Heart's Desire* by Edward Hoagland, and *The Clown in the Belfry: Writings on Faith and Fiction* (1992) by Frederick Buechner.

Dr. Peter Kavanagh for extracts from "Miss Universe," "Wet Evening in April," "A Christmas Childhood," "Advent," "Canal Bank Walk," and "Is" from *The Complete Poems of Patrick Kavanagh*, edited by Dr. Peter Kavanagh, (1972), The Peter Kavanagh Hand Press, New York.

Macmillan, London for the poem "Stations" from *Mass for Hard Times* by R. S. Thomas.

Mitchell Beazley and H. A. Williams for the extract from *Poverty, Chastity, and Obedience* by H. A. Williams.

W. W. Norton & Company, London, for the stanzas from "i thank You God for most this amazing" reprinted from *Complete Poems 1904–1962* by e. e. cummings, edited by George J. Firmage. Copyright © 1950, 1978, 1991 by the Trustees for the e. e. cummings Trust and George James Firmage.

Oxford University Press for the poem "Yesterday Lost" from *Collected Poems of Ivor Gurney* (1982) edited by Kavanagh and the extract from *Venus Observed* (1970) by Christopher Fry.

Penguin Books, London, for the quotes from *City of the Mind* (1992) and *Cleopatra's Sister* (1993) by Penelope Lively.

Phaidon Press, London, for the extracts from *The Image and the Eye* and *Art and Illusion* by Professor E.H. Gombrich.

Random House, New York, for poems from *The Selected Poetry of Rainer Maria Rilke* by Rainer Maria Rilke, ed. & trans. by Stephen Mitchell (1982).

Alastair Reid for the poem "Growing, Flying, Happening" from *Weathering* (New York: E.P. Dutton, 1978).

George Sassoon for part of the poem "Testimony" by Siegfried Sassoon.

SCM Press, London, for extracts from *The Go-Between God* (1972) and *The Christlike God* (1992) by John Taylor.

R.S. Thomas for poems from his book *Frequencies and Laboratories of the Spirit*.

Every effort has been made to trace copyright owners, and the publishers apologize to anyone whose rights have inadvertently not been acknowledged. This will be corrected in any reprint.

Notes

I BY WAY OF EXPLANATION

1. Alastair Reid, "Growing, Flying, Happening," in *Weathering* (New York: E. P. Dutton, 1978).

2. *Letters to a Young Poet*, published in *Selected Letters 1902–1926* (London: Quartet Encounters 1988), 417.

3. *The Clown in the Belfry* (HarperSanFrancisco, 1992), 103.

4. *Heart's Desire* (London: Collins Harvill, 1988), 265.

5. Annie Dillard, *The Writing Life* (London: Picador, 1985), 79.

6. Ezra Pound, "And the days are not full enough," *Collected Shorter Poems* (London: Faber & Faber, 1968).

7. Quoted in James Roose-Evans' *Inner Journey, Outer Journey* (London: Rider 1987), 25.

8. G. K. Chesterton, *Autobiography* (London: Burns Oates, 1937), 94–5.

9. Annie Dillard, *The Writing Life*, 68.

10. Alan Ecclestone, *The Scaffolding of Spirit* (London: Darton, Longman & Todd, 1987), 16.

11. *Introducing David Jones: A Selection of his Writings*, edited by John Matthias (London: Faber & Faber, 1980), 128.

12. Dag Hammarskjöld, *Markings* (London: Faber & Faber, 1964), 64.

13. Abraham Joshua Heschel, *I Asked for Wonder* (New York: Crossroad, 1988), vii.

II THE MYSTERY THAT IS ME

1. Letter to the Times, 7 February 1970.

2. *Hamlet*, Act 3, scene 2, ll. 365–6.

3. *Much Ado about Nothing*, Act 2, scene 3, ll. 58–60.

4. William Blake, "A Memorable Fancy" in *The Marriage of Heaven and Hell*, II, 69–70.

5. Peter Hughes at a Westminster School Service in Westminster Abbey, 1993.

6. D. H. Lawrence: from an essay, "Hymns in a Man's Life."

7. George Steiner: *Real Presences* (London: Faber & Faber, 1989), 4 and 229.

8. Ibid., 3.

9. Ibid., 49.

III THE TRANSFIGURED COMMONPLACE

1. The phrase is that of the poet Douglas Dunn who writes that he has "a rendezvous / To keep with the transfigured commonplace."

2. John V. Taylor, *The Go-Between God* (London: SCM Press, 1972), 45.

3. W. B. Yeats, "Vacillation," in The Poems (London: J. M. Dent & Sons, 1990).

4. From "Black Rook in Rainy Weather" in *The Collected Poems of Sylvia Plath* (London: Faber & Faber, 1981).

5. George Steiner, *Real Presences* (London: Faber & Faber, 1989), 153.

6. Philip Toynbee, *End of a Journey* (London: Collins, 1981, and Bloomsbury, 1988), entry for 26 October 1979.

7. John V. Taylor, *The Go-Between God*, 11–13.

8. Rainer Maria Rilke (J. B. Leishman, trans.), *The Possibility of Being*, (London: Hogarth Press, 1964), 108.

9. John V. Taylor, *The Christlike God* (London: SCM Press, 1992), 25.

10. P.J. Kavanagh, "Images of Heaven and Hell," Radio 3. Reprinted in *People and Places* (London: Carcanet 1988), 174–5.

11. Rosamond Lehmann, *The Swan in the Evening* (London: Collins, 1967), 114–115.

12. Leo Tolstoy, *Anna Karenina*, (London: Penguin Books, 1988), 428.

13. Philip Toynbee, *End of a Journey*, 28 October 1979.

14. Victor Gollancz, *My Dear Timothy* (London: Gollancz 1952), 25–6.

15. Mark Rutherford, *More Pages from a Journal* (Oxford: The Clarendon Press, 1910).

16. J.W.N. Sullivan, *But for the Grace of God* (London: Jonathan Cape, 1932), 62–3.

17. Rosemary Sutcliff, *Blue Remembered Hills: A Recollection* (London: Bodley Head, 1983), 132.

18. Elizabeth Jennings, "A Proustian Moment" in *Collected Poems* (London: Carcanet, 1986).

19. Thomas Merton, *Confessions of a Guilty Bystander* (London: Sheldon Press, 1977), 153–4.

20. William Wordsworth, *The Prelude*, Bk. V, ll. 604–5.

21. C.S. Lewis, *The Weight of Glory* (London: Geoffrey Bles, 1949), 24.

22. C.S. Lewis, *Surprised by Joy* (London: Geoffrey Bles), 209.

23. Ruth Pitter, *Collected Poems* (London: Macmillan, 1968), xi.

24. Ibid., "Sudden Heaven."

25. Aldous Huxley, *The Doors of Perception* (London: Chatto & Windus, 1954), 27.

26. A.M. Allchin, *The World is a Wedding* (London: Darton, Longman & Todd, 1978), 55.

27. Rainer Maria Rilke, Letter to Ilse Erdmann, 31 January 1914.

28. George Steiner, *Real Presences*, 179.

29. John Fowles, Daniel Martin (London: Triad/Panther 1978), 120–1.

IV THE GIVEN AND THE GLIMPSED

1. T.S. Eliot, "The Dry Salvages," II, l. 45; *Four Quartets* (London: Faber & Faber, 1944).

2. Ludwig Wittgenstein (G.H. von Wright and G.E.M. Anscombe, eds., G.E.M. Anscombe, trans.), *Notebooks 1914–1916* (Oxford: Basil Blackwell, 1961), 74.

3. From Solzhenitsyn's Nobel lecture, 1970, translated by F.D. Reeve, (New York: Farrar, Straus & Giroux, 1972).

4. Wallace Stevens, "Six Significant Landscapes," *Collected Poems* (London: Faber & Faber, 1955), 75.

5. A.N. Wilson, *A Bottle in the Smoke* (London: Sinclair-Stevenson, 1990), 108–9.

6. William Blake, "Auguries of Innocence," ll. 125–6.

7. Susan Hill, *Air and Angels* (London: Sinclair-Stevenson/Mandarin paperback, 1991), 263.

8. Frederick Buechner, *The Alphabet of Grace* (San Francisco: HarperSanFrancisco, 1970), 74–6.

9. William Blake, "Auguries of Innocence," ll. 57–60.

10. Christopher Fry, *The Dark is Light Enough*, Act 2, in *Collected Plays* (Oxford: Oxford University Press, 1971).

11. Saul Bellow, *Mr. Sammler's Planet* (London: Penguin, 1972), 147.

12. Philip Toynbee, *Part of a Journey* (London: Collins, 1981), entry for 21 January 1978.

13. Franz Kafka, *The Great Wall of China: Reflections* (London: Penguin, 1991).

14. Cardinal Suhard, Archbishop of Paris in the late forties.

15. Frederick Buechner, *Now and Then* (New York: Harper & Row, 1983), 87.

V THE OTHERNESS AND NEARNESS OF GOD

1. Gregory of Nyssa, Catechetical Oration 25.

2. From *The Book of Hours*, "I find you, Lord, in all things" in *Selected Poetry of Rainer Maria Rilke*, edited by Stephen Mitchell (New York: Vintage International, 1989), 5.

3. From "Miss Universe" in *The Complete Poems of Patrick Kavanagh*, edited by Peter Kavanagh, (New York: The Peter Kavanagh Hand Press, 1972).

4. From *The Age of Anxiety*, final sequence in *The Collected Poems of W. H. Auden* (London: Faber & Faber, 1976), 408.

5 William Temple, *Christian Faith and Life* (London: SCM Press, 1931), 24.

6. Quoted in his obituary in *The Independent*.

7. Augustine, *Confessions*, Bk. X, Ch. 27, 38.

8. Augustine, *The City of God*, Bk. XI, Ch. 29.

9. William Ullathorne, *The Little Book of Humility and Patience* (London, 1908).

10. John Updike, *Self-Consciousness* (London: Penguin Books, 1990), 218.

11. See note 2.

VI THE CREATION AS SACRAMENTAL:
THE HOLY IN THE COMMON

1. Paul Claudel, *The Tidings Brought to Mary* (Paris: Éditions Gallimard, 1912).

2. Quoted on title page of Patrick White's *The Solid Mandala* (London: Penguin, 1969).

3. From Meister Eckhart's first sermon, quoted as one of the epigraphs in Patrick White's *The Solid Mandala* (London: Penguin, 1969).

4. Philip Toynbee, *End of a Journey*, entry for 7 March 1979.

5. From "The Discourses of the Elder Zossima" in *The Brothers Karamazov*, Bk. 6, Ch. 3.

6. From "Word made flesh" in the *Collected Poems of Kathleen Raine* (London: Hamish Hamilton, 1956).

7. Cormac McCarthy, *All the Pretty Horses* (New York: Albert A. Knopf, 1992).

8. Quoted in *Henri Matisse*, edited by Ingo F. Walther, trans. Michael Hulse (Cologne: Benedikt Taschen Verlag GmbH, 1986).

9. "God's Grandeur" in *The Poems of Gerard Manley Hopkins* (Oxford: Oxford University Press, 1952).

10. Isaiah 6:3.

11. William Law, *Selected Mystical Writings*, ed. Stephen Hobhouse (London: Barrie & Rockcliffe, 1948).

12. R.S. Thomas, from "Emerging" in *Frequencies* (London: Macmillan, 1978), 41.

13. E.M. Forster, *Howard's End* (London: Penguin, 1989), 112.

14. T.S. Eliot, from "The Rock, IX" in *Collected Poems 1909–1962* (London: Faber & Faber, 1963).

15. Christopher Fry, *The Firstborn* (Oxford: Oxford University Press, 1970), 100.

16. Edwin Muir, from "The Labyrinth" in *Collected Poems* (London: Faber, 1960), ll. 65–6.

17. Billy Yellow, Navajo Medicine Man, speaking in a BBC 2 film about native American life.

18. Bruce Chatwin, *The Songlines* (London: Picador, 1987), 314.

19. Laurens van der Post, *The Heart of the Hunter* (London: Penguin, 1965).

20. Chief Seattle, quoted in *Millennium* by David Maybury-Lewis (London: Viking, 1992), 59.

21. Angela Tilby, *Science and the Soul* (London: S.P.C.K., 1992), 32.

22. Emily Dickinson, *The Complete Poems* (London: Faber & Faber, 1970), 401.

23. Iris Murdoch, *Metaphysics as a Guide to Morals* (London: Chatto & Windus, 1992), 475.

VII THE MEANING OF WONDER

1. Emily Dickinson, *The Complete Poems* (London: Faber & Faber, 1970), 577.

2. Thomas Traherne, from *Centuries* (London: The Faith Press, 1960), I, 37.

3. John de Dondis, 14th century, quoted in J. S. Collis, *The Worm Forgives the Plough* (London: Charles Knight, 1973), 170.

4. Philip Tonybee, *Part of a Journey*, entry for 15 February 1978.

5. Siegfried Sassoon, from "Testimony" in *Collected Poems* (London: Faber & Faber, 1947).

6. W. H. Auden, *Making, Knowing, and Judging*, Inaugural Lecture at the University of Oxford, 11 June 1956.

7. Wordsworth, "Lines composed a few miles above Tintern Abbey," ll. 95–102.

8. "The Cuckoo at Laverna," l. 71.

9. William Blake, *Auguries of Innocence*, ll. 111–4.

10. Antoine de Saint-Exupéry, *The Little Prince* (London: William Heinemann, 1945), 77.

11. John Stewart Collis, *The Worm Forgives the Plough* (London: Charles Knight, 1973), 43.

12. Abraham Joshua Heschel, *God in Search of Man* (London: Jason Aronson, 1987), 74–5.

13. Michael Faraday, *Lectures*, 1863.

14. Richard Wilbur, "For Dudley" in *Walking to Sleep* (London: Faber & Faber, 1971).

15. Angela Tilby, *Science and the Soul* (London: S.P.C.K., 1992), 151.

16. Pablo Casals, quoted in *Song of the Birds*, compiled by Julian Lloyd Webber (London: Robson Books, 1985).

17. Barry Lopez, *Arctic Dreams* (London: Picador, 1980).

18. Ibid., xx, xxvii.

19. Ivor Gurney, "Yesterday Lost" in *Collected Poems of Ivor Gurney*, edited by P. J. Kavanagh (Oxford: Oxford University Press, 1982).

20. From a letter to The Reverend Dr. Trusler, 1799.

21. Philip Toynbee, *Part of a Journey*, various entries.
22. Philip Toynbee, *End of a Journey*, entry for 20 April 1981.
23. Ibid., entry for 16 May 1981.

VIII THE WONDER OF YOU

1. St. Augustine, *Confessions*, Bk. X, eh. 8, 15.

2. Thomas Traherne, lines from "The Salutation" in *Collected Poems* (Oxford: Oxford University Press, 1966).

3. Misattributed to Isaac Newton, though cited in *Human Nature: An Interdisciplinary Biosocial Perspective* (1978, I[7-12], 47) and quoted in Des MacHale, *Wisdom* (London: Prion Press, 2002), no earlier publication of such a statement is known to exist.

4. e.e. cummings, *Selected Poems 1923–1958* (London: Faber & Faber, 1958), 76.

5. Deepak Chopra, *Unconditional Life* (New York: Bantam Books, 1991), 75.

6. Ibid., 76–7.

7. Michael White, article in *The Independent Magazine*, 10 July 1993.

8. Henry Quastler, quoted by Ernst Gombrich in *The Image and the Eye* (London: Phaidon, 1982), 50.

9. John Ruskin, quoted in John Stewart Collis' *Living with a Stranger* (London: MacDonald and Jane's, 1978), 111.

10. Ibid., 112.

11. Ibid., 149–150.

12. Jacquetta Hawkes, *Man on Earth* (London: The Cresset Press, 1954), 129.

13. Penelope Lively, *Moon Tiger* (London: André Deutsch, 1987), 68.

14. William Golding, *Darkness Visible* (London: Faber & Faber, 1979), 231.

IX THE WONDER OF THE WORLD ABOUT YOU

1. Emily Dickinson, *The Complete Poems* (London: Faber & Faber, 1970), 155; three stanzas of poem no. 327.

2. Albert Einstein, from *The World as I See It* (New York: Philosophical Library, 1949).

3. Charles Dickens, *Hard Times* (London: Penguin Classics, 1985), 54.

4. Martyn Skinner, from *Old Rectory* (London: Michael Russell, 1984).

5. Tom Stoppard, *Arcadia* (London: Faber & Faber, 1993), 47–8.

6. Annie Dillard, *Living by Fiction* (New York: Harper & Row/Perennial Library, 1982/1988), 55.

7. Christopher Fry, *Venus Observed* (Oxford: Oxford University Press, 1970), 175.

8. John Stewart Collis, *The Vision of Glory* (London: Charles Knight, 1972), 10.

9. Kieran Egan, *Primary Understanding: Education in Early Childhood* (London: Routledge, 1988), 193.

10. Jacquetta Hawkes, *Man on Earth* (London: The Cresset Press, 1954), final page.

11. Bede Griffiths, *A New Vision of Reality* (London: Harper-Collins/Fount, 1992), 149.

12. John Polkinghorne, article in *The Tablet*, 23 January 1993.

13. Angela Tilby, *Science and the Soul* (London: S.P.C.K., 1992), 199–200.

14. Thomas Hardy, "Proud Songsters," no. 816 in *The Complete Poems* (London: Papermac/Macmillan, 1976).

X THE SPONTANEOUS WONDER OF THE CHILD

1. This is from a letter of Rilke quoted in *Requiem and Other Poems*, translated by J. B. Leishman (London: Hogarth Press), but I have not been able to trace it in the published letters. [Since this

book's original publication, readers can find the source in *Letters of Rainer Maria Rilke: 1892–1910*, translated by Jane Bannard Greene and M. D. Herter Norton (New York: W. W. Norton, 1945), 59.]

2. C. E. Montague, *The Right Place: A Book of Pleasures* (London: Chatto & Windus, 1926), 219.

3. Delmore Schwartz, from "Seurat's Sunday Afternoon along the Seine" in *Selected Poems* (London: Summer Knowledge/New Directions, 1938).

4. Penelope Lively, *City of the Mind* (London: Penguin, 1992), 86–7, 183.

5. Penelope Lively, *Next to Nature, Art* (London: Penguin, 1984), 79–80.

6. Rilke, *Duino Elegies*, eighth elegy, *Selected Poetry*, edited and translated by Stephen Mitchell (New York: Vintage International, 1989), 193.

7. Edwin Muir, *An Autobiography* (London: The Hogarth Press, 1954), 25.

8. Thomas Traherne, *Centuries* (London: Faith Press, 1963), III. 3.

9. George Steiner, *Real Presences*, 190–1.

10. David Cecil, *Visionary and Dreamer* (London: Constable, 1969), 35.

11. Penelope Lively, *Cleopatra's Sister* (London: Viking, 1993), 74.

12. Quoted in an address on Paul Nash given by The Rt. Rev. Peter Walker in Great St. Mary's Church, Cambridge, 20 July 1981.

13. John Ruskin, *Modern Painters 1843*, quoted in Ernst Gombrich: *Art and Illusion* (London: Phaidon Press, 1977), 250.

14. Ibid., 258, 261.

15. Quoted in Collis, *Living with a Stranger*, 94.

16. Marghanita Laski, *Everyday Ecstasy* (London: Thames & Hudson, 1980), 29.

17. A. S. Byatt, essay in *The Pleasure of Reading*, edited by Antonia Fraser (London: Bloomsbury, 1992), 131.

18. John Updike, *Self-Consciousness*, 235.

19. William Blake, from a letter to Dr. Trusler, 1799.

20. *A Memorable Fancy*, l. 14.

21. *A Vision of the Last Judgment*, Descriptive Catalogue, 1810.

22. "The Elixir," *A Choice of George Herbert's Verse* (London: Faber & Faber, 1967).

23. Jonathan Dove, from an article in *Christian* (1993), 3.

24. Donald Nicholl, *Holiness* (London: Darton, Longman & Todd, 1981), 149.

XI THE MEANING OF BEAUTY

1. Kathleen Raine, "A Sense of Beauty" in *Resurgence*, no. 164, January 1986.

2. Edna St. Vincent Millay, "God's World" from *Collected Poems* (New York: Harper & Row, 1956).

3. Eric Newton, *The Meaning of Beauty* (London: Longmans, Green & Co., 1950), 125.

4. Kathleen Raine, "A Sense of Beauty" in *Resurgence*, no. 114, January 1986.

5. I am grateful to the Royal National Theatre for permission to reproduce this sketch.

6. Simone Weil, from "Forms of the Implicit Love of God" in *Waiting on God* (London: Routledge & Kegan Paul, 1951), 101.

7. "A Master of Zen Buddhism," quoted in *The Buddhist Sects of Japan* by E. Steinilber-Oberlin (London: Allen & Unwin, 1938), 113.

8. Oscar Wilde, *The Decay of Lying*, 1889.

9. Max Beerbohm, *Zuleika Dobson* (London: Penguin, 1952), 159.

10. Oscar Wilde, from "De Profundis," printed in *Selected Letters*, edited by Rupert Hart-Davis (1979), 237.

XII THE ROLE OF THE ARTIST IN ENABLING US TO SEE

1. Rilke, *Tuscan Diary 1898*, quoted in Rainer Maria Rilke by H.F.

Peters (New York: McGraw Hill, 1960), 188.

2. John Berger, *The White Bird*, writings edited by Lloyd Spencer (London: Hogarth Press, 1988), 9.

3. Jacques Maritain, *Art and Scholasticism* (London: Sheed & Ward, 1930), 127.

4. E. H. Gombrich, *Art and Illusion*, 329.

5. Picasso to Jean Leymarie, 1966.

6. John Fowles, *The French Lieutenant's Woman* (London: Panther Books, 1970), 86.

7. Philip Toynbee, *Part of a Journey*, entry for 4 December 1977.

8. Francis Hoyland, *A Painter's Diary* (Reading: Educational Explorers, 1967), 55.

9. Ibid., 58.

10. John Constable, *English Landscape 1830–32*, quoted in *Art and Illusion*, 149.

11. Quoted in *Art and Illusion*, 98.

12. John Banville, *The Book of Evidence* (London: Minerva, 1990), 104–5.

13. Andrew Graham-Dixon, "The Sacrament of Holy Oils" in *The Independent*, 12 February 1993.

14. *The Letters of Vincent van Gogh*, edited by Mark Roskill (London: Fontana, 1983), Letter to Theo, September 1888.

15. Rilke, Letter to Clara Rilke: 13 October 1907 in *Selected Letters 1902–26*.

16. Andrew Harvey, *A Journey in Ladakh* (London: Fontana, 1987), 5.

17. Ibid., 174.

18. Elizabeth Jennings, from "Rembrandt's Late Self-Portraits" in *Collected Poems* (London: Carcanet, 1987).

19. George Steiner, *Real Presences*, 179.

20. Iris Murdoch, *Metaphysics as a Guide to Morals*, 8.

21. Sister Wendy Beckett, *Art and the Sacred* (London: Rider, 1992), 9.

22. Wallace Stevens, lines from "The Man with the Blue Guitar

I" in *Collected Poems* (London: Faber & Faber, 1984). I am indebted to Bishop Peter Walker for drawing my attention to these lines; as for much else.

23. Ibid., XXXII.

XIII LIGHT AND COLOUR

1. Genesis 1:3–4.
2. Eva Figes, *Light* (London: Hamish Hamilton/Fontana, 1983/ 1990), 115–117.
3. Patrick Heron, interview in *The Independent*, 27 July 1993.
4. Quoted in *The Impressionists at First Hand*, edited by Bernard Denvir (London: Thames & Hudson, 1987), 48.
5. Ibid., 180.
6. Ibid., 187.
7. Ibid., 186.
8. Quoted in Diane Ackerman, *A Natural History of the Senses* (London: Chapmans, 1990), 267.
9. Eric Newton, *The Meaning of Beauty*.
10. Vincent van Gogh, *The Letters of Vincent van Gogh*, Letter to Theo, May 1888.
11. Ibid., Letter to Theo, July 1884.
12. Ibid., Letter to Theo, June 1888.
13. Ibid., Letter to Theo, August 1888.
14. Ibid., Letter to Theo, October 1888.
15. Julian of Norwich, *Revelations of Divine Love* (London: Penguin, 1966), Ch. 5.

XIV POETRY AND MUSIC AS THE LANGUAGE OF WONDER

1. Psalm 33:9 (Psalm set for today, Trinity Sunday).
2. W. H. Auden, *Making, Knowing, and Judging*, 33.
3. Geoffrey Grigson, *The Private Art: A Poetry Notebook* (London:

Allison & Busby, 1982), 8, 153.

4. Joseph Conrad, *The Nigger of the Narcissus*, preface, 1898.

5. Patrick Kavanagh, *People and Places*, "Wet Evening in April."

6. George Steiner, from *The Hollow Miracle in Language and Silence* (London: Faber & Faber, 1965).

7. Jeanette Winterson, essay in *The Pleasure of Reading*, 248.

8. Seamus Heaney, Sonnet 3 from "Clearances," an eight-sonnet sequence in *The Haw Lantern* (London: Faber & Faber, 1987).

9. Geoffrey Grigson, *The Private Art*, 113.

10. Seamus Heaney, *The Government of the Tongue* (London: Faber & Faber, 1988), 13.

11. Ibid., 106–7.

12. Ibid., 23.

13. Poem by Sir Waiter Raleigh. Written on the eve of his execution and found in his Bible in the gate-house at Westminster.

14. Graham Swift, *Ever After* (London: Picador, 1992), 71.

15. *King Lear*, Act V, Sc. 3, ll. 8ff.

16. Samuel Beckett, *Waiting for Godot* (London: Faber& Faber, 1956), 51, 96.

17. Lines from "The Fall of Rome" in *Collected Poems*.

18. A. E. Housman, "The Name and Nature of Poetry" in *Collected Poems and Selected Prose* (London: Penguin, 1988), 369–70.

19. W. B. Yeats, *The Poems*, "Memory."

20. Graham Swift, *Ever After*, 234.

21. Seamus Heaney, "The Placeless Heaven" in *The Government of the Tongue*, 8.

22. Seamus Heaney, "The Sense of Place" in *Preoccupations* (London: Faber & Faber, 1980), 142.

23. Patrick Kavanagh, *People and Places*, from "Is."

24. Ibid., from "Advent."

25. Ibid., from "Advent."

26. Ibid., from "A Christmas Childhood."

27. Ibid., from "Canal Bank Wall."

28. Ted Hughes, *A Choice of Shakespeare's Verse*, afterward quoted

by Seamus Heaney in *Preoccupations* (1980), 91.

29. David Blamires, *David Jones, Artist and Writer* (Manchester: Manchester University Press, 1971), 1–2.

30. Quoted in *A Way of Life: Kettle's Yard*, compiled by Jim Ede, (Cambridge: Cambridge University Press, 1984), 232–3.

31. Theodore Roethke, From "Informity," ll. 18–20, in *The Collected Poems* (London: Faber & Faber, 1968).

32. Ibid., l. 34.

33. Ibid., from "Her Becoming (Meditations of an Old Woman)," last lines of section 3.

34. Ibid., from "What can I Tell My Bones?" l. 28 from section 3.

35. Ibid., from "The Shape of the Fire," section 5.

36. Nathan A. Scott Jr., *The Wild Prayer of Longing* (New Haven: Yale University Press, 1971), 118.

37. Bernard Levin, *Enthusiasms* (London: Jonathan Cape, 1983), 171.

38. George Steiner, *Real Presences*, 19 and 218.

39. Janet Baker, *Spirituality and Music*, The Eric Abbott Memorial Lecture, 1988.

40. Hans Küng: *Mozart* (London: S.C.M. Press, 1992), 19.

41. Ibid., 34.

XV ENTR'ACTE: JOURNALS AND DIARIES, AND KETTLE'S YARD

1. Quoted in Grigson, *The English Year* (Oxford: Oxford University Press, 1984), v.

2. Goethe, "Song from the Watch Tower," translated by David Luke.

3. The words of an elderly cousin of Kilvert's.

4. Francis Kilvert, *Diary*, edited by William Plomer in three volumes (London: Jonathan Cape, 1969).

5. The *Journals* of Dorothy Wordsworth.

6. Geoffrey Grigson, *The English Year: From Diaries and Letters*

(Oxford: Oxford University Press, 1984).

7. Jim Ede, *A Way of Life: Kettle's Yard* (Cambridge: Cambridge University Press, 1984), 55.

8. Ibid., 122.

XVI RILKE AND THE GIVING OF ATTENTION

1. Rilke, Letter to Witold Hulewicz, 13 November 1925.

2. Kathleen Raine, *The Land Unknown* (London: Hamish Hamilton, 1973), 5.

3. Letter to the Princess Marie von Thurn and Taxis-Hohenlohe, 25 July 1921.

4. W. H. Auden, "Sonnets from China XIX" in *Collected Poems* (London: Faber & Faber, 1976).

5. Rilke, *Duino Elegies*, the Ninth Elegy, ll. 29–36.

6. Ibid., "Archaic Torso of Apollo," ll. 3, 14.

7. Rilke, Letters on Cézanne, 10.

8. Rilke, "Turning-Point," ll. 1–3, 8–25.

9. Letter to Magda von Hattingberg, 17 February 1914.

10. From *Duino Elegies*, the First Elegy, ll. 23–25.

11. Ibid., the First Elegy, ll. 56–60.

12. Ibid., the Seventh Elegy, ll. 34–5, 39.

13. Ibid., the Ninth Elegy, ll. 10–19, 69–73.

14. See note 3.

XVII HOPKINS AND THE "INSCAPE" OF THINGS

1. W. H. Auden, Sonnets from China, I.

2. Gerard Manley Hopkins, "As Kingfishers Catch Fire."

3. C. S. Lewis, Surprised by Joy (London: Geoffrey Bles, 1955), 187–8.

4. From "Red Geranium and Godly Mignonette" in *Selected Poems* (London: Penguin, 1950).

5. Gerard Manley Hopkins, *Sermons and Devotional Writings*, edited by Christopher Devlin S.J. (Oxford: Oxford University Press, 1959), 123.

6. Gerard Manley Hopkins, *Journals*, May 1870.

7. Gerard Manley Hopkins, *Selected Prose*, edited by Gerald Roberts (Oxford: Oxford University Press, 1980), entry for 8 April 1873.

8. Hopkins, from "Pied Beauty," in *Selected Poems* (London: Penguin, 1950).

9. Czeslaw Milosz, from "The Blacksmith's Shop" in *Province* (New York: The Ecco Press, 1991).

10. From "The Wreck of the Deutschland" in *Selected Poems*.

11. From "As Kingfishers Catch Fire" in *Selected Poems*.

12. Kathleen Raine, *Farewell Happy Fields* (London: Hamish Hamilton, 1973), 2–3.

13. Sylvia Plath, "Pheasant," in *The Collected Poems of Sylvia Plath* (London: Faber & Faber, 1981).

14. *Hamlet* V, ii, ll. 232–5.

15. Philip Toynbee, *Part of a Journey*, entry for 13 November 1977.

16. Hopkins, *Sermons*.

17. Sam Keen, *Apology for Wonder* (New York: Harper & Row, 1969), 30.

18. Annie Dillard, *Teaching a Stone to Talk* (London: Picador, 1982), 13–14.

XVIII PEOPLE AND OBJECTS: THEIR SINGULAR PARTICULARITY

1. Philip Toynbee, *Part of a Journey*, entry for 10 March 1978.

2. Thomas Traherne, *Centuries*, II, 66.

3. Brian Keenan, *An Evil Cradling* (London: Hutchinson, 1992), 68–9.

4. David Blamires, *David Jones: Artist and Writer*, 60.

5. George Orwell, "In Front of Your Nose" in *Tribune* 22 March

1946.

6a. Martin Buber, *I and Thou* (Edinburgh: T & T Clark, 1937/ 1966), 53, 112.

6b. Quoted, without context, in Victor Gollancz, *More for Timothy* (London: Gollancz, 1953), 107.

7. Simone Weil, "Reflections on the Right Use of School Studies," in *Waiting on God* (London: Fount Paperbacks 1977), 53.

8. Frederick Franck, *The Zen of Seeing* (New York: Random House, 1973), 104.

9. Br. Roger, Prior of Taizé, *Festival* (Taizé: Les Presses de Taizé, 1973), 133–4.

10. The Paradise of the Fathers.

XIX GIVING ATTENTION AND SO LEARNING TO LOVE

1. Revelation 4:8.

2. Matthew 19:19.

3. Henri de Tourville, *Letters of Direction*.

4. Alun Lewis, from *Collected Poems of Alun Lewis*, edited by Cary Achard (Bridgend: Seren Books, 1994).

5. St. Bernard, *On the Love of God* (London: A.R. Mowbray, 1950), chapters 8–11, passim.

6. Thomas Merton, *The Last of the Fathers* (New York: Harcourt, Brace, 1954), 52.

7. Helen Oppenheimer, *The Hope of Happiness* (London: S.C.M. Press, 1983), 94.

8. W. B. Yeats, *Autobiographies* (London: Macmillan, 1955).

9. Arthur Miller, *Death of a Salesman*, Act I in *Plays: One* (London: Methuen Drama, 1993), 162.

XX THE CHRISTLIKENESS OF GOD

1. John V. Taylor, *The Christlike God*, 132.

2. George Steiner, *The Death of Tragedy* (London: Faber & Faber, 1961), from the Epilogue.

3. Printed at the head of the service sheet at the Service of Thanksgiving for Bishop Joe Fison in Salisbury Cathedral, 1972.

4. Sister Wendy Beckett, "Divine Intervention," Sunday *Times*, 21 February 1993.

5. John 1:18.

6. John 14:9.

7. Gustave Flaubert, *Madame Bovary*, Pt. II, chapter 12.

8. Peter Schaffer, *The Gift of the Gorgon* (London: Penguin Viking, 1993), 60–61.

9. Helen Waddell, *Peter Abelard* (London: Constable, 1946), 201.

10. Psalm 139:8.

11. Paul Tillich, *The New Being* (London: SCM Press, 1956), 18.

XXI "COME AND SEE"

1. Mark 8:18.

2. Matthew 6:22.

3. John 9:25.

4. Mark 8:24.

5. George Steiner, from "A Kind of Survivor" in *Language and Silence*.

6. John 1:14.

7. Frederick Buechner, *Wishful Thinking* (London: Collins, 1973), 30.

8. 2 Corinthians 4:6.

9. 1 Corinthians 12:3.

10. John 20:22.

11. J. V. Taylor, *The Go-Between God*, 19.

12. Dante, *The Divine Comedy*, Paradiso, xxxiii, 145.

13. Galatians 2:20.

14. Ephesians 3:17.

15. Hopkins, "As Kingfishers Catch Fire."

16. Ephesians 1:18.

17. St. Augustine, *The City of God.*

18. R. S. Thomas, "The Bright Field" in *Laboratories of the Spirit.*

19. "Where do we go from here?" printed in *The Listener* (8 August 1974), 177–8.

20. Four lines from "Stations" in R. S. Thomas, *Mass for Hard Times* (London: Bloodaxe Books, 1992).

XXII PRAYER AS GIVING ATTENTION TO GOD

1. H. A. Williams, *Poverty, Chastity, Obedience* (London: Mitchell Beazley, 1975), 111.

2. Evelyn Underhill: *Mysticism* (London: Methuen, 1942), 300.

3. St. Augustine: *Sermons* (de Script N.T.), 88 v. 5.

4. Alan Ecclestone, essay in *Spirituality for Today*, edited by Eric James (London: S.C.M. Press, 1968), 39.

5. From a radio programme for primary schools.

6. Anthony Bloom, *Meditations on a Theme* (London: Mowbray, 1972), 28.

7. Hugh Lavery, *Reflections* (London: Mayhew McCrimmon, 1978), 68.

8. Iris Murdoch, *The Sovereignty of Good* (London: Routledge & Kegan Paul, 1970), 55.

9. Thomas Merton, *Zen and the Birds of Appetite* (New York: New Directions, 1968), 49–50.

10. Peter Shaffer, *Five Finger Exercise*, Act I, sc. 2 in Three Plays (London: Penguin, 1976), 51.

11. T. S. Eliot, From "East Coker," III ll. 23–28 in *Four Quartets* (London: Faber & Faber, 1944).

12. Evelyn Underhill, *Mysticism*, 234.

13. Ibid., 301–2.

14. Edwin Muir, *An Autobiography*, 246.

15. Simone Weil, *Waiting on God*, 153.

16. Simone Weil, "Essay on the Right Use of School Studies with

a view to the Love of God," in *Waiting on God* (London: Fount Paperbacks, 1977).

17. Rilke, *Duino Elegies*, the Eighth Elegy, ll. 711–76.

18. Psalm 118:24.

19. Kierkegaard, *Christian Discourses*.

20. A story told me by Nadir Dinshaw.

21. Dennis Potter, interview with Melvyn Bragg, Channel 4, April 1994.

XXIII LIVING THE EUCHARIST

1. W. H. Auden, final six lines from "Precious Fire" in *Collected Poems*, 450.

2. A Carthusian, *The Way of Silent Love* (London: Darton, Longman & Todd, 1993).

3. From *Four Quartets*, "The Dry Salvages," V, ll. 17–19.

4. Emily Dickinson, lines from no. 1684 of *The Complete Poems*, 687.

5. Annie Dillard, *Pilgrim at Tinker Creek* (London: Jonathan Cape, 1975), 2–3.

6. Ibid., 271.

7. Charles Péguy, quoted by Alan Ecclestone. See XXII, note 3.

8. These words have often been attributed to St. Augustine, though I have failed to trace the source. Professor Henry Chadwick writes to me: "The words are a very free paraphrase and development of Augustine's ideas . . . no doubt he would be pleased to be credited with so noble a sentiment. . . ."

9. Stephen Bayne, from a sermon preached as Bishop of Olympia in the Polish National Catholic Cathedral, Buffalo, New York, 11 May 1958.

10. T. S. Eliot, "The Rock," VII.

11. Meister Eckhart, quoted in Helen Waddell, *Mediaeval Latin Lyrics* (London: Gollancz, 1976), 37.

12. Frederick Buechner, *Wishful Thinking*, 23.

XXIV POSTSCRIPT

1. See LETTER 1, note 8.
2. P.J. Kavanagh, *People and Places*, 178.
3. Seamus Heaney, *The Government of the Tongue*, 107.
4. Michael Ignatieff, article in *The Observer*, 7 January 1990.
5. Richard Wilbur, "The Beautiful Changes," in *New and Collected Poems* (London: Faber & Faber, 1989).

Bibliography

Here is a list of books I have found rewarding in preparing over the years to write this book, although not every book referred to in the Notes appears here.*

Ackerman, Diane. *A Natural History of the Senses.* London: Chapmans, 1990.

Allchin. A. M. *The World is a Wedding.* London: Darton, Longman & Todd, 1978.

Auden, W. H. *Making, Knowing, Judging.* Oxford: The Clarendon Press, 1956.

Auden, W. H. *Collected Poems.* London: Faber & Faber, 1976.

Beckett, Wendy. *Art and the Spiritual.* London: Rider, 1992.

Berger, John. *The White Bird.* London: Hogarth Press, 1988.

Berger, Peter L. *A Rumour of Angels.* London: Pelican, 1969.

Blake, William. *The Complete Poems.* London: Longmans, 1972.

Blamires, David. *David Jones, Artist and Writer.* Manchester, UK: Manchester University Press, 1971.

Bloom, Anthony. *Meditations on a Theme.* London: Mowbray, 1972.

Brook, Peter. *The Empty Space.* London: Penguin, 1990.

Buechner, Frederick. *The Alphabet of Grace.* New York: HarperCollins Publishers, 1970.

Buechner, Frederick. *The Clown in the Belfry.* New York: HarperCollins Publishers, 1992.

Buechner, Frederick. *Now and Then.* New York: Harper & Row, 1983.

Capps, Walter Holden. *Seeing with a Native Eye*. New York: Harper & Row, 1976.

A Carthusian. *The Way of Silent Love*. London: Darton, Longman & Todd, 1993.

Chatwin, Bruce. *The Songlines*. London: Picador, 1987.

Chopra, Deepak. *Unconditional Life*. New York: Bantam Books, 1991.

Collis, John Stewart. *Living with a Stranger*. London: MacDonald & Jane's, 1978.

Collis, John Stewart. *The Vision of Glory*. London: Charles Knight, 1972.

Collis, John Stewart. *The Worm Forgives the Plough*. London: Charles Knight, 1973.

Denvir, Bernard (Editor). *The Impressionists at First Hand*. London: Thames & Hudson, 1987.

Dickinson, Emily. *The Complete Poems*. London: Faber & Faber, 1970.

Dillard, Annie. *Pilgrim at Tinker Creek*. London: Jonathan Cape, 1975.

Dillard, Annie. *Teaching a Stone to Talk*. London: Picador, 1984.

Dillard, Annie. *The Writing Life*. London: Picador, 1985.

Dooling, D. M. and Paul Jordon-Smith (Editors). *I Become Part of it: Sacred Dimensions in Native American Life*. London: HarperCollins Publishers, 1992.

Dowell, Graham. *Enjoying the world: The Rediscovery of Thomas Traherne*. London: Mowbray, 1990.

Ecclestone, Alan. *Yes to God*. London: Darton, Longman & Todd, 1975.

Ecclestone, Alan. *The Scaffolding of Spirit*. London: Darton, Longman & Todd, 1987.

Ede, Jim. *A Way of Life: Kettle's Yard*. Cambridge, UK: Cambridge University Press, 1984.

Egan, Kieran. *Primary Understanding*. London: Routledge, 1988.

Eliot, T.S. *Four Quartets*. London: Faber & Faber, 1944.

Figes, Eva. *Light*. London: Hamish Hamilton, 1983.

Fowles, John. *Daniel Martin*. London: Jonathan Cape, 1977.

Franck, Frederick. *The Zen of Seeing*. New York: Random House, 1973.

Fraser, Antonia (editor). *The Pleasure of Reading*. London: Bloomsbury, 1992.

Fry, Christopher. *Collected Plays I & II*. Oxford, UK: Oxford University Press, 1971 and 1972.

Gibbard, Mark. *Prayer and Contemplation*. London: Mowbray, 1976.

Golding, William. *Darkness Visible*. London: Faber & Faber, 1979.

Gollancz, Victor. *From Darkness to Light*. London: Victor Gollancz, 1956.

Gollancz, Victor. *The New Year of Grace*. London: Victor Gollancz, 1961.

Gollancz, Victor. *My Dear Timothy*. London: Victor Gollancz.

Gombrich, E.H. *Art and Illusion*. London: Phaidon, 1977.

Gombrich, E.H. *The Image and the Eye*. London: Phaidon, 1982.

Griffiths, Bede. *A New Vision of Reality*. London: Fount Paperbacks, 1992.

Grigson, Geoffrey. *The Private Art, a Poetry Notebook*. London: Allison & Busby, 1982.

Grigson, Geoffrey. *The English Year*. Oxford, UK: Oxford University Press, 1984.

Hammarskjöld, Dag. *Markings*. London: Faber & Faber, 1964.

Harvey, Andrew. *A Journey in Ladakh*. London: Jonathan Cape, 1983.

Hawkes, Jacquetta. *Man on Earth*. London: The Cresset Press, 1954.

Heaney, Seamus. *Preoccupations*. London: Faber & Faber, 1980.

Heaney, Seamus. *The Government of the Tongue*. London: Faber & Faber, 1988.

Heaney, Seamus. *New Selected Poems*. London: Faber & Faber, 1990.

Hepburn, R. W. *Wonder and Other Essays*. Edinburgh, UK: Edinburgh University Press, 1984.

Heschel, Abraham Joshua. *I Asked for Wonder*. New York: Crossroad, 1988.

Heschel, Abraham Joshua. *God in Search of Man*. Northvale, NJ: Jason Aronson, 1987.

Hoagland, Edward. *Heart's Desire*. London: Collins Harvill, 1991.

Hopkins, Gerard Manley. *Selected Prose*. Oxford, UK: Oxford University Press, 1980.

Hoyland, Francis. *A Painter's Diary*. Reading, UK: Educational Explorers, 1967.

Huxley, Aldous. *The Doors of Perception*. London: Chatto & Windus, 1954.

James, William. *The Varieties of Religious Experience*. London: Penguin, 1983.

Jennings, Elizabeth. *Collected Poems*. London: Carcanet, 1986.

Jones, John. *The Egotistical Sublime: A History of Wordsworth's Imagination*. London: Chatto & Windus, 1954.

Johnston, William. *Lord, Teach us to Pray*. London: Fount Paperbacks, 1990.

Jones, Alan. *Soul Making*. London: S.C.M. Press, 1985.

Kavanagh, P. J. *People and Places*. London: Carcanet, 1988.

Keen, Sam. *Apology for Wonder*. New York: Harper & Row, 1969.

Keenan, Brian. *An Evil Cradling*. London: Hutchinson, 1992.

Kilvert, Francis. *Diaries*. Jonathan Cape. London: 1969.

Küng, Hans. *Mozart: Traces of Transcendence*. London: S.C.M. Press, 1992.

Laski, Marghanita. *Ecstasy*. London: Cresset Press, 1961.

Laski, Marghanita. *Everyday Ecstasy*. London: Thames & Hudson, 1980.

Lavery, Hugh. *Reflections*. London: Mayhew-McCrimmon, 1978.

Lewis, C.S. *Surprised by Joy*. London: Geoffrey Bles, 1955.

Lewis, C.S. *The Weight of Glory*. London: Geoffrey Bles, 1949.

Lively, Penelope. *Next to Nature, Art*. London: Penguin, 1984.

Lively, Penelope. *Moon Tiger*. London: André Deutsch, 1987.

Lively, Penelope. *City of the Mind*. London: Penguin, 1992.

Lopez, Barry. *Arctic Dreams*. London: Picador, 1986.

Martin, Robert Bernard. *Gerard Manley Hopkins: A Very Private Life*. London: HarperCollins, 1991.

Matthias, John (editor). *Introducing David Jones*. London: Faber & Faber, 1980.

Maybury-Lewis, David. *Millennium*. London: Penguin Viking, 1992.

Maxwell, Meg and Verena Tschudin. *Seeing the Invisible*. London: Penguin, 1990.

Merton, Thomas. *Confessions of a Guilty Bystander*. London: Sheldon Press, 1977.

Montague, C.E. *The Right Place*. London: Chatto & Windus, 1924.

Murdoch, Iris. *Metaphysics as a Guide to Morals*. London: Chatto & Windus, 1992.

Muir, Edwin. *An Autobiography*. London: Hogarth Press, 1954.

Muir, Edwin. *Collected Poems*. London: Faber & Faber, 1960.

Newton, Eric. *The Meaning of Beauty*. London: Longmans

Green, 1950.

Nicholl, Donald. *Holiness*. London: Darton, Longman & Todd, 1981.

Nouwen, Henri. *Thomas Merton: Contemplative Critic*. New York: Triumph Books, 1991.

Oppenheimer, Helen. *The Hope of Happiness*. London: S.C.M. Press, 1983.

Peters, H. F. *Rainer Maria Rilke: Masks and the Man*. Seattle, WA: University of Washington Press, 1960.

Pitter, Ruth. *Collected Poems*. London: Macmillan, 1968.

Plath, Sylvia. *Collected Poems*. London: Faber & Faber, 1981.

Raine, Kathleen. *Collected Poems*. London: Hamish Hamilton, 1956.

Raine, Kathleen. *William Blake*. London: Thames & Hudson, 1970.

Raine, Kathleen. *Farewell Happy Fields*. London: Hamish Hamilton, 1973.

Raine, Kathleen. *Living with Mystery*. Ipswich, UK: Golgonooza Press, 1992.

Rilke, Rainer Maria. *Selected Letters: 1902–1926*. London: Quartet Encounters, 1988.

Rilke, Rainer Maria. *Selected Poetry*. Edited and translated by Stephen Mitchell. New York: Vintage International, 1989.

Rilke, Rainer Maria. *Letters on Cézanne*. London: Jonathan Cape, 1988.

Robinson, Edward. *The Language of Mystery*. London: S.C.M. Press, 1987.

Roethke, Theodore. *The Collected Poems*. London: Faber & Faber, 1968.

Roose-Evans, James. *Inner Journey, Outer Journey*. London: Rider, 1987.

Roskill, Mark (Editor). *The Letters of Vincent van Gogh*. London: Fontana Paperbacks, 1963.

Schmemann, Alexander. *The World as Sacrament*. London: Darton, Longman & Todd, 1966.

Shaffer, Peter. *The Gift of the Gorgon*. London: Penguin Viking, 1993.

Sherrard, Philip. *The Sacred in Life and Art*. Ipswich, UK: Golgonooza Press, 1990.

Simon, Madeleine. *Born Contemplative*. London: Darton, Longman & Todd, 1993.

Smith, Cyprian. *The Way of Paradox: Spiritual Life as Taught by Meister Eckhart*. London: Darton, Longman & Todd, 1987.

Steiner, George. *Real Presences*. London: Faber & Faber, 1989.

Steiner, George. *The Death of Tragedy*. London: Faber & Faber, 1961.

Stevens, Wallace. *Collected Poems*. London: Faber & Faber, 1955.

Sutcliff, Rosemary. *Blue Remembered Hills*. London: Bodley Head, 1983.

Swift, Graham. *Ever After*. London: Picador, 1992.

Taylor, John V. *The Go-Between God*. London: S.C.M. Press, 1972.

Taylor, John V. *The Christlike God*. London: S.C.M. Press, 1992.

Thomas, R.S. *Selected Poems*. London: Hart-Davis, MacGibbon, 1973.

Thomas, R.S. *Later Poems*. London: Macmillan, 1983.

Tilby, Angela. *Science and the Soul*. London: SPCK, 1992.

Tillich, Paul. *The New Being*. London: SCM Press, 1956.

Toynbee, Philip. *Part of a Journey*. London: Collins, 1981.

Toynbee, Philip. *End of a Journey*. London: Bloomsbury, 1988.

Traherne, Thomas. *Centuries*. Oxford, UK: The Clarendon
  Press, 1960.
Underhill, Evelyn. *Mysticism*. London: Methuen, 1942.
Updike, John. *Self-Consciousness*. London: Penguin, 1989.
Waddell, Helen. *Peter Abelard*. London: Constable, 1946.
Weil, Simone. *Waiting on God*. London: Routledge & Kegan
  Paul, 1951.
White, Patrick. *The Solid Mandala*. London: Penguin, 1969.
Wilbur, Richard. *New and Collected Poems*. London: Faber &
  Faber, 1989.
Wright, Frank. *The Pastoral Nature of the Ministry*. London:
  S.C.M. Press, 1980.
Yancey, Philip and Paul Brand: *Fearfully and Wonderfully Made*.
  London: Marshall Pickering, 1993.
Yeats, W.B. *Collected Poems*. London: Everyman, 1990.

*Publisher's Note: Since the publication of the original edition
of this book, a number of titles listed in the Bibliography are
now, unfortunately, out of print. Most of these titles can, however, be found via searches on the Internet through
Amazon.com and a number of secondhand booksellers' Web-
sites, such as Alibris, Bookfinder, Powells and the like.

fractals ?

p.36

p.18

p.25

Ecclesiastes

CPSIA information can be obtained at www.ICGtesting.com
Printed in the USA
LVOW07s0128140514

385694LV00001B/139/P

9 781936 9124